SIBLING RELATIONSHIPS ACROSS THE LIFE SPAN

SIBLING RELATIONSHIPS ACROSS THE LIFE SPAN

VICTOR G. CICIRELLI

Purdue University
West Lafayette, Indiana

PLENUM PRESS • NEW YORK AND LONDON

Library of Congress Cataloging-in-Publication Data

On file

BF
723
.S43
C53
1995

ISBN 0-306-45025-9

© 1995 Plenum Press, New York
A Division of Plenum Publishing Corporation
233 Spring Street, New York, N.Y. 10013

10 9 8 7 6 5 4 3 2 1

Printed in the United States of America

Preface

When one begins to examine the existing literature dealing with siblings, one soon becomes aware that many separate domains of sibling research exist and that there is little connection between them; for example, sibling relationships in early childhood, genetic and environmental influences on individual differences between siblings, dysfunctional sibling relationships, adult sibling helping relationships, sibling violence and abuse, and so on.

The author's aim in writing this book was to attempt to bring together for the first time studies from diverse areas of sibling research into a single volume. The book is a summary and integration of the various domains of sibling studies, extending across the life span where studies exist to make this possible.

Although many gaps in the sibling research literature within and between domains of study and over the life span still exist, it is hoped that this book will motivate others to help fill in the gaps by suggesting directions where further research is needed.

Following a brief introduction, the book begins by presenting a broad theoretical framework for sibling research, followed by a discussion of methodological problems confronting the sibling researcher. Other chapters review research on sibling relationships in childhood and adolescence, and in adulthood and old age. Cross-cultural evidence for the universality of the sibling relationship is examined and cultural differences noted. A hermeneutic study of the relationships of a single family of adult siblings, their spouses, and their parents provides new understandings of how adult sibling relationships are maintained. Next, sibling helping relationships are examined across the life span, as well as the cooperative relationships between adult siblings as they endeavor to help their aging parents.

The latter portion of the book is devoted to special topics concerning sibling relationships: those where a sibling is chronically ill, disabled, or mentally retarded, those where there is sibling conflict, violence, and abuse, those where a sibling relationship is incestuous or sexually abusive, those where a sibling has died, and those dysfunctional sibling relationships where some form of therapy is needed. An epilogue attempts to make the case for integration of sibling research across the life span, suggesting that approaches used and topics studied in one portion of the life span might profitably be applied to other portions, and proposing that life span attachment theory could provide a unifying theoretical basis for sibling relationships across the life span and account for diverse sibling phenomena.

The book is intended for a broad academic audience, including researchers, professionals, clinicians, and students. Although it was not the author's intention to produce a textbook, the book might be used as a supplementary text for advanced undergraduates and graduate students in courses on family relationships that include the study of siblings. Finally, the book may have appeal to a more general audience of individuals who are interested in the topic of sibling relationships.

VICTOR G. CICIRELLI

Contents

Chapter 1
Introduction: The Importance of Sibling Relationships   1

Unique Characteristics of Sibling Relationships   2
Meanings and Distinctions   3
The Importance of Studying Sibling Relationships   5
Demographic Changes 10
Concluding Comments 11

Chapter 2
A Life Span Perspective for Sibling Research 13

Life Span Time Frame 14
Development and Aging 15
Kinship 17
Sibling Constellation 18
Structure and Process 19
Person and Context 20
Partial Systems 24
A Perspective for Sibling Research 25

Chapter 3
Methodological Approaches and Issues in Studying Siblings .. 27

Identifying Sibling Populations and Selecting Samples 27
Methods of Data Collection 34

Sources of Sibling Data 38
Conclusion 40

Chapter 4
Siblings in Childhood and Adolescence 41

Developmental Changes in Sibling Relationships 41
Explaining Individual Differences in Siblings and in Their
    Relationships 46
Conclusion 52

Chapter 5
Siblings in Adulthood and Old Age 53

Existence of the Sibling Relationship in Adulthood 53
Aspects of the Sibling Relationship 55
Changes in Sibling Relationships 60
Effects of Siblings on Well-Being 63
Theoretical Explanations for Adult Sibling Relationships 65

Chapter 6
Sibling Relationships in Cross-Cultural Perspective 69

Universality of Sibling Relationships 69
Identification of Siblings 71
Differences in Sibling Structure 72
Sibling Caretaking in Childhood 75
Marriage Arrangements of Siblings 79
Sibling Relationships in Adulthood 81
Effects of Cultural Change on Sibling Relationships 82
Conclusion 84

Chapter 7
Understanding Sibling Relationships: A Hermeneutic
   Approach 87

Study Procedure 88
Background Characteristics of Family Members 89
Family Climate 90

Influence of Sibling Structure   92
Sibling Perceptions of One Another   95
Spouses' Perceptions of the Siblings   99
Sibling Communication and Contact 101
Conclusion 105

Chapter 8
Sibling Helping Relationships 109

Sibling Help in Childhood and Adolescence 110
Sibling Helping Relationships in Adulthood 114
Sibling Helping Relationships in Old Age 115
Conclusion 122

Chapter 9
Siblings as Caregivers of Elderly Parents 123

Which Siblings in the Family Help and How Much? 123
Decision Making by Adult Siblings 127
Factors Influencing Sibling Help 128
Effects of Parent Caregiving on Adult Siblings 131
Conclusion 135

Chapter 10
Siblings with Mental Retardation, Illness, or Disability 137

Some Preliminary Considerations 137
Siblings in Childhood and Adolescence 139
Siblings in Adulthood 144
Conclusion 149

Chapter 11
Sibling Conflict, Aggression, Violence, and Abuse 151

Definitions and Distinctions 151
Prevalence of Conflict, Aggression, Violence, and Abuse 157
Developmental Course of Conflict, Aggression, Violence,
    and Abuse 159

Factors Associated with Sibling Conflict 160
Factors Associated with Siblings' Conflict Management Modes . . 164
Factors Associated with Outcomes and Consequences of Conflict 165
Conclusion 167

Chapter 12
**Sibling Sexual Experiences: Normal Exploratory Behavior,
Nonabusive Incest, and Abusive Incest** 169

Normal Sexual Behavior 169
Normal Sibling Sexual Behavior in Childhood and Adolescence . . 170
Incest 170
Prevalence of Nonabusive and Abusive Sibling Incest 173
Effects of Sibling Incest 176
Factors Associated with Sibling Incest 180
Conclusion 184

Chapter 13
Loss of Siblings through Death 185

Loss in Childhood 186
Loss in Adolescence 192
Loss in Adulthood and Old Age 196
Conclusion 198

Chapter 14
Siblings and Psychotherapy 201

Sibling Therapy as an Adjunct to Family Therapy 202
Sibling Therapy as an Adjunct to Individual Therapy 203
Sibling Therapy Used Alone 204
Sibling Therapy in Childhood and Adolescence 206
Sibling Therapy in Adulthood and Old Age 209

Chapter 15
Epilogue 215

Integrating Research across the Life Span 215
Attachment Theory: A Unifying Theory for Life Span Sibling
    Research 222

References 225

Author Index 247

Subject Index 253

Introduction: The Importance of Sibling Relationships

A large literature concerning siblings can be found in any research library, but most of past research has been concerned with the effects of birth order, family size, and gender on individual differences in various intellectual and personality characteristics. Although this is still an important domain of research, in recent years considerable attention has been focused on the interpersonal relationships between siblings and the factors influencing such relationships.

The progress of research aimed at understanding sibling relationships has been relatively slow compared to that of research on spousal and parent–child relationships, largely because the full impact of sibling relationships on the developing individual has only recently been realized. Previous thinking assumed that parents were the primary influence on an individual's behavior and development in childhood and adolescence, with peers becoming the primary influence in adulthood and old age. Any long-range effects of siblings stemming from childhood were regarded as negligible, and siblings were considered to have little contact with each other in the later stages of life. More recently, sibling interactions were found to be important influences in themselves. The emergence of family systems theory, in which parent–parent, parent–child, and sibling relationships are all seen as functioning as part of an interdependent system, has spurred a renewed interest in sibling relationships.

UNIQUE CHARACTERISTICS OF SIBLING RELATIONSHIPS

Sibling relationships have attributes in common with all interpersonal relationships, but they also have certain unique characteristics:

First, the relationship with a sibling is usually the longest relationship that an individual will experience in the total lifetime. This appears to be true even among half-, step-, and adoptive siblings, whose relationships usually begin early enough in life to have a longer time course than relationships with parents, spouses, offspring, or most other friends and relatives. Thus, duration itself can be an important factor in determining the impact of the relationship.

Second, the sibling relationship is ascribed rather than earned, that is, brotherhood or sisterhood is a status that is obtained by birth (or by legal action, as in the case of step- and adoptive siblings). Although there may be a dissolution of an active sibling relationship under certain circumstances, there is no dissolution of the sibling status. This situation presents the possibility of the existence of a continuing bond between separated siblings. Given the opportunity, it may be possible to revitalize this important relationship in a way which may not be possible with disaffected peers or friends.

Third, the sibling relationship in childhood and adolescence is more one of intimate daily contact as siblings interact within the home, in contrast to sibling relationships in adulthood where intimacy is maintained at a distance by telephone communication, letters, and periodic visits. As a result, the sibling relationship in adulthood is more subject to change or disruption as a result of external forces and unexpected life events.

Fourth, the relationship between siblings is often seen as one of relative egalitarianism. Obviously, however, some power or status differences may exist between brothers and sisters (or between full, half-, step-, and adoptive siblings), based on age, size, intelligence, knowledge, social skills, economic success, other achievements, influence with parents, and so on. However, in the majority of cases, there is usually equivalence in siblings' feelings of acceptance for one another, which allows them to relate as equals.

Fifth, siblings' lives have in common a long history of shared as well as nonshared experiences. Shared experiences contribute to siblings' similarity whereas nonshared experiences contribute to their individual differences. However, a reciprocal interaction between siblings' shared and nonshared environments may further contribute to individual differences. On the other hand, communication between siblings about their lives, either directly or indirectly (through a parent or others), may produce empathy and vicariously shared experiences, facilitating greater similarity. In short, siblings' similarities and differences cannot be attributed to shared or nonshared environments as if these environments were totally independent of each other, or as if sibling communication and vicarious sharing of experiences did not exist. Sibling interactions and relationships are part of a larger context existing over the life span which simultaneously and paradoxically may continue to make siblings more similar in some ways while also continuing to make them more different in others.

MEANINGS AND DISTINCTIONS

Meaning of a Sibling

Almost all sibling research has been done with full siblings with little or no attention given to half-siblings, stepsiblings, adoptive siblings, or fictive siblings. Given the growing prevalence of blended families, it is important to clarify the distinction between these terms. Traditionally, full siblings are defined as two individuals who have both biological parents in common. Half-siblings are individuals who have only one biological parent in common. Stepsiblings are individuals who have no biological parents in common, but who are linked by virtue of the marriage of a biological parent of one to a biological parent of the other (as in blended families following divorce and remarriage). Adoptive siblings are individuals whose sibling status is established when they are is legally adopted into a family. Fictive siblings are nonfamily members who have been accepted into the family as siblings based on desirability or custom rather than on the basis of blood ties or legal criteria. In some cultures fictive siblingship may be sentimental or honorary, but in other cultures (Cicirelli, 1994a; M. Marshall, 1983a; Weisner, 1989a) fictive siblings have all the privileges and obligations of biological family members. (Other types of quasi-sibling relationships arising from various alternative family life-styles are yet to be defined.)

Meaning of a Relationship

The personal relationship perspective (Duck, 1992; Hartup, 1975; Hinde, 1981; Huston & Robins, 1982; Kelley et al., 1983) provides the background for the definition of a relationship as the interdependency of two individuals as manifested in their interactions (actions, verbal and nonverbal communication), which influence their beliefs, knowledge, attitudes, and feelings toward each other and which in turn influence their further interactions. The cognitive and affective dispositions are long lasting and relatively stable, and they account for the continuing influence of individuals in their absence, for continuation of the relationship over periods where there is no behavioral interaction, and for the motivation to make contact after a separation. A relationship involves two individuals; events and relationships with other individuals provide the context in which the original relationship is embedded. Many types of relationships exist (marital, romantic, parent–child, work, friendship, and so on), defined by differences in attributes that characterize the relative independence or interconnectedness of the individuals involved.

Relationships involve varying degrees of closeness. Very close relationships have a high degree of interdependency or mutual influence, attachment, intimacy, and emotional involvement. However, many apparently close relationships differ in their degree of actual closeness. People may go through the motions or ritual behaviors of a close relationship while feeling distant rather than deep emotional involvement, attachment, or intimacy. Thus, it may be difficult at times to determine the existence of close relationships.

Meaning of a Sibling Relationship

The distinguishing characteristic of a sibling relationship is the interdependency of two children in a family who either (1) share some degree of common biological origin (full siblings, half-siblings); (2) share a relationship defined legally (stepsiblings, adoptive siblings); or (3) share some degree of commitment or socialization to the norms of sibling roles in a particular culture (fictive siblings). In all cases, relationships between siblings are ascribed rather than voluntary, they include some history of intimate family experiences; they are enduring, perhaps lasting a lifetime, and they are more or less egalitarian.

The following definition of a sibling relationship has been adapted from earlier work (Cicirelli, 1985b): Sibling relationships are the total of the interactions (physical, verbal, and nonverbal communication) of two or more individuals who share knowledge, perceptions, attitudes, beliefs, and feelings regarding each other, from the time that one sibling becomes aware of the other. A sibling relationship includes both overt actions and interactions between the sibling pair as well as the covert subjective, cognitive, and affective components of the relationship. The implication is that sibling relationships can continue to exist when the siblings are separated by distance and time without ongoing sibling interaction.

As with other relationships, sibling relationships can vary. For example, some siblings may have a relationship of long duration with much contact, closeness, and commitment, while others may have a purely formal relationship with little or no contact or interest in one another. Full siblings may feel a greater commitment to the relationship than do siblings of other types. Such considerations indicate the need to assess existing relationships carefully before generalizing research results from one type of sibling relationship to another or to siblings in general.

Meaning of Sibling Characteristics

Sibling characteristics are the attributes that define a sibling. However, there is an issue concerning the stability and origin of such characteristics. Some researchers believe that these attributes are dispositions within the sibling (i.e., similar to traits, they exist regardless of time or situation). Other researchers believe that such attributes are relational (i.e., reside in the perceptions of those siblings interacting with each other, and can change depending upon the situation). Which view of sibling characteristics is used depends on the researcher's overall metamodel and theoretical perspective. In this book, both positions are accepted, depending upon the particular characteristics and part of the life span involved. For example, certain temperamental attributes of a sibling may be considered dispositional, whereas other sibling attributes may be viewed as relational, with the ongoing perception of the sibling the result of many reciprocal interactions with the sibling in various contexts.

THE IMPORTANCE OF STUDYING SIBLING RELATIONSHIPS

The present book was undertaken in an effort to emphasize the importance of studying sibling relationships throughout the life span and to examine existing research on a variety of topics dealing with the sibling relationship.

Early Sibling Studies

A historical review of sibling studies is not within the scope of the present volume. However, for a discussion of major themes in early sibling research the interested reader is referred to such sources as Bank and Kahn (1982b), Cicirelli (1978), Lamb (1982), Schibuk (1989), Schvaneveldt and Ihinger (1979), and Sutton-Smith and Rosenberg (1970); for more recent themes and issues, the reader is referred to Cicirelli (1985b, 1991, 1993c) and Dunn (1993). Examining sibling themes in historical perspective from the earliest sources in myth, Biblical references, and the like to the present produces an appreciation of the significance of sibling relationships. Early themes of sibling rivalry were reflected in the psychodynamic formulations of Freud and Adler, while Adler's (1959) emphasis on the importance of birth order was accompanied by a large empirical literature of birth order and sibling structure effects on siblings' intellectual and personality characteristics. Somewhat more recently, effects of relationships between siblings and factors explaining these relationships began to be studied and are still being explored today.

Influence of Siblings

Researchers have begun to realize that siblings have a major impact on one another's behavior and development through mutual socialization, helping behaviors, cooperative tasks and activities, and simple companionship, as well as through aggressive and various other negative behaviors. This impact may be relatively independent of the impact of parents and other family members on the siblings, or the impact of the siblings on the total family system.

Siblings have an influence on one another's behavior, learning, and development throughout the life span that is relatively independent of their genetic potential. This influence can be short- or long-term, direct or indirect, and can involve basic socialized learning as well as idiosyncratic learning. Direct influence takes place when one sibling interacts with another to change some aspect of behavior, or one sibling communicates certain ideas, skills, expectancies, or attitudes that affect the immediate or future behavior of the other. Indirect influence occurs when a direct effect of a sibling interacts with some other variable to bring about a change later in time, or when one sibling influences another family member who in turn influences another sibling. Short-term influence of siblings takes place in the immediate present; long-term effects are found when one sibling learns certain characteristics, expectancies, or skills from another sibling that in turn influences future learning or behavior. Socialized learning is concerned with the norms, rules, or common ways of society, whereas idiosyncratic learning refers to knowledge that has a unique significance for the individual.

Siblings influence each other throughout their common life spans. In addition, the younger may influence the older even before the younger sibling's birth as a result of expectancies communicated from parents regarding the new sibling. Similarly, after the death of a sibling, the survivor may not only grieve for a period of time but also be influenced by memories of the sibling.

Siblings within the Family System

The advent of family systems therapy (e.g., S. Minuchin, 1974) underscored the importance of sibling relationships within a total family system made up of parent–parent, parent–child, and sibling subsystems. In addition to the influence of parents on their children within the parent–child subsystem of the family, relationships between siblings constitute a major subsystem of the family which directly influences the siblings involved and indirectly influences the other subsystems. It is essential to understand the workings of these subsystems, as well as those of coalitions of siblings within the sibling subsystem or coalitions involving certain siblings and a parent, if one is to fully comprehend the processes by which the family functions.

A recent trend in sibling research has been the application of behavioral–genetic methods to the study of the family system (e.g., Anderson, Hetherington, Reiss, & Howe, 1994; Dunn, Stocker, & Plomin, 1990b). Such methods attempt to determine the extent to which similarities and differences in siblings' characteristics and behavior can be attributed to genetic similarity, shared experience (such as certain parental behaviors), and various sources of nonshared experience including differential parental treatment and sibling behaviors. Longitudinal studies in this area are still in progress, but should yield valuable insights into processes in the family system.

Particularly in adulthood, the dyadic relationship between a pair of siblings can assume great importance apart from the system as a whole. Physical or psychological distance between a sibling pair and other family members, or the overlap of certain siblings' interests, is a situation in which a dyad functions in relative independence of other portions of the family system. Yet, the dyad's relationship to the remainder of the system is an essential background condition for the dyadic relationship.

Most of the research into family systems has dealt with families where the siblings are children or adolescents. It is also important to understand how sibling relationships function as part of a larger family system in adulthood. As yet, there is little research information bearing on adult family systems of this sort.

Sibling Relationships across the Life Span

The fact that the sibling relationship is one of extraordinary longevity means that it is important to study this relationship not only in early childhood, but through all the life stages across the life span. Researchers are just now beginning to determine how the relationship is affected by various life cycle changes as well as by critical life events. Taking a life span perspective enables one to see implications of early events for later relationships and to appreciate the natural cycle of change in the sibling relationship.

Universality of Sibling Relationships

Examining sibling relationships across many cultures leads to an appreciation of the importance of siblings to human family life. Siblings' lives are closely intertwined throughout life in many nonindustrialized societies, with carefully defined duties and responsibilities. In contrast, more aspects of sibling relationships in industrialized societies are voluntary, yet sibling relationships remain of significance throughout life for most individuals.

Sibling Helping Relationships

As siblings interact with one another throughout life, help tends to be exchanged in a variety of ways. Such help can include an older sibling's help to a younger one in early play activities, help with school tasks in middle childhood and adolescence, help with dating and other social activities in adolescence, help with household tasks and child rearing in adulthood, and help during illness in old age. Although older adults rarely need sibling help, existing research indicates that having sibling help potentially available provides a source of security.

Siblings' Parent Caring Activities

During the midlife task of caring for aging parents, the relationship between the siblings takes on renewed salience. If the siblings can forge a cooperative and mutually supportive alliance to make family decisions where needed and to carry out required caregiving duties, their relationship is strengthened and becomes closer. On the other hand, if some siblings abdicate from the task or quarrel over what should be done and who should do it, the resulting bitterness can result in a weakening of the sibling relationship or permanent estrangement. Because siblings at midlife must deal with competing responsibilities of jobs, marriage, children, and community activities in addition to their responsibilities to parents, and because siblings are often geographically separated, the mechanics of cooperating for caregiving are often exceedingly difficult.

Siblings with Chronic Illness or Cognitive Disability

Although only a small portion of families are affected, a sibling who suffers from a chronic illness or cognitive disability can have a great effect on other siblings in the family and on the family system as a whole. Parents tend to be preoccupied with the afflicted child and give their other children little attention. The normal siblings in the family, especially sisters, are typically assigned extra home or caregiving duties, leaving them less time for their own activities. The relationship of normal siblings with the afflicted one is also affected. Where there is an older mentally retarded sibling, the usual age roles are reversed, with the normal younger sibling acting as the wiser, more knowledgeable one. Overall, when one sibling has a chronic illness or cognitive disability, the activities that can be shared with a normal sibling can be quite limited, depending on the seriousness of the condition. If the afflicted sibling has a condition that is socially embarrassing or to which a stigma is attached, normal siblings often withdraw from interaction with the sibling; on the other hand, they may be teased or ostracized by others in the community. Whether a close sibling relationship exists in these families depends to a large extent on the dynamics of the total family as well the extent of the afflicted child's disabilities. In many families, the sibling relationship as well as the responsibility of normal siblings for the care of a chronically ill or cognitively disabled sibling extends throughout life, with the normal sibling accepting the full burden of care when a parent becomes too old or dies. It is clear that unusual demands are placed upon the sibling relationship in such cases.

Conflict and Violence

Some degree of conflict between siblings seems to be an unavoidable part of family life during the childhood years. It can be argued that sibling conflict can be a valuable childhood experience, as the participants learn to take the perspective of the other, argue their positions, negotiate to settle differences, and so on. Whether the siblings settle things on their own or whether parents set limits to the conflict and help the children to negotiate agreements, mild sibling conflicts that are successfully resolved prepare the children for interaction with peers and others throughout life. However, when sibling conflict escalates into violent interactions or the physical or mental abuse of a weaker sibling by a stronger, the sibling relationship becomes maladaptive and can be seriously harmful. Although only a minority of siblings have violent or abusive relationships, the study of factors in the family system in general and sibling relationships in particular that lead to violence and abuse is extremely important.

Sibling Sexual Relationships and Sexual Abuse

As in the case of sibling conflict, some sexual curiosity and sexual play between siblings in the early years appears to be a normal part of development. The frequency with which such early experience progresses to more intense sexual relationships between siblings or to sibling sexual abuse is not well known, nor are the dynamics of the family system. Such relationships tend to be shrouded with secrecy in the light of societal incest taboos. However, existing clinical information indicates that when one sibling engages in coercive or abusive sexual practices with another, the victim can suffer long-lasting emotional scars. This is a topic that merits further inquiry.

Effects of Sibling Death

Because sibling relationships are part of the total family system, the death of a sibling has effects throughout the system. When sibling loss occurs in childhood and adolescence, parents often fail to communicate their feelings about the death, leaving sibling survivors without emotional support as they attempt to deal with their grief. In such cases, siblings can suffer lasting maladjustment. Because they are more mature, siblings are better able to cope with the loss of one of their group in adulthood and old age. However, siblings often function throughout adulthood as a potential source of help and emotional support, so that sibling loss can be keenly felt. Additionally, the death of a sibling can sever perhaps the only remaining link to the family system of their childhood and youth, and can force the survivors to deal with their own mortality.

Siblings and Psychotherapy

For those who have dysfunctional family relationships leading to maladaptive sibling relationships or to mental illness of one or more siblings, siblings can play an important role in psychotherapeutic treatment. In family therapy, the dynamics of the relationships within the family system can be explored and efforts made to influence the system. Including siblings in the therapy can frequently lead to a more rapid identification of problem areas, and sibling cooperation can be helping in effecting change in the system.

DEMOGRAPHIC CHANGES

The impact of siblings on one another may grow in the future given changing family patterns. Although current predictions are that future families will have fewer children, the number of single-parent families is increasing. Siblings will increase in importance in families where no second parent exists. Also, the number of reconstituted families formed by remarriage after one or more divorces is increasing rapidly, with concomitant increases in the number of half-, step- and adoptive siblings. A recent report using 1991 census data (Usdansky, 1994) indicated that approximately 14% of white and Hispanic children and 20% of black children live in such blended families. Major demographic changes of this type will have a profound impact on relationships within the total family and sibling relationships in particular. Another emerging trend with an impact on sibling relationships in adulthood is the increasing number of older people in the society. Responsibilities of caregiving for longer living parents will bring siblings closer together in midlife, especially if society cannot provide adequate community care for the increasing numbers of elderly.

CONCLUDING COMMENTS

In general, the thesis of this book is that siblings influence one another's characteristics, cognitive and personal–social behavior, development and aging, and adjustment as they influence and are influenced by the larger family system and external social context of which they are a part. This influence continues over the life span from childhood to old age.

As major topics of interest regarding siblings are considered throughout the book, various questions that have occupied researchers in this area will be examined. Among them are the following:

1. What is the meaning or nature of a sibling relationship? What are its important qualities? Are there different types of sibling relationships? Does the nature of sibling relationships change from childhood to adolescence to adulthood to old age?
2. What characteristics do siblings in the same family have in common? How are they different? What accounts for the commonalities and differences (in terms of genetic heritage and shared and nonshared environments)?
3. What are the changes in sibling characteristics (those common to siblings as well as those on which there are individual differences) over the life course? What accounts for these changes over time?
4. From the perspective of family systems theory, how do spousal or parent–child relationships influence the characteristics of siblings? How do they influence sibling relationships? In turn, how do sibling relationships influence other interpersonal relation-

ships within the family? How do the relationships between siblings influence relationships to peers?

5. How do sibling relationships influence siblings' behavior and development?

6. How does growing up with a sibling who is physically or mentally disabled, sick, or abusive influence a normal sibling? How does the relationship with normal siblings affect a sibling who is physically or mentally disabled, sick, or abusive? What is the course of the relationship over the life span?

7. Do close sibling relationships compensate for inadequate parent–child relationships?

8. What is the influence of a sibling's death on surviving siblings?

9. To what extent do siblings help one another, playing supportive roles, at various parts of the life span?

10. How do adult siblings function as a caregiving system to help care for aging parents?

11. How important are individuals' perceptions and interpretations of their relationships with siblings, parents, and other family members?

12. What explains the continuation of sibling relationships over the life span?

Before proceeding to take up such topics, a general perspective for sibling research will be discussed in Chapter 2, followed by a consideration of methodological issues in carrying out sibling research in Chapter 3.

CHAPTER 2

A Life Span Perspective
for Sibling Research

This chapter is an attempt to provide a framework for the purpose of guiding future sibling research. Obviously, each existing research study reported in this book has had its own rationale, whether based on some theoretical notion, or an inductive empirical approach.

A frame of reference or perspective is less broad than a metamodel but more general than a theory or model. It is useful in identifying and organizing the phenomena to be studied in a systematic manner. For example, the study of children is based on a certain perspective involving the concepts of birth and chronological age, and the idea that development increases or changes with age. Given birth as a reference point, one can count the number of years lived since birth, divide the time into segments, and label them as infancy, early childhood, and childhood. This allows the researcher to perceive and organize the data in a given field of research within some basic classification scheme as a starting point for carrying out future research studies. Another example using an opposite perspective should help make this more clear. One can take a different perspective involving the concept of death and the idea of decline as one moves closer to death. Given death as a reference point, one can establish a time scale of nearness to death by combining scores from average life expectancy tables with the weighting of other variables known to influence longevity to determine an individual score (such scores can eventually be validated by the actual death of the individual). One could then establish categories representing different degrees of nearness to death as a basis for classifying aging individuals in the process of late life decline. The researcher could then carry out studies to determine how adequately individuals function relative to their nearness to death. Such a perspective could conceivably be applied to study change in children and younger adults as well as in older adults. In summary, viewing individuals either in terms of increasing chronological age or increasing nearness to death provides a time framework within which data in developmental psychology can be organized for further investigation.

The author has formulated a perspective involving a collection of concepts that is hoped to be of value in guiding researchers' organization of data for sibling research. Concepts included in this perspective are discussed below.

LIFE SPAN TIME FRAME

The life span is the total time of an individual's life from conception to birth to death. A life span perspective is the longest possible time period from which to view siblings in order to understand their sibling relationships.

The total life span is the reference point from which to view and evaluate changes in sibling relationships, and it also allows one to interpret the significance of these relationships at different points in the life span. The interpretation of sibling relationships may be different at different time periods relative to any past behavior that may exist as well as projected future behavior. For example, suppose that two brothers have been very close during childhood, adolescence, and young adulthood. They have sacrificed for each other, helped each other get through college, and developed a thriving business together. Now in their early 40s, they are both happily married with children, and continue to enjoy each other's company. Gradually, they become bored with success, begin drinking, taking drugs, becoming more incompetent at work, having family conflicts, and finally their own relationship begins to deteriorate. They now have many conflicts, leading to hatred, and eventually dissolution of the relationship. For the next 40 years of their lives, they no longer speak to each other.

In contrast, suppose that two brothers have had a dysfunctional home life in their early upbringing, and until their early 40s, they had conflict and negative feelings for each other, rarely speaking or interacting. Finally, economic necessity brought them together in a family business, and for the first time, they made a real attempt to understand each other. Their positive feelings for each other grew, and for the next 40 years, they developed a strong and positive bonding for each other. The latter years of their lives are happy in terms of "brotherly love." The question becomes, Who had the most successful sibling relationships, the siblings with a positive relationship in the first 40 years of life, or the siblings with a positive relationship in the last 40 years of life? Obviously, a judgment has to be made. But without viewing their lives within a total time span, one may not have a sufficiently broad time perspective to consider all the factors that are significant in making such a judgment.

A life span time perspective has other advantages; for example, one can understand better the generation gap between siblings of different age spacing, one can be more sensitive to long-range effects of earlier experiences on sibling relationships. Also, by thinking analogically, one may perceive similarity of problems for siblings in different parts of the life span which will help to understand them. For example, conflicts in adolescent siblings may help understand conflicts in middle-aged siblings. In short, a life span time frame may have the heuristic value of better understanding sibling relationships by relating them to the past, and also their future possibilities.

DEVELOPMENT AND AGING

Development and aging are two concepts that have been difficult to define, either individually or in relation to each other. There are four basic ways in which the relationship of the two concepts can be conceptualized:

First, *development* and *aging* can be viewed as synonymous terms, although different approaches have been used. Both can be reduced to systematic rather than random change (Baltes, 1987), or to sustained learning (Kausler, 1991), or one can consider the concepts essentially synonymous but arbitrarily use the label *development* to represent change in the early part of the life span and *aging* to represent change in the latter part of the life span, considering the terms simply as labels identifying the location of change (Perlmutter, 1988).

Second, aging can be regarded as part of, or subsumed under, the more general concept of development. This is the position taken by various personality theorists who view aging as simply a name for qualitatively described stages of change in the latter part of the life span (Erikson, 1968).

Third, development and aging are viewed as relatively independent and distinct concepts. This view is the traditional biological approach to development and aging which has been extended to the psychological level by many psychologists. This view is represented in the cognitive area, as declines in cognitive functioning are demonstrated (Salthouse, 1991).

Fourth, the concept of development is viewed as part of the concept of aging. This view has been rarely promoted but it represents the author's viewpoint (Cicirelli, 1993c, in press). In actual use, by adopting multiple perspectives, the first and second conceptualizations are sometimes accepted simultaneously by certain researchers, whereas others appear to accept the third and fourth conceptualizations.

In regard to the third position, which considers development and aging as related but relatively distinct concepts of change, and employs different mechanisms to account for them, then aging change can be defined as decremental, deteriorative change in the individual, with decreasing potential over time to reverse such change, and with a concomitant decrease in adaptation to the environment. Extending this viewpoint further, the third position can be merged conceptually with the fourth to regard development as part of aging in an ultimate sense. In other words, death is the ultimate end point, and "healthy" development is merely a means of delaying the onset, duration, and rate of aging. This is not a pessimistic position or one in which plasticity is not possible. If one thinks of increasing life expectancies from ages in the 70s to the 80s and average life spans moving into the 90s (as indicated by Social Security Administration data), then it is possible to think of the present maximum life span of 120 eventually becoming more of a reality for many individuals. Thus, most individuals can expect a long life in which much improvement can occur before decline. Also, research has demonstrated that in certain dimensions or characteristics, individuals continue to develop well into their 60s and 70s, and both practitioners and researchers can now help older individuals restore some mental and physical functions at later ages. Even when certain key mental functions do decline (such as processing speed and fluid intelligence), occupational success and adaptation to everyday living may well continue into the 80s and 90s through the use of compensatory strategies and sustained motivation to achieve.

Although optimism regarding development can continue for many decades of life as a result of using various methods for retraining skills and reversing decline, eventually there is some threshold where decline becomes inevitable, irreversible, and universal, accompanied by a decrease in individual differences. Logically, if this were not the case, then no one would die except by accident, murder, or acute illness. However, the threshold of decline may occur later and later if life-styles change; it may be possible to delay the onset of decline until age 100, 110, or beyond. Eventually, there are limits to development, unless some form of genetic engineering in the next century is able to modify the biological foundations of life.

From such a perspective, the course of sibling relationships should be studied not only in terms of their formation and maintenance, or premature dissolution, but in terms of aging relationships in the latter part of the life span. Fundamental to the concept of relationship is some kind of interdependence between two individuals with each having some kind of impact on the other. With regard to relationships between elderly centenarians, this impact declines. There appears to be less contact, less thinking about the other, and less intensity of feelings for the other. The two individuals' frailty and lack of energy at an advanced age may lead toward an indifference toward each other. That is, like the two aging individuals themselves, the sibling relationship itself eventually goes through a process of aging and dying during which the relationship slowly fades away. (Such speculations are based on only a few case studies at this time.)

KINSHIP

Many researchers today think in terms of carrying out sibling research within the context of the family. Usually, sibling researchers conceptualize the family as a family system in which three subsystems exist: spouse-spouse, parent-child, and sibling-sibling. This particular breakdown of subsystems is based on the traditional, middle-class nuclear family which may not fit very well for many modern families, such as single-parent families, families with an only child but also a fictive sibling from the neighborhood, and minority families where cousins may be regarded as siblings. Even the concept of extended family does not seem sufficient to describe such cases. It may be more appropriate to use the concept of kinship, for the following reasons. Among younger parent cohorts, many reconstituted families exist due to the large number of divorces and remarriages in recent decades. This means that many families now include, in addition to children who are full biological siblings, children who are partial biological siblings (half-siblings), and children who have no biological relationship (stepsiblings and adoptive siblings). Sibship of the latter types usually involves continued connections to a biological parent who is now part of another reconstituted family (and possibly continued connections to siblings of the original family who are in the custody of the other parent).

When studying siblings in middle adulthood and old age, most are found to be married. In such cases, sibling relationships are likely to be influenced by spouses and various in-laws. Finally, sometimes more extended kin may need to be considered as part of the family system, such as grandparents, cousins, aunts, uncles, nieces, and nephews. In many families, some of these kin reside together or live in close proximity to the nuclear family and may be an important part of the family system; extended family groups tend to be more frequent in certain ethnic groups or certain types of countries. In short, siblings and sibling relationships may be better understood from the perspective of kinship than from the perspective of the nuclear family, especially among certain populations.

SIBLING CONSTELLATION

A sibling constellation is defined as a hierarchical network of sibling positions in the family that identifies the status of each sibling relative to other siblings within a family. The positions in the network are defined or determined in terms of the number of siblings (or size of the network), the birth order associated with each position, gender, age level (chronological age), and age spacing between siblings. Additionally, one might consider additional variables describing the sibling constellation such as the ratio of female to male siblings and the ratio of younger to older siblings, especially in large families where a wide age spacing separates two subsets of siblings.

Some researchers (e.g., G. Brody & Stoneman, 1990; Dunn, 1992; Lamb, 1982) have criticized earlier researchers' attempts to relate sibling structure variables to individual differences in sibling characteristics, pointing out that study findings have been moderate and inconsistent and do not reveal the processes leading to individual differences. These are legitimate criticisms but they are not a sufficient justification for ignoring the contribution that the sibling structure concept can make to sibling research. (Even the critics do not seem able to do without the use of such sibling structure variables as gender and relative age in their own research.) One or more sibling structure variables (such as birth order, relative age, and gender) have been used in many previous studies in an attempt to relate structure to individual differences in personality, behavior, achievement, and so on. As previously stated, study results have been weak and inconsistent, particularly those dealing with effects of birth order. One reason for inconsistent findings may be that most researchers have considered only one component at a time (such as birth order or age spacing) when carrying out such studies. When interactions of all the structural components are considered simultaneously, their relationship to sibling characteristics may be stronger and more consistent (e.g., Cicirelli, 1978). However, such an approach requires large samples in order to sample all the combinations of structural components and form appropriate subgroups for analysis. Obtaining such samples is not always easy to accomplish.

Beyond this, sibling structure variables can be used in explanatory research. This point can be illustrated with reference to chronological age.

As with sibling structure, most descriptive research with chronological age indicates weak or moderate relationships and inconsistent results. When age is included as a variable in explanatory studies, it is recognized that age in itself does not cause anything, but that age-related variables certainly do. Analogously, the researcher can think in terms of constellation-related variables that play a mediation role and can be used for explanatory purposes. The researcher may have certain expectations or hypotheses that constellation-related variables may mediate differences in sibling characteristics which in turn will influence sibling relationships. For example, even if only one component of sibling structure (for example, birth order) is used in sibling research involving a sample of children from different families, the researcher might hypothesize that certain expectancies or role enactments are associated with being the oldest or youngest sibling. This might then lead to a study to assess not just the direct effects of birth order but its indirect effects as siblings behave in a certain manner that fulfills others' expectations for a given birth order role. Sibling constellation variables could serve as exogenous variables in causal models linked to intervening variables which correlated highly with the dependent variable. In such a case, the sibling constellation may be viewed as having an indirect effect on the dependent variable, depending on the path coefficients that exist.

In general, sibling constellation variables might have greater use in descriptive research if all structural variables were included in the same study so that their interactive effects on the dependent variable could be determined. For explanatory research, they could be used in causal models along with constellation-related variables to determine their indirect effects. The point being stressed here is that they have not been given a sufficient test of their usefulness.

Above and beyond these considerations, constellation variables may be helpful simply to organize sibling data as a starting point for further research. The sibling constellation sets the stage for sibling subgroups to be considered in research studies.

STRUCTURE AND PROCESS

For many sibling researchers, process has become paramount in their research. Understanding process or the mechanisms underlying sibling relationships provides greater explanatory power and increases prediction as well as the possibility of control or intervention.

However, the author has a somewhat different viewpoint. Early in the life span, process seems to have priority over structure; that is, the processes underlying interactions between sibling dyads will influence dyad members' behavior and lead to the development of certain mental and personality characteristics. Later on, sibling interaction processes and structure have a reciprocal influence, with some kind of a balance between them. For example, existing mental characteristics modify sibling interactions, and the interactions in turn modify the mental characteristics. However, by old age the reciprocal influences of interaction and structure may no longer be in balance, but rather exist in an imbalance in which structure has priority over process. This does not mean that process no longer influences structure, but it may be highly imbalanced in favor of structure. Imagine if you can, both your spouse and yourself as being 95 years old and married for 70 long years. After such a long time period, each knows fairly well what to expect of the other, what the other is going to say and do. Similarly, after many years of interacting and communicating, the siblings' characteristics solidify, and may evoke stereotypic responses from one another during interactions; thus interaction has little likelihood of altering characteristics. Previous research (Cicirelli, 1993a) found such stereotypic responding between adult children and elderly parents; by analogy, the same would seem to apply to sibling relationships among elders who are in their 80s and 90s. In this sense, structure regulates process. Accordingly, researchers studying sibling relationships should view the reciprocal interaction between process and structure differently at different stages of the life span.

PERSON AND CONTEXT

The author has deliberately avoided referring to the "person in context" in the heading above. It seems that the person–context view of many researchers is extremely important, and is certainly becoming the dominant view in developmental psychology, especially given the popularity of life span developmental psychology (Baltes, 1987).

Perhaps the most important implication of such a view for studying sibling relationships is the usual statement that sibling relationships must be understood with the context of the family (or within certain extrafamilial contexts). When this statement is made, it implicitly assumes a particular meaning associated with the use of context (independent of the size, or boundaries to the context). The author also agrees with this viewpoint, but it may not be a sufficiently wide perspective. From a multiple-perspective viewpoint, they may best be studied at certain times within the family context or family system, but at other times, sibling relationships may best be studied in an additive combination with the influence of other family members, or even in a decontextualized situation. To make the author's position more clear, the reader is asked to follow his thinking in a brief digression.

Environment and context are sometimes used synonymously, but at the outset they need to be distinguished. Environment is defined as the surroundings that lie outside the boundary of the body skin and that have an impact on the individual. Context is the surroundings that lie outside the boundary of the psyche or mental functioning of the individual and have an impact on the latter. Context may include biochemical, physiological, and other levels of variables within the individual as well as those outside the individual. Context, either as synonymous with environment or distinct from it, is an aspect of all metamodels or world views: mechanism, organicism, and contextualism. Thus, context and contextualism are not the same, as sometimes presumed.

Contextualism as a world view itself needs to be subdivided into two subtypes: pure contextualism and quasi-contextualism. In pure contextualism, multilevels of systems or organized variables exist, ranging from the physiological level of the individual to the physical, social, cultural, and historical environment. The individual is viewed as a system made up of subsystems each with its own properties, and simultaneously part of a larger system at the same or a different level but now manifesting different properties. For example, an individual may show (or be perceived as showing) aggressive properties (or behavior) with his or her job supervisor but may show submissive properties or behavior (or be perceived as such) when functioning within the family system. Most important, a reciprocal interaction exists between variables at the same level and also between levels. This state of affairs results in such complex reciprocal interactions that the individual's behavior is unique from moment to moment; that is, it is not predictable or reproducible (Cicirelli, 1993b; Ford & Lerner, 1992). At the present time, this world view cannot serve as a metaphor for the scientific study of human behavior. From the perspective of pure contextualism, one cannot state that the study of sibling relationships must be carried out within the family context. For now, pure contextualism may be quite suitable for describing certain phenomena, using case studies carried out on a post hoc basis (for example, reconstructing the damage of a hurricane as a result of the unpredictable reciprocal interactions of many variables). Perhaps pure contextualism could serve someday as a metaphor for chaos theory, if it turns out that there is not always an underlying determinism to the indeterminism.

Quasi-contextualism (Cicirelli, 1993b) is the term applied by the author to the world view that many researchers call contextualism. It is what Ford and Lerner (1992) call partial contextualism. In quasi-contextualism, change takes place, but the existing or ongoing organization of the individual system limits the degree of novelty or uniqueness that can occur. If it were otherwise, there would be no continuity to the system. In quasi-contextualism, a degree of reproducibility exists, and the laws of probability can be used to achieve some degree of predictability. Thus, sibling relationships should be studied within the context of family not only to be understood as part of a larger system, but to understand the degree of probability that the same sibling relationships will occur in that ongoing organized system.

Context considered from the world view of organicism is more synonymous with the environment. It is separate from the boundary skin of the individual, and is passive in its effect on the individual. Instead the individual actively uses or modifies the passive context. The individual is the active system, with reciprocal interactions between subsystems within the skin of his or her own body, using input from the environment as needed for behavior and development. In this case, studying sibling relationships within the context of the family could also occur. However, the context consisting of other family members is not seen as active but simply provides resources as needed by the siblings. This situation could be illustrated with adult siblings who interact with each other in the family context of submissive and noncaring parents who communicate or interact very little with the siblings except to provide resources if requested.

The ongoing organization within the individual also includes a developing or mature ego which attains autonomy or integration (Loevinger, 1976). An individual who reaches the high level of maturity (a strong ego) which leads to greater autonomy will transcend the surroundings, and tend to control or regulate the network of relations of which he or she is a part.

Context in the mechanistic world view is also synonymous with the environment and independent of the individual. In contrast, however, the environment is viewed as active, acting on a passive individual. (Passive here does not mean inert, but means that regardless of brain or intrapsychic activity, the individual is ultimately controlled by the environment.) In the mechanist view, sibling relationships could be studied within the context of the family but there would not be a reciprocal interaction. The sibling relationship would be molded and shaped by the dominance of the parents.

Many psychologists have felt that the major metamodels are mutually exclusive, and cannot be combined or integrated in any fashion without destroying the unique meanings or assumptions about the world and man inherent in each model. However, such world views are based on defining basic concepts as mutually exclusive in the tradition of Aristotelian logic

(Pepper, 1942). It would seem, though, that basic concepts do not have to be defined in the traditional sense of representing either this or that. Arguments using dialectical logic (Riegel, 1979), fuzzy logic (McNeill & Freiberger, 1993), and prototype concept (Kausler, 1991) have made it clear that individuals do not necessarily think and deal with conjunctive concepts only. A concept can be defined that includes opposites, such as a disjunctive concept. Therefore, these newer notions of concepts allow one to define a metaphor involving alternate viewpoints. For example, one might think of a world view of mechanistic-organicism in which both apply to phenomena, either simultaneously or in sequence. This seems to be the case with Freudianism and information theories, as neither can be derived in clear-cut fashion from either metamodel alone. One also might think of mechanism and organicism as being integrated under a larger more complex category, and conceived as variants of contextualism. Or, another possibility is a mechanistic-quasi-contextualism world view. For example, researchers have carried out studies demonstrating the effects on a dependent variable of both individual and contextual variables (including cultural variables) and their interactions. In this sense, both types of variables and their interactions involve linear causality and are antecedent to the effect. However, these variables and their statistical interactions with contextual variables are antecedent to the effect on the dependent variable, and involve one-way or linear causality. The use of recursive path analysis with many complex relations between individual and contextual variables would be an example of this approach. (If nonrecursive path analysis were used, one then might have an example of a quasi-contextualist approach.) Such research is not justified by either a mechanistic or quasi-contextualist metaphor alone, although it is sometimes mistaken for a contextualist approach. It is what the author would call a mixed metaphor, that is, a mechanistic-quasi-contextualism.

The author's own metamodel has been labeled organistic quasi-contextualism. Basic to this metaphor is the sequential applicability of world views to different parts of the life span, from organicism to quasi-contextualism and again back to organicism. At certain threshold points in the time dimension, different metamodels in the sequence are evoked, requiring a shift in perspective by the researcher. In this viewpoint, the world views are still mutually exclusive but, given the total time span of the individual's life, they are integrated in a fixed sequence with overlapping at threshold points where shifts in world views occur. It is the author's view that until late childhood or early adolescence, the organicist metamodel is most appropriate with its emphasis on genetic–maturational factors. When a certain biological threshold of growth is reached, certain genes are "turned off" and quasi-contextualism emerges as the most appropriate world view until late in life (approximately 85 years of age), when genetic–maturational factors emerge to control senescence. At this threshold point, organicism again becomes the dominant metamodel for this segment of the life span (Cicirelli, 1993b). This metamodel is an integration of a unidirectional and irreversible programmed theory of development and aging derived from organicism with a multidirectional and reversible approach to development and aging derived from quasi-contextualism. Such an approach will lead to different research questions in different parts of the life span.

PARTIAL SYSTEMS

A system consists of various components which interact with each other in a reciprocal manner. When one component is disturbed, it will affect other components, which in turn affect still others in a reciprocal manner. There are direct reciprocal interactions between components, and also feedback loops indirectly affecting various other components.

Different types of systems exist. A basic distinction is between closed systems and open systems. Also, there are subtypes of closed and open systems (e.g., a homeostatic system is a closed system derived from an organicist metamodel; a chaos system is an open system which might be derived from a quasi-contextualistic metamodel).

The author conceptualizes a subtype of open system called a hierarchical semiautonomous system. In this system, all the components do not have equal status. For example, if the body is a system, and a leg is amputated, the system will reorganize itself but continue to function. However, if the brain is destroyed, the system will collapse. By analogy, in a young family, a sibling may die but the family will reorganize itself and continue to function. But if the mother and father die, the family will be destroyed; the siblings will be dispersed to live with others. In short, some components of the system are more important than others for the survival of the system.

The system is semiautonomous because all the parts may not always interact in a reciprocal manner or with feedback loops, or because the effect of one component may be so weak or delayed in its feedback that for all practical purposes it is nonfunctional in the given situation. For example, there may be five siblings in a system, with four of them involved in continuing communication regarding some issue, totally ignoring the fifth sibling. When the fifth sibling attempts to communicate, he or she is ignored. Even the presence of the fifth sibling has no particular effect at the moment. In this case, the family has not reorganized or shifted boundaries; all the siblings are still part of the system. But the system may be operating temporarily as if one sibling is absent or nonexistent.

If hierarchical and partially autonomous open systems exist, then there may be times when sibships of more than two siblings develop varied relationship patterns. For example, if a sibling subsystem composed of three siblings is hierarchical in nature, then it may function as a triadic sibling relationship only when sibling A is present or involved. If only sibling A is not present, B and C have no impact on each other. Or, if the system is partially autonomous, then sibling C's behavior may have no effect on the system (be functionally nonexistent) at times, only to emerge as part of the subsystem periodically in different situations. Thus, the sibling triad's relationship may vacillate between different interactions or patterns.

Also, the concept of hierarchical and semiautonomous systems can apply to sibling relationships within the context of the total family. For example, the father in the family may be so dominant that sibling relationships between an older sibling dyad may be totally shaped by him, with the mother and other children having little influence. A semiautonomous family can exist where there is little or no interaction or communication between an older sibling dyad and the parents and other children. In this case, the older sibling dyad functions as a sibling relationship but not as a functioning component interacting reciprocally with other parts of the total family system.

A PERSPECTIVE FOR SIBLING RESEARCH

In summary, studying sibling relationships within the context of the family may be more fruitful if the researcher considers a perspective that includes a life span time perspective, involves both development and aging during the course of the life span, considers relationships within wider kinship systems as well as within the nuclear family, and considers partial family systems as well as the entire family system. The researcher needs to consider interactions of sibling constellation variables, and regards the balance between structure and process changing over the life span (e.g., process predominating over structure early in the life span, an approximate reciprocal balance between structure and process in the middle part of the life span, and structure regulating process in the latter part of the life span).

CHAPTER 3

Methodological Approaches and Issues in Studying Siblings

A major aim of the present chapter is to acquaint the reader with some of the methodological difficulties inherent in undertaking studies of siblings and their relationships.

IDENTIFYING SIBLING POPULATIONS AND SELECTING SAMPLES

On the surface it would appear to be a simple matter to identify a population of siblings for study and to draw a sample from this population. On more careful consideration, however, the researcher must give serious thought to just how siblings and sibling characteristics (e.g., family size) should be defined and delimited for purposes of the study (see Chapter 6 for a discussion of the differing definitions of siblings in other cultures). In the past, most sibling studies involved only full biological siblings residing with both parents, although some studies included half-siblings, stepsiblings, and adoptive siblings.

Changes over time in the family size distribution of different age cohorts (as well as the distribution of birth orders, age spacing, and gender combinations) in the population may also be of concern for researchers. Eggebeen (1992) examined census data for five cohorts of black and white children from 1940 to 1980. Successive cohorts showed a rise in the number of siblings from 1940 through the 1950s, followed by sharp declines through the 1960s and 1970s. Proportions of firstborn and only children increased through 1980; there were changes in distributions of gender composition as well. Researchers in the future may find relatively few larger families. Such considerations affect researchers wishing to compare sibling relationships across the life span, particularly if dyads have been sampled without regard to sibship size.

Full Siblings

A first question in carrying out studies of full siblings is who should be included as a sibling. For instance, supposing that the biological parents have their two children who are full siblings residing at home with them, but as teenagers they had another child which was given up for adoption and never seen again. Should this child be regarded as a sibling; is this a two-child or a three-child family? Similarly, is a fetus which miscarried or which died in the birth process to be regarded as a sibling? Most researchers would not so regard it, but Leon (1990) has shown that perinatal sibling loss of this type can have a negative effect on the remaining siblings in the family (see Chapter 13). If a sibling in a three-child family died at some point after birth, are the remaining siblings to be included in a study of two-child families? Alternatively, if a sibling has resided with someone else since the early years (such as a grandmother), but is known by other siblings residing with the parents, should this sibling be included for study? Researchers employing strict criteria would limit study populations of siblings to full biological siblings living (or reared) in nuclear families with the parents married to each other. However, only 56% of children now live in traditional nuclear families of this sort (Usdansky, 1994). On the other hand, some researchers define siblings very loosely, using only the criterion that a sibling pair have the same biological parents. Whether they live with a single parent, or in split custody or other living arrangements, or have other types of siblings, may be excluded from consideration.

Half-Siblings, Stepsiblings, and Adoptive Siblings

Because prevalence of these sibling types is increasing, sibling researchers are beginning to show an interest in studying the interactions between them. Overall, some 14% of American children now live in blended families (Usdansky, 1994).

Beer (1989) has pointed out the methodological complexities involved in studying stepfamilies. He identified eight different types of remarriages (based on whether a single, widowed, or divorced man married a single, divorced, or widowed woman, and excluding the new marriage of two singles). For each of these remarriage types there are three possible types of parent–child patterns (he brings his children to the marriage, she brings her children to the marriage, and both bring children to the marriage), making 24 stepfamily types in all. Should further children be born into such a remarriage, the half-sibling relationships complicate the picture still further, as does the presence of adopted children. Additionally, questions of whether these half-siblings and stepsiblings have lived together and for how long bring further complexities. When serial marriages take place, the possibilities are staggering. Whether or not siblings remain together through divorces and remarriages or are separated in split custody arrangements can have an important effect on the sibling relationship. Beer regards these blended families as "a process with a changing cast of characters living in a household at any one time" (p. 9). Thus, the membership boundaries of blended families are not very clear. At present, there are no guidelines for researchers attempting stepsibling research. The researcher must decide whether to restrict the study to only certain types of stepsibling or half-sibling relationships or to allow all the possible family structure configurations to freely vary. Those who have studied blended families usually attempt to set up some operational criteria for which sibling dyads should be included.

Reiss et al. (1994) discussed the difficulties of sampling from such a population. They wanted to study stepsiblings and half-siblings in families with at least two children of the same gender between the ages of 10 and 18 who had an age spacing of no more than 4 years; in addition, the children were to reside in a stepfamily where the duration of the remarriage was at least 5 years. Using a U. S. Census survey of 63,000 families that provided the needed family information, only .05% met these researchers' criteria for stepsiblings and only .1% met the criteria for half-siblings. (Ultimately these researchers abandoned any thought of representative sampling for cost considerations, and obtained a sample by approximate methods in other ways.)

Limiting studies to full siblings may be justified to some extent with the present older cohort since divorce and remarriage was not so common during the period in which they were reared. However, as demographic changes continue in our society, studying only full siblings not only may become a more serious sampling problem in the future, but may become less relevant to understanding all types of siblings as socializing and helping agents across the life span.

Sampling Sibling Structure Variables

As noted earlier, each sibling has a given status position in the sibling constellation of the family, defined for each sibling by number of siblings and birth order, gender, and age spacing from other siblings.

In planning a study, researchers have several choices of how to handle these variables. Most use one or more structure variables as a criterion for sampling. If sibling dyads are to be studied, researchers typically specify an age or age range (or school grade level) for the selection of one sibling and then select another on the basis of relative age or within a given age spacing. Gender of each sibling can also be considered in sampling or else used as a classification variables for analysis. If a target child at a given age level is selected for study, the researcher needs to decide whether to select dyads consisting of the target child and an older sibling, the target child and a younger sibling, or to include both. Sutton-Smith and Rosenberg (1970) pointed out that, where one child is of a given age, there are eight distinct sibling dyad configurations possible in a two-child family, considering gender of each child and relative age (older, younger) of the sibling with respect to the target child: first grade boy with older brother, first grade boy with older sister, first grade girl with older brother, first grade girl with older sister, first grade boy with younger brother, first grade boy with younger sister, first grade girl with younger brother, and first grade girl with younger sister. If this seems like a tedious enumeration, the reader is reminded that the family environment for the first grade child is different in each case. Koch (1954, 1955, 1956) carried out studies sampling children from each of the eight subgroups, and Sutton-Smith and Rosenberg studied the 24 possible subgroups of the three-child family. The number of possible subgroups goes up geometrically as family size increases. Small wonder that many researchers choose to study only dyads in the two-child family, and others sample dyads based on only a few criteria of sibling structure and allow other structural variables to vary freely or measure them for use in data analysis.

Unfinished and Incomplete Sibships

There are two other concerns for researchers studying siblings. The first, the question of unfinished sibships, applies primarily to young children. At the time when a sibling dyad is selected for study, especially from a small family, the parents may or may not have the intention of having other children. Often, if two daughters are born first, parents wish to keep trying for a boy. Some parents have the intention of having a large family from the outset of their marriage. Thus, these sibships are viewed as unfinished. It can be argued that parenting styles will be different in these unfinished sibships than in cases where the parents view the sibship as finished or complete. Obviously, additional children could be born in either case. However, interested researchers might assess parents' intentions regarding further children and determine their effect in analysis.

The second concern is the question of sibships that are incomplete by virtue of the death of one or more of the siblings. Although such sibships are found throughout the life span, they are more prevalent in adulthood and old age. Particularly when studying sibling relationships in old age, the problem is whether it is possible to find sufficient samples of siblings from complete sibships to carry out a study.

The prevalence of incomplete sibling sets can be a serious problem in studies of older adults, as not all members of a sibling set survive from childhood on. (If study findings are to be used for comparison with findings obtained from complete sibships at younger ages, this can be an important consideration.) Most individuals in the mid-old (ages 75–84) and old-old (ages 85 and older) groups have experienced the death of some members of their sibling set. It is also true that a greater percentage of deceased siblings of older people are men, so that if one studies sibling relationships in very late life, one may be studying the relationship between sisters who are the remaining members of their sibling sets.

Another concern centers on practical reasons for the paucity of sibling studies in middle and old age, and the resulting limitations on sample representativeness. Sibling research in infancy, childhood, and adolescence is easier to do as it typically is carried out either within the nuclear family setting or within school environments, making possible observation studies of face-to-face interaction, laboratory or field experiments, and longitudinal studies under stable conditions. However, in the latter part of the life span, siblings no longer live in the same household as they did in childhood and adolescence, making it not only more difficult to identify sibling pairs and to contact them, but also to bring them together to participate in any research project. One or both members of a sibling pair may be unwilling to participate, finding it threatening to reveal any information regarding themselves in relation to their sibling, feeling that such research is an invasion of their privacy, or holding antiresearch attitudes. In the case of elderly siblings, some may be too ill, frail, or immobile to participate. Even if willing to participate, scheduling problems may be insurmountable. Such problems not only limit recruiting of samples but the types of data collection and research design that can be used, particularly in longitudinal studies. Observational studies or laboratory or field experiments may be totally unfeasible, forcing the researcher to depend upon interviews or questionnaires.

As a result, the process of building up a body of knowledge about sibling relationships in middle and old age has been slower and has resulted in serious gaps. One consequence of the many limitations on research is the continuing need to simply establish the existence of certain phenomena in regard to sibling relations in middle and old age, further delaying the formulation of any theory regarding sibling relationships.

An emerging problem for the study of middle-aged siblings of the baby boomer cohort (and for the study of elderly siblings in the future) will be finding sufficient samples of full siblings reared in intact nuclear families to further develop the body of knowledge concerned with full siblings. Limiting studies to full siblings can be justified with the present older cohort since parental divorce and remarriage were not so common during the period in which they were reared. Given the divorce and remarriage rates of recent decades, the norm is slowly shifting to families composed of half-siblings, stepsiblings, adoptive siblings, and fictive siblings. In the future, studies involving only full siblings may become less important than those involving all types of siblings as socializing and helping agents across the life span.

Which Sibling Dyad Should Be Selected for Analysis?

Sometimes researchers collect interview or self-report data from a given sibling (or target sibling) with regard to relationships with all the siblings in the family, regardless of sibship size, but select only one relationship for analysis. Alternatively, they may obtain data regarding the target sibling's relationship with just one sibling in the family regardless of birth order or gender. Such research designs tend to appear in studies of older families, where there is a large range of sibship sizes, the sibships are incomplete, and some sibling dyads are geographically separated. It is not possible to apply selection criteria based on structural variables consistently when surviving sibling sets are incomplete. Methodological problems arise in each case.

One problem concerns the case where data are obtained regarding a target sibling's relationship with all other siblings in the family. (Thus, an individual from a five-child family would report on his or her relationship with each of four siblings.) If the researcher wished to use data regarding all the dyads in data analysis (e.g., data from 80 interviewees reporting on 240 sibling dyads), clearly the dyads would not be independent. Furthermore, subjects with different numbers of siblings would be unequally represented in the overall data set. No good solution to this dilemma exists. One possible solution is to construct an average score representing the target sibling's relationship with all siblings in the family, or with all siblings of a given sex (Cicirelli, 1989a). However, if there is a large variation in the scores pertaining to the various siblings in a family, the use of an average score would be conceptually misleading. (Further, if an average relationship score is taken as the unit of analysis, the "average" would have a larger variance in small families than in large ones.) Another approach is to select only one of the target sibling's brothers or sisters for the study, such as the firstborn, the closest in age, the geographically closest, or the one to whom the target sibling is affectionally closest. A variant on this approach is to randomly sample only one of the target sibling's siblings for use in analysis. This is probably the best approach, but the sample tends to overrepresent firstborn and second-born siblings. The author has compared data from the same group of target siblings regarding their sibling relationships, with one analysis using the random selection method and the other using data obtained regarding the target child's relationship to the affectionally closest sibling, and found that results did not differ appreciably. (Problems and approaches involved in selecting one dyad per family for study *before* gathering data are similar.)

Selecting Siblings from Special Populations

Special problems arise when researchers wish to study sibling relationships in special groups: families with an ill, disabled, or mentally retarded sibling; families with abusive siblings; families with incestuous siblings; families with a mentally ill sibling; and families where a sibling has died. Most of these conditions are relatively infrequent, except for death of siblings in later adulthood and old age. Researchers who would like to specify certain sibling structure characteristics as criteria for inclusion in a sample from such populations, typically find that to do so might make a sufficiently large sample for study extremely difficult to find. Even with relaxed sampling criteria, researchers often have to resort to opportunistic rather than random sampling methods, obtaining samples through special interest groups (such as Compassionate Friends to locate children who have lost siblings through death), hospitals and clinics (for mental and physical illness and disability), courts (for physical and sexual abuse), and so on. Most researchers realize that the samples are far from ideal, but the value of the information obtained is judged to be worth some sacrifice in quality of sampling methods.

Design and Sampling Considerations in Studies of Shared and Nonshared Environments

The classic twin studies used to determine the relative contributions of genetic similarity and the environment to the explanation of individual differences in sibling characteristics are well known to most developmental psychologists (e.g., Scarr & Grajek, 1982). In these studies, differences in characteristics of pairs of monozygotic and dizygotic twins were compared with those of pairs of nontwin siblings and with unrelated pairs of children.

More recent studies have enlarged this design in order to examine the contribution of shared and nonshared environments to explaining individual differences above and beyond genetic similarity (e.g., Reiss et al., 1994). By considering siblings from three types of families involving different degrees of shared environments (stepfamilies with no twins, nonstepfamilies with no twins, and nonstepfamilies with twins), these researchers were able to identify four levels of genetic similarity. "Blended" stepsiblings from stepfamilies had 0% genetic similarity; half-siblings from stepfamilies had 25%; full siblings from stepfamilies, full siblings from nonstepfamilies, and dizygotic twins from non-stepfamilies had 50%; and monozygotic twins from non-stepfamilies, 100%). Problems involved in locating samples of stepsiblings and half-siblings in the study by Reiss et al. have already been discussed. It should be noted, however, that in order to sample siblings of the given types, other family structure criteria had to be ignored (family size, birth order, gender) or relaxed somewhat (age and age spacing). (Methods of measurement and data analysis will not be discussed here; the interested reader is referred to Reiss et al., as well as to Deal, Halverson, and Wampler, 1994 and Rovine, 1994).

METHODS OF DATA COLLECTION

A variety of methods for collecting data about sibling relationships are at the disposal of the sibling researcher, among them experiments, observations, interviews and questionnaires, and ethnographic methods. Each has advantages and disadvantages, and each may yield only partial information. Different methods may also differ in reliability and validity; for example, Dunn, Stocker, and Plomin (1990a) found greater test–retest reliability for maternal interview data than for either of two types of observational measures. Certainly more studies of this type are needed. To gain a more complete picture, many studies use two or more methods. For example, a given study of school-aged siblings might combine administration of tests or self-report instruments with interviews, and observations of sibling interactions.

Experiments

Less use has been made of experiments involving siblings than of such methods as observation, interview, and administration of test instruments. However, experiments have been used in studies of sibling teaching (e.g., Azmitas & Hesser, 1993; Cicirelli, 1972, 1973, 1974). In these studies, the learning of some particular information or skill by a child when taught by an older sibling is compared with the learning of a child taught by an older peer; a measure of task achievement is used as the dependent variable. Typically, observations of the interactions of older and younger siblings and of child and peer while working on the learning task are also used. Experiments are useful to establish the unique influence of siblings on one another (as compared to a peer or other family member).

Tests and Self-Report Instruments

A variety of tests, self-report, and rating instruments are available for use in obtaining information about sibling and family relationships and sibling interactions; for example, the Sibling Relationship Questionnaire (Furman & Buhrmester, 1985), or the Conflict Tactics Scale (Straus, 1979). Depending on their reliability and validity, such instruments can be very useful to assess aspects of relationships not easily examined by other methods. A drawback of such instruments is that the perspective of only one family member is obtained unless the researcher administers the instrument to both members of the dyad in a given relationship. In some studies, a parent is asked to respond concerning the relationship of young siblings, which can introduce error as well as bias into the data. A parent may be unaware of aspects of the siblings' relationship, or may perceive events either more positively or more negatively than is actually the case. For instance, McHale and Gamble (1989) found that mothers rated warmth and aggression in siblings' interactions more positively than observational data indicated.

Interviews and Questionnaires

Perhaps the most frequently used methods of obtaining information about sibling relationships are interviews and questionnaires. In both cases, either structured or open-end questions may be used; administration of self-report instruments can be incorporated within the interview schedule or questionnaire as well. Face-to-face interviewing is costlier than use of questionnaires, but offers the researcher the advantage of being able to probe to obtain complete information where needed and to resolve any ambiguity or misunderstanding of a question by a respondent. (For some cases, telephone interviews can be used and are less costly.) Also, interview is more appropriate for use with young children who are unable to read or to read well enough to complete a questionnaire, as well as for older people who have poor vision, hearing problems, or inability to write. In some cases, anonymous questionnaires may be more appropriate if the researchers wish to probe siblings' interactions with regard to some sensitive topic, such as sexual behavior or drug use.

Observations

Observational methods are often used in studies of sibling and parent–child interactions, so that researchers can obtain evidence about ongoing family processes. Two types of observation studies are often carried out with siblings: Observations of interaction behaviors in relation to a structured task, and observations of spontaneous interactions in the home setting. However, a number of important methodological problems exist.

Observations of a structured task (such as young siblings working on a task with building blocks, or adolescent siblings discussing a particular topic) may elicit particular behaviors of a desired type. However, they tend to lack ecological validity whether carried out in the laboratory or at home. On the other hand, if observers of spontaneous interactions sample only a brief period of behavior, sibling behavior in this interval may not be typical. The researcher runs the risk of observing no sibling interactions at all during a single observation period or observing an intense interaction that rarely occurs. With either type of observation method, researchers face the problem of choosing how many periods of behavior to observe and for how long a time. Regarding observations of spontaneous interactions at home, the time of day tends to be linked to particular types of family behaviors. For example, observations during early morning periods when children are getting ready for school may elicit different types of interactions than an after-school play period or the dinner hour. Observers who schedule many sessions usually try to schedule them at different times to sample as wide a variety of behaviors as possible. Similarly, researchers using structured tasks may sample additional types of tasks, or carry out the observations in several settings (such as laboratory, home, school, or playground).

In the abstract, researchers would like to sample a large number of occasions and settings in order to get valid and reliable data. However, cost is a major limiting factor to the number of observations that can be carried out, including the cost of the observation sessions themselves as well as the cost of data coding and analysis. A second limiting factor is whether participants are willing to undergo more than a few observation sessions.

A second methodological problem connected with sibling and family observations concerns the reactivity of the observations, that is, whether the presence of the observer changes the behavior to be observed. Studies that have compared relatively unobtrusive observational methods with more obtrusive methods have usually not found differences, and have concluded that reactivity is not a problem. However, there is no easy way of knowing whether or not there might have been reactivity with both methods. A recent study by Jacob, Tennenbaum, Seilhamer, Bargiel, and Sharon (1994) investigated reactivity in home observations of parents and children aged 10 to 18 by comparing a highly salient method of having the family activate a tape recorder during the dinner hour with a highly unobtrusive method of having tape recorders stationed at various places in the home activate at random times (they analyzed dinnertime interactions in both conditions). In addition, they investigated the hypothesis that reactivity in distressed families would differ from that in normal families by comparing three groups: normal families, families with an alcoholic father, and families with a depressed father. They coded behavioral exchanges from one family member to another (mother to father, father to mother, mother to child, child to mother, child to child, etc.) as positive, negative, or information sharing. Only 2 of the 28 ANOVAs conducted showed a significant difference between the salient and unobtrusive observation conditions, and both involved exchanges between the parents. Only 1 ANOVA (for positive exchanges from mother to child) showed a significant interaction between observation condition and distress group such that mothers in the depression group showed more positive exchanges to the child than mothers in the alcoholic and nondistressed groups in the salient observation condition, and less positive exchanges than the other two groups in the unobtrusive condition. On the basis of the findings of Jacob et al., it does not appear that reactivity is a major problem, and certainly not for interactions between young siblings. However, to be sure of obtaining a truly unobtrusive observation, one would need to use a hidden microphone or videorecorder, a method obviously unethical for researchers.

Finally, there may be difficulty in interpreting the meaning of observational data. A given behavioral exchange may have different meanings for the researcher and for the siblings involved. For example, the researcher may observe a boy hitting his younger brother on the arm and interpret it as aggression, the boy may interpret it as a sign of camaraderie, and the younger brother may interpret it as part of a history of abuse. Thus, researchers must be very careful to examine discrete observations in the context of the overall patterns in the relationship when making interpretations.

Ethnographic Methods

Probably the greatest use of ethnographic methods is in cross-cultural research into sibling relationships, where the researcher is interested in learning about aspects of the culture that may affect sibling relationships, as well as about the relationships themselves (see Chapter 6). In addition to observation of sibling dyads and families, and interviews with family members, ethnographers consult elders in the society, government agencies, and written materials as appropriate. It is a very broad approach, and takes a great deal of skill to isolate major themes of sibling relationships within a given culture. The researcher must be sure that the meaning and interpretation he or she attaches to given behaviors noted in a particular culture is the meaning and interpretation attached to the behavior by residents indigenous to that culture.

Other Methods

Additional methods that can be used for the study of sibling relationships include guided reminiscence with sibling dyads, autobiographical records, clinical records, and case histories.

SOURCES OF SIBLING DATA

In most cases, the primary and best source of information about the relationship between two or more siblings comes from the siblings themselves. However, when children are very young, parents (typically mothers) are usually interviewed because the children cannot provide needed information themselves; occasionally older siblings are interviewed. In addition, information is sometimes obtained from other family members and relatives, teachers, doctors and other professionals, and peers. (Of course, direct observations can be used whatever the age of the siblings.)

Studies of sibling relationships in adulthood and old age sometimes obtain information from parents (when siblings are geographically distant), spouses (see Chapter 7), adult children, or from doctors and other professionals.

Each source of information has certain methodological drawbacks. As a source of interview data, siblings themselves may be too immature, lacking in insight, or too inarticulate to be able to provide more introspective sorts of data about feelings, motives, and the like. Parents and older siblings can provide their own perspectives on a given sibling relationship, but they may be unaware of many events occurring between the siblings. Further, their interpretation of the relationship may be biased by social desirability considerations, by gender bias, by favoritism for one child, or perhaps by scapegoating of another child. Teachers, doctors, and other professionals usually see siblings only in a limited context. Peers, particularly in adulthood, may not know both siblings well enough to respond about their relationship.

Types of Sibling Relationship Information and Associated Problems

Depending somewhat on the source of data about sibling relationships, three different types of information are obtained: information about overt behaviors, information about covert characteristics of siblings or the sibling relationship, and retrospective information about earlier aspects of the relationship.

Information about overt behaviors comes primarily from observational studies of ongoing behaviors of siblings. (Questions regarding the number and length of observations and the observation settings have already been discussed.) In addition, researchers must decide which behaviors to observe, which behaviors to code for analysis, what constitutes a unit of behavior, and whether to consider behaviors as independent or as a related sequence of events (for example, sibling A does something, sibling B does something next, and so on). Contingencies involved in sequences of behaviors are more difficult to analyze but provide fuller information about the relationship. Another approach is to use trained judges to rate observation protocols (or videotapes) on more general qualities of sibling interactions; such judgments can be somewhat subjective, however, unless criteria are objectively defined.

Information about covert aspects of siblings or of the sibling relationship, such as feelings or attitudes about the sibling or the relationship, typically comes from interview data or use of self-report instruments and is subjective in nature. For information about the sibling relationship, data ideally should be gathered from both siblings in a dyad so that the perspectives of both can be compared to determine to what extent there is congruence of views and where mismatched perceptions occur. Mismatches are relatively common and are of interest to detect. Various means of handling dyadic data (difference scores, a total dyad score, etc.) need to be considered, depending on the purpose of the analysis.

The third type of information consists of retrospective reports, typically obtained in interviews with one sibling or a parent. Retrospective data about sibling relationships suffers from the same problems of all retrospective data: memory problems and subjective interpretations. Of course, the more objective the events being reported, the more reliable it is likely to be. One means of improving on retrospective data is to obtain information from both siblings in a dyad (and perhaps from a parent as well), so that memories can be cross-checked and differences in perspective noted.

CONCLUSION

It has not been possible to touch on all methodological issues involved in sibling research here. Rather the aim has been to make the researcher beginning to work in this area aware of some of the issues and problems so that some pitfalls can be avoided. It is clear that in most cases not every sibling structure variable can be assessed or controlled. In research studies, the most that can be done is to specify carefully the conditions under which a sibling sample was obtained, the characteristics of the sample, and the reasons for the choices of measures and data gathering methods used. In addition, when interpreting findings, the researcher and reader of such research must bear in mind the possible effects of uncontrolled and unassessed sibling structure variables through their effects on nonshared environmental conditions such as differential parenting and social role expectancies.

CHAPTER 4

Siblings in Childhood and Adolescence

Studying sibling relationships in the first portion of the life span is important, whether they are studied in infancy, early childhood, childhood, or adolescence. Siblings can be major influences in one another's lives because each sibling lives in an environment which is different by virtue of the influence of the other siblings as well as that of various other family and extrafamilial factors.

In the present chapter, two major questions will be explored: How do relationships between siblings develop and how do they change over time through childhood and adolescence? What accounts for individual differences between siblings and their relationships?

DEVELOPMENTAL CHANGES IN SIBLING RELATIONSHIPS

Every relationship has a formation phase, a maintenance phase, and a dissolution phase. The sibling relationship is no exception. It begins in early childhood, and continues to grow and change throughout childhood and adolescence until it reaches a maintenance phase in early adulthood once the siblings are launched as independent adults. Under normal circumstances, the sibling relationship does not undergo either maintenance or dissolution in childhood and adolescence. In this chapter, therefore, we will examine only the formation phase, beginning with the initiation of the relationship and tracing its growth through adolescence.

Formation of the Sibling Relationship in Early Childhood

A sibling relationship begins when one sibling first becomes aware of the existence of the other. Usually this occurs at birth when the older sibling first comes into contact with the younger sibling, but in many cases the mother begins preparing the older sibling for the arrival of the younger one at some point in her pregnancy (Dunn & Kendrick, 1982b). For some children, the birth of a younger sibling is a shock and they have a difficult period of adjustment. However, Dunn and Kendrick found that the adjustment was easier if the older sibling was prepared for the event in advance.

Dunn and Kendrick (1982a, 1982b, 1982c) observed sibling pairs from the birth of the younger, when the older sibling was between 18 months and 2 years of age, until the younger sibling was 14 months of age. Although there was considerable variability in the reactions of the siblings to each other, and some behaviors were negative, there was evidence of positive behaviors and feelings. They observed warm and affectionate behavior of the older sibling toward the younger sibling (55% of the older's approaches to the younger were of this type) and friendly behavior on the part of the younger sibling toward the older (70% of the infant's approaches to the older sibling were of this type). Further, 95% of the older siblings were eager to help care for the baby; aggressive acts toward the baby were uncommon. The reactions of older siblings whose mothers talked to them about the baby as a person with feelings had a more positive relationship with the baby than those whose mothers did not do so.

A series of studies of very young siblings (Abramovich, Corter, & Lando, 1979; Abramovich, Corter, and Pepler, 1980; Abramovich, Corter, Pepler, & Stanhope, 1986; Abramovich, Pepler, & Corter, 1982) found that older siblings were usually the leaders in the sibling interactions, showing prosocial behaviors as well as some aggression, threats, and struggles over objects with their younger siblings. The younger siblings showed a marked tendency to imitate the older. Teti (1992) observed that the older sibling gains in social skills in interacting with the younger at this stage of development, but that the younger sibling gains cognitively by imitating the older.

Dunn and Kendrick (1982c) found that the older sibling initiated attempts at communication with the younger, and when the younger sibling began to talk, the older sibling was able to interpret what the infant was trying to say and to infer the infant's feelings and desires. Additionally, the older siblings simplified their speech to the infants, used repetition, and as appropriate made other accommodations to the younger sibling's developing language abilities. Ervin-Tripp (1989) also found that older siblings showed a great deal of accommodation to the young child's low level of language competence, including gesturing and demonstrating, repeating, speaking louder, paraphrasing, eliciting imitation, and speed. They also solicited repetitions of words or phrases by the young child, and interpreted and expanded the young child's utterances.

The growing relationship between young siblings can be interpreted in terms of attachment theory (Ainsworth, 1972, 1989; Bretherton, 1992; Bowlby, 1979, 1980). To the extent that an infant finds or experiences comfort and security in the presence of the attachment figure, the infant forms a secure attachment and an "internal working model" or mental representation of that attachment figure as responsive and supportive. Hereditary predispositions of mother and infant initiate interactions between them, which in turn, maintain the nurturing of the mother and attachment of the infant to the mother.

Attachment is not restricted to the mother (although this is typically the strongest bond); multiple attachments to other individuals who are responsive and supportive to the child (e.g., father, siblings) can also develop. Various researchers have concluded that young children's behaviors toward their older siblings imply a sibling attachment (Bank, 1992; Bank & Kahn, 1982a, 1982b; Dunn & Kendrick, 1982b). Bank theorizes that for a sibling bond to develop there must be both access of the siblings to one another and a vacuum of parental care. In the mother's absence, both siblings may cling to one another for comfort. In this sense the sibling attachment bond can be reciprocal, but the younger sibling's attachment to the older is stronger than vice versa. Obviously, not every sibling relationship involves a secure attachment bond. The older sibling can reject the younger, or fail to provide nurturing behaviors, or be inconsistent, so that a weak, ambivalent, or disturbed attachment results. Convincing empirical evidence of the young child's attachment to the older sibling was provided by Stewart (R. Stewart, 1983; R. Stewart & Marvin, 1984). Over half of a group of older siblings aged 30 to 58 months were observed to provide caregiving and nurturance to their younger siblings when they showed distress when the mother was leaving the playroom. In addition, the infants showed attachment behaviors by approaching and maintaining proximity to the older sibling when the mother was away but not doing so when the mother was present. Further evidence comes from a study by Samuels (1980), who placed an infant and an older sibling in an unfamiliar backyard when the mother was seated at the edge of the yard. When the sibling was present, the infants left their mother sooner and explored more, showed less distress, and were more independent. In this setting, the older sibling served as a source of security for the younger.

Changes over Time

As the sibling pair increases in age, the younger sibling becomes a more active participant in the relationship and the older sibling takes more interest in the younger sibling and in their relationship (Brown & Dunn, 1992; Munn & Dunn, 1988). When the younger sibling is about 3 or 4 years old, the sibling relationship becomes more important. The younger sibling begins to take part in the more active play of the older sibling, and also begins to engage in conflict on occasion. Also, the younger sibling begins to take part in the mother's interactions with the older sibling and thus participate more fully in family life (Dunn & Shatz, 1989).

Although sibling relationships early in life are characterized by considerable variability in interaction behaviors, there appears to be a moderate degree of stability in both the positive and negative aspects of the relationship. Over a longitudinal period of 4 years ranging from preschool to middle childhood periods, Dunn (1992) reported statistically significant stabilities in the positive aspects of the relationship of .40 for the younger sibling and .60 for the older sibling; for the negative aspects of the relationship, stabilities were .28 for the younger sibling and .43 for the older sibling. Thus certain aspects of the relationship appear to persevere over time, but there also appears to be some change.

The period from early childhood to middle childhood is a time of transition in sibling relationships. The older child enters the world of school and peers earlier than the younger one, with a consequent reduction in the access of siblings to each other for interaction. On the other hand, older siblings often take on a pioneering function so that when the younger sibling is ready to enter school, the older sibling is able to help the younger with school related problems. Bryant (1992) found that younger siblings go to an older sister or brother for advice about topics that they feel uncomfortable discussing with the parents. As they become older, the siblings are more often away from the supervision of the mother or other caregiver. On the one hand, siblings may develop a closer relationship under such circumstances, on the other, greater freedom from supervision leaves the younger sibling more vulnerable to physical or sexual abuse by the older.

Less is known about what happens to sibling relationships in adolescence than during other periods. Buhrmester and Furman investigated the course of sibling relationships during the late childhood and adolescent years (Buhrmester, 1992; Buhrmester & Furman, 1987, 1990), looking at qualities of warmth and closeness, status and power, and conflict. Overall, same sex siblings reported greater warmth and closeness in this period than opposite sex siblings. Conflict was greater at closer age spacings between the siblings. Not surprisingly, in the younger portion of the age range, the older sibling held greater power and status in the relationship than the younger, but at age 11 or 12, the amount of nurturance given to the younger sibling by the older declined markedly while the younger sibling's nurturance to the older increased somewhat. The power differential between the siblings also became narrower, as the older siblings were no longer given caretaking duties by the parents. Buhrmester viewed these changes as a trend toward greater egalitarianism in the relationship. Overall, rivalry and conflict peaked in early adolescence, but dropped off by late adolescence; however, this trend was reported primarily by younger siblings, with older siblings reporting little change in conflict. Throughout the period, siblings reported a decline in the intensity and involvement of the relationship as more time was spent on peer relationships.

Vandell, Minnett, and Santrock (1987) reported an increase in the power exerted by the younger siblings on their older siblings as they approached adolescence, with corresponding increases both in the positive emotional tone of the relationship and conflict.

In the author's retrospective study of the developmental course of the sibling relationship (Cicirelli, 1994b), middle-aged sibling pairs representing the four gender combinations were asked to rate both positive and negative qualities of their relationship in childhood, adolescence, young adulthood, and middle adulthood. Overall, positive qualities of the relationship (such as enjoyment, trust, confiding, understanding) declined sharply in adolescence and then increased in adulthood. This teenage dip was sharpest in the relationship between pairs of sisters, whereas pairs of brother reported a flatter trajectory (trends were intermediate for the brother–sister pairs). Although the shape of the trajectories for older and younger siblings did not differ, the younger siblings viewed their relationship a little less positively throughout than did the older siblings. The negative qualities of the relationship (such as arguing, competition and rivalry, and antagonism) rose to a peak in adolescence and then declined in adulthood. There was little difference in the form of the trajectories for older and younger siblings, or for the four sex combinations. When asked to explain why their sibling relationships had changed, most attributed the changes in adolescence to the general upheaval at that stage of life, when one or the other sibling became more adventurous outside the family ("acted wild") and emotions were unpredictable. Siblings found it difficult to accept changes in the other's behavior or personality. The subsequent improvement in relationships by young adulthood was attributed to increasing maturity and the ability to accept each other as they were.

Because knowledge about the course of sibling relationships in middle childhood and adolescence is limited, and findings are conflicting in some respects, the question of how the relationship changes over this period of life is far from settled.

EXPLAINING INDIVIDUAL DIFFERENCES IN SIBLINGS AND IN THEIR RELATIONSHIPS

Many individual differences exist between the characteristics (such as personality and cognitive characteristics) of various siblings in the family, as well as in the characteristics of the relationships between different sibling dyads. Some characteristics appear to be quite stable (e.g., temperament) and others change over time in a normative or unique manner which may involve developmental or aging change. Also, sibling characteristics have antecedents and consequences (or long-range effects).

Recent studies reviewed in the earlier portion of this chapter indicate that the various sibling status variables describing the family constellation influence the sibling relationship in complex ways. Whether there is a developmental trend in the effects of such variables as relative age, gender, and age spacing remains unclear.

Over the history of sibling research, many researchers have tried to explain why individual differences in siblings and sibling relationships exist. Some of the directions that this research has taken will be discussed below.

Direct Effects of Sibling Constellation Variables

The earliest attempts to explain sibling differences in terms of the sibling constellation were numerous studies of the effects of sibling birth order. In general, such attempts were based on the idea that the firstborn sibling was favored in terms of attention and family resources in comparison with later born siblings. At the time of Schooler's (1972) devastating critique of this research, well in excess of a thousand studies had been published. These studies were characterized by nonrandom sampling, few controls, and conflicting findings.

Nonetheless, Zajonc and Markus (1975) attempted to explain sibling differences in intelligence and achievement in terms of birth order, family size, and age by means of an elaborate confluence theory involving an exponential growth curve. The theory held that the child's intellectual development will be influenced by the average intelligence of others in the family in terms of mental age. For the firstborn, this average will be high, but with the confluence of the lower mental ages of succeeding siblings the average will go down. Thus, later-born siblings will grow up in a relatively impoverished intellectual environment and will have less intelligence than early borns in their own family. The theory described aggregated data quite well, but was not successful when applied to data where the individual was the unit of analysis.

Sutton-Smith and Rosenberg (1970) and Toman (1976) attempted to explain sibling personality characteristics and interaction behaviors in terms of such variables as family size, birth order, relative age, gender, and age spacing. Whereas Toman developed detailed portraits of individuals in a given position in their sibling constellation (even suggesting that marriages were more successful when the partners had the proper match of sibling status variables), the work of Sutton-Smith and Rosenberg set the stage for later research by exploring the status variables in relation to sibling interactions and interactions with other family members.

Some later researchers have attempted to study sibling relationships apart from considerations of sibling structure (number of siblings, age level, age spacing, gender, birth order, ratio of young to old, ratio of female to male), reasoning that these variables themselves are neither causal nor highly related to sibling characteristics or relationships. However, consideration of the role of structural variables helps to identify sibling structure-related variables that do exist in a causal or mediator relationship to outcome variables (e.g., parental expectations for siblings in relation to birth order).

To reiterate, sibling structure variables have been used in past studies as if they were causal factors of individual differences. When the results of using sibling structure variables in this manner led to inconsistent results, many researchers concluded that they are no longer worth investigating, and research should focus instead on family process.

However, sibling structure should be looked upon as an organizational framework, as age is for developmental psychology. Sibling structure is not a cause but a condition that sets the conditions within which other causal factors operate. Just knowing the age of an individual stimulates a search for age-related causal factors. The same is true for sibling structure variables. However, they do guide researchers to look for relevant structure-related variables that are related to characteristics of siblings and characteristics of sibling relationships.

Sibling Deidentification

Yet another attempt to explain differences in sibling characteristics used relative sibling birth order positions as mediators for a process involving a hypothesized defense against sibling rivalry (Schachter, 1982, 1985; Schachter & Stone, 1987). College students from two- and three-child families were asked to judge whether they were alike or different from their siblings on 13 bipolar personality traits. Judgments of being different from the sibling were regarded as sibling deidentification. "First pairs" (a firstborn and second born) showed greater deidentification than "second pairs" (a second born and third born). Deidentification was least for "jump pairs" (first and third born). Schachter theorized that first pairs should be most rivalrous since they had undiluted competition before the third child arrived; jump pairs would be least rivalrous due to the presence of the intervening sibling. Deidentification was viewed as a socially accepted way of dealing with feelings of rivalry by developing areas of the self that do not compete with the sibling's strong points. Despite some empirical validation of Schachter's theory, it is limited in its application.

Critical Life Events

Some sibling characteristics have been explained by the impact of various critical events on the developing siblings (Dunn, 1984). Dunn argued that the occurrence of a critical event in the life of a child alters that child's world in a significant way; the child's response to this altered world may change feelings, beliefs, and ways of acting and relating to others. She used the birth of a sibling to illustrate the effect of a critical event on the life of the older child. Other events, such as illness or hospitalization of a family member, death of a parent or a sibling, and divorce and remarriage are other examples of critical events that can exert a large effect on sibling characteristics and sibling relationships.

Split custody arrangements following divorce can have serious consequences for the sibling relationship, at times effectively dissolving it (Kaplan, Hennon, & Ade-Ritter, 1993). On the other hand, children may respond to the upheaval and stress of a parental divorce either by externalizing or internalizing behavior. Kempton, Armistead, Wierson, and Forehand (1991) compared the behavior of adolescents with and without siblings following divorce, finding that adolescents without siblings had more problems. It appears that the presence of siblings helps to serve to buffer the impact of the stress of divorce. Presumably the siblings may draw closer to share their feelings and concerns and to give each other comfort.

Hetherington (1988) carried out a 6-year longitudinal study of sibling relationships in middle childhood following divorce and remarriage. Siblings in nondivorced families were compared with those in divorced families and in stepfamilies. Siblings in stepfamilies exhibited the most problems, showing fewer positive behaviors and more negative behaviors than the other groups. However, boys in divorced families were more aggressive and rivalrous than any other groups of children. The presence of a stepfather was associated with poor sibling relationships, although things got better with time. In the longer-remarried families, the level of aggression had diminished to the level found in nuclear families.

A sibling's death (see Chapter 13) is another critical incident that can have profound effects on the surviving siblings, with younger children having more problems due to their limited understanding and limited repertoire of coping strategies. Diminished parental attention during the mourning period can intensify problems.

Genetic Differences in Characteristics

Certain genetically transmitted sibling characteristics can greatly influence the sibling relationship. One that has been investigated by a number of researchers is temperament, which can influence the degree of hostility and conflict between siblings. In general, children who are active, intense, or unadaptable in temperament have more conflicted relationships (Boer, 1990; Brody & Stoneman, 1987; Brody, Stoneman, & Burke, 1987; Stocker, Dunn, & Plomin, 1989). The match between the temperament of the two children is also important (Munn & Dunn, 1988). If both siblings have an intense and unadaptable temperament, hostilities are almost sure to erupt. On the other hand, if a child with a difficult temperament is paired with a sibling who is easygoing and adaptable, their relationship is likely to be better.

Differential Parenting and the Systems Approach

The nature–nurture issue is one that has occupied developmental psychologists since the inception of the field and has relevance for the study of sibling differences. With the application of the methods of behavioral genetics (twin studies, adoption studies) to the problem of sibling differences (Scarr & Grajek, 1982) and years of ensuing research, it has gradually become clear that not only does genetic similarity fail to explain sibling differences in personality, psychopathology, and cognition, but the environment shared by siblings also provides little explanation of such phenomena. Two excellent recent reviews of this literature (Dunn & Stocker, 1989; Hoffman, 1991) are available for the interested reader. Authors of both reviews conclude that environmental influences not shared by siblings must therefore account for the differences. It is immediately clear that siblings may experience different environments outside the home (different playmates, different teachers, and so on). However, it is not quite so obvious that the environments experienced by different siblings within the home may also differ as a result of differential parental treatment, sibling interactions themselves (including the children's perceptions and interpretations of each other's behaviors), and events experienced by one sibling but not the other (Dunn & Stocker, 1989).

Using naturalistic observation, Dunn found significant differences in the responsiveness, attention, affection, control, and play behaviors of mothers toward their two children (Dunn & Munn, 1986b; Dunn, Plomin, & Daniels, 1986; Stocker, Dunn, & Plomin, 1989). Mothers' differential treatment of young siblings has also been reported by Brody, Stoneman, and Burke (1987), and by Bryant and Crockenberg (1980). Older children (Furman & Buhrmester, 1985) and adolescents (Daniels, 1986; Daniels, Dunn, Furstenberg, & Plomin, 1985) have themselves reported experiencing differential parental treatment. The differences in parental treatment were found to be associated with siblings' adjustment and relationships to each other when one sibling perceived himself or herself as the deprived or unfavored child. Siblings were also observed to behave differently to each other, with older siblings tending to be initiators of behavior and younger siblings followers (Abramovich, Corter, Pepler, & Stanhope, 1986; Brody et al, 1987; Dunn & Munn, 1986b; Rodgers & Rowe, 1988). In a recent longitudinal study of siblings in middle childhood (Brody, Stoneman, & McCoy, 1994), child temperament as well as family cohesion and expressiveness, father–child relationship quality, and father's differential treatment of siblings were all associated with dimensions of the quality of the sibling relationship. When the father had a warm relationship with the children and did not provide differential negative treatments, when parents perceived family relationships as close, and when the children did not have different temperaments, the sibling had a more positive relationship and less conflict. Similarly, Conger and Conger (1994) found that when parental hostility was directed differentially to adolescent siblings, the one treated in the most hostile fashion showed the most delinquent behavior two years later.

The situation may be somewhat more complex than presented above. Hoffman (1991) points out that the child is an active interpreter of his or her environment, as well as an elicitor of parent and sibling behaviors. As a result, parent and sibling influences may not produce characteristics similar to their own in the child, but the opposite, depending on the child's interpretation. Further, child age at the time of a given event, child gender, and physical appearance (attractiveness, resemblance to a parent, and so on) also tend to influence personality development. Finally, the magnitude of sibling differences seems to be a function of the particular variables measured, with greater sibling similarity on such things as attitudes and values than on personality traits.

As part of the family system, a sibling dyad may share certain experiences and interactions that affect their relationship and their personalities quite apart from the rest of the family system. Certainly differential parental treatment is only one part. Teti (1992) regards siblings themselves as potent agents of socialization on one another. Changes in the sibling subsystem should have an effect on parent–child relationships. However, existing research in this area examines one-way and not reciprocal influences between elements in the system.

Shared and Nonshared Evironments

The traditional approach to the study of siblings is to use between or across-family environmental measures. Family environmental measures (parental affection, control, numbers of toys, intellectual stimulation provided, authoritarian treatment, and the like) are related to adjustment, personality, and intelligence scores of one child in the family. This traditional approach to studying family environment neglects the within-family environmental influences. Behavior–environment relationships found with the between-family approach usually has been small. This suggests that within-family environmental influences operate to make siblings different. A key premise of this research is that environmental experiences that are shared in common by siblings (aspects of the physical environment of the home, certain parental treatments) will not explain why they are different; they could only explain why they are alike. It is only the different things that siblings experience that contribute to making them different from one another. Dunn and McGuire (1994) point out that it is what a child perceives to be different that is important, regardless of whether or not two siblings are exposed to the same environmental event. Additionally, within the sibling subsystem itself, a given action by one sibling is perceived differently because each views it from his or her own perspective.

On the basis of behavioral genetic evidence, variance due to within family influences has been estimated to account for approximately 30 to 50% of environmental variance in cognitive traits (Plomin, Chipuer, & Neiderhiser, 1994; Rowe & Plomin, 1981), and approximately 80 to 90% of the environmental variance in personality traits. In Chapter 3, the sampling method employed in a study in progress (Reiss et al., 1994) was discussed. This method will enable the researchers to make a better estimate of the contribution of genetic factors, shared environmental experiences, and nonshared environmental experiences to the explanation of the variance in sibling characteristics.

Earlier studies of individual differences within the family did not go beyond the study of the family constellation variables of birth order, age, and sex of siblings. However, these variables explained between 1 and 10% of the variance in achievement and ability scores (Plomin & Foch, 1981; Scarr & Grajek, 1982). (It should be pointed out that these earlier studies did not investigate interaction effects of constellation variables.)

In an early study of the relationship between environmental differences within the family and sibling behavioral differences, Daniels, Dunn, Furstenberg, and Plomin (1985) analyzed data on a nationally representative sample of 346 adolescent sibling pairs. It was found that the sibling who experienced more maternal closeness, more say in the family decisions, and more peer and sibling congeniality, as reported by both the parents and the siblings, also showed better psychological adjustment as reported by parents, self, and teachers. The Daniels et al. study was limited in that the within family measures were created indirectly from between family measures scored individually for each sibling.

In the same vein, Dunn, Stocker, and Plomin (1990b) examined the adjustment of 4- and 7-year-old sibling dyads as a function of differential maternal treatment. When the mother was more affectionate to the younger sibling, the older child had more internalizing behavior; when the mother exerted greater control of the older sibling, it predicted both internalizing and externalizing problems as assessed by teachers.

The important lesson to be learned from studies of a nonshared environment is that researchers need to look at the environmental influences that are specific to each child and not general to an entire family (Plomin et al., 1994).

CONCLUSION

Trying to find an explanation for why siblings growing up in a given family have the characteristics they do and interact the way they do is a difficult task indeed. Researchers using different theories and approaches to the problem have amassed a great deal of evidence over time, some of it conflicting. However, in explaining why siblings are alike and different, each area of research has a grain of truth to offer.

Considering what the relationship between siblings has to contribute to each other's development, one is left with several outcomes of their interactions. Among these are sibling socialization of one another independently of parental influences, long-range changes in sibling characteristics, and changes in the relationship over time with maintenance of stability during the adult years.

CHAPTER 5

Siblings in Adulthood and Old Age

Although the topic of sibling relationships in adulthood and old age has received relatively little research attention in the past, an increase in research interest in this area over the past decade has paralleled the surge in research on sibling relationships in childhood and adolescence. However, studies of adult siblings have been, for the most part, broadly focused empirical explorations. These research findings will be examined in this chapter.

EXISTENCE OF THE SIBLING RELATIONSHIP IN ADULTHOOD

Once adolescents reach adulthood and leave the family home to establish their own households, are relationships with siblings continued or are they abandoned? Most people are familiar with siblings who have maintained close relationships throughout life, as well as those who have had no further contact with siblings in adult life. Obviously, if one is going to study sibling relationships in adulthood and old age, an important preliminary concern is to determine whether adults maintain some kind of contact with their siblings in sufficient numbers to make the study of sibling relationships a relevant topic. A related concern is whether, in view of rising death rates in later adulthood and old age, older adults have surviving siblings in sufficient numbers for study.

Findings of survey studies show that, for most older individuals, siblings do exist and maintain contact until very late in life (Cicirelli, 1979, 1980b, 1981; Clark & Anderson, 1967; Rosenberg and Anspach, 1973; Shanas, 1973; Shanas, Townsend, Wedderburn, Friis, Milhoj, & Stehouwer,

1968). Percentages of people over age 60 having at least one living sibling ranged from 78% for the Cicirelli sample to 93% for the sample reported by Shanas et al.; however, the Cicirelli sample represented the older portion of the age range more heavily than did others.

In an age-stratified sample of 300 older people and their adult children (Cicirelli, 1979, 1981), 85% of the middle-aged adults had at least one living sibling (88% had siblings in their birth families), compared to 78% of those over age 60. Looking at each age range more specifically, those in the 60 to 69 group reported an average of 2.9 living siblings, those in the 70 to 79 age group reported 2.2 living siblings, and those aged 80 and over reported 1.1 living siblings. These groups originally had averages of 4.6, 4.9, and 4.2 siblings in their family of origin. Some 26% of the elders had a sibling living in the same city, and 56% had a sibling within 100 miles. Thus most of the elders studied had living siblings, with the majority having some accessibility to at least one sibling.

Some 17% of the older respondents saw their most frequently contacted sibling weekly or more often, while 33% saw their sibling at least monthly; the modal frequency of visiting was several times a year. Although the remainder saw their siblings less frequently, very few respondents actually lost contact with a sibling. In addition, the frequencies of telephoning were similar to frequencies of visiting (Cicirelli, 1979, 1980b). These same studies indicated that the majority of older people saw their siblings at least several times a year, and very few actually lost contact with each other.

Using a national probability sample of some 7,700 respondents over the entire age range in adulthood, White and Riedmann (1992a) examined sibling contact in families where the respondent had at least one living full sibling. About half reported seeing or talking with their sibling at least monthly. Contact was greater between pairs of sisters than in mixed-gender dyads, with brother–brother pairs having the least contact. As might be expected, proximity was an important factor in sibling contact, with the most frequent contact occurring between siblings living within 2 miles of each other. However, living within a 300-mile radius was also associated with more frequent sibling contact than when siblings lived at greater distances. Respondents who were the oldest child in the family reported more sibling contact than those who were younger. Having adult children was negatively related to sibling contact, whereas having a living parent was related to increased sibling contact. When sibship and family characteristics were controlled, respondents with higher income and education had more contact with their siblings.

The same study provided information on ethnic group differences in sibling contact as well as contact in blended families. African-American respondents saw their siblings significantly more often than did non-Hispanic whites or Mexican Americans; Asian Americans saw their siblings significantly less. Stepsiblings and half-siblings, too, continued to keep in touch with each other in adulthood, although contact was less frequent than for full siblings (Pulakos, 1990; White & Riedmann, 1992b).

ASPECTS OF THE SIBLING RELATIONSHIP

Researchers studying sibling relationships in adulthood and old age have focused on several aspects of the topic. Some of these are essential characteristics or attributes of any relationship, whereas others are particular to adult siblings, and still others reflect idiosyncratic interests of particular researchers.

Affectional Closeness

Early investigations of the quality of the sibling relationship centered around feelings of closeness and rivalry, although both concepts were loosely defined. Adams (1968) reported that a majority of young and middle-aged adults still felt close to their siblings, even though they were living independently. Despite reduced contact with their siblings, older adults reported greater feelings of closeness with siblings than did younger cohorts (Cicirelli, 1980b, 1982, 1985a; Ross & Milgram, 1982). In regard to their most frequently contacted sibling, 65% of older adults reported feeling close or very close (Cicirelli, 1979, 1980b). In addition to feelings of closeness, siblings tend to serve as confidants for one another in middle adulthood and old age (Connidis & Davies, 1990).

In White and Riedmann's large national study (1992a), affection was operationally defined as considering a sibling to be among one's closest friends. Results indicated that having a sister and having a living parent were significant factors in sibling affectional feelings, but being married was negatively related. Greater proximity was positively related to affection; however, when amount of contact was controlled the relationship was negative, suggesting that siblings who lived close but didn't see each other didn't get along well. Sibling closeness was lower in blended families (White & Riedmann, 1992b), not only for relationships with half-siblings and stepsiblings, but for full sibling relationships in such families as well. Although siblings in some families can become closer in response to difficulties in the parental system (Bank & Kahn, 1982a, 1982b), disruption of the original nuclear family appears to have more negative effects on the sibling relationship in most cases.

Rivalry

The question of whether rivalry between siblings declines in adulthood or continues to exist is one that has been much debated. Cross-sectional age trends for feelings of sibling rivalry indicated a decline in rivalry reported by older cohorts (Cicirelli, 1985b). Sibling rivalry assessed through self-report measures appears not only to be low throughout adulthood and old age but to be lower for older than for younger cohorts, with rivalry greatest between pairs of brothers and least between cross-sex siblings (Cicirelli, 1980b, 1985b). However, evidence from studies that used clinical interview techniques or projective methods (Bedford, 1989a; Gold, 1986, 1989b; Ross and Milgram, 1982) suggests that the prevalence of sibling rivalry may be considerably greater in adulthood than previously thought, with little decrease with age. Using extended clinical-type interviews, Gold found a higher incidence of rivalry than revealed in self-report studies, with pairs of elderly brothers showing greater envy and resentment than other sibling dyads. Recent work by Bedford, using a projective measurement technique (1989a), revealed that up to 71% of adults in a wide age range reported feeling sibling rivalry at some point in their lives, with 45% still feeling rivalrous in adulthood. Older adults revealed as much sibling rivalry and conflict as did younger adults. Although Ross and Milgram's findings indicate that most rivalrous siblings seek to repair their relationships by later adulthood and old age, Bedford's work suggests that some feelings of rivalry persist into old age.

Despite any underlying rivalrous feelings, most older adults value their relationships with siblings and have developed ways of interaction that avoid conflict and overt rivalry. As a result, hostility, aggression, and violence between siblings in adulthood and old age are relatively rare. Not surprisingly, a higher percentage of conflict was reported when relationships involved half-siblings and stepsiblings than when relationships involved only full siblings (White & Riedmann, 1992b).

Indifference

Some adult siblings have little or no contact with each other and have little feeling for each other (either positive or negative). In short, they may be characterized as indifferent, apathetic, or disinterested (Cicirelli, 1985b; Gold, 1989b; Scott, 1990), disowned (Bank & Kahn, 1982b), or disaffiliated (Matthews, Delaney, & Adamek, 1989). Sibling pairs with indifferent relationships occur in from 5 to 11% of all sibling relationships. Factors leading to indifferent relationships have not been studied. However, one can speculate that a wide age spacing, geographic separation, and failure to develop secure attachments early in life may all contribute.

Companionship

According to Goetting's (1986) analysis of the developmental tasks of siblings over the life cycle, providing companionship and emotional support constitutes an important function of sibling relationships over the entire life span. Scott (1983) examined companionship activities reported by siblings and found that visits, reunions, and happy family occasions were the most frequent sibling activities reported, followed by various types of recreational activities (home, commercial, and outdoor), and by shopping, church attendance, and miscellaneous other activities. When proximity was controlled, frequency of these sibling activities compared quite favorably with similar activities with children. Various authors have found that most relationships in old age are companionate in nature (Adams, 1968, Cicirelli, 1982, 1985a; Johnson, 1982; Troll, Miller, & Atchley, 1978).

For some siblings, interaction goes beyond the typical companionate activities, family occasions, and family concerns to include participation in a family-owned business. As yet, most information about siblings in family businesses tends to be anecdotal or clinical in nature, coming to national attention via the media when the accomplishments of the siblings themselves are noteworthy (the Rockefellers, the Hunts), or when particularly acrimonious business disagreements threaten or disrupt the partnership (the Basses). According to Carroll (1988), some 12 million businesses in the United States are family-owned, although the number of these in which siblings are partners or coworkers is not known. Family issues and business issues are inextricably interwoven in such ventures. Sibling interactions on day-to-day business matters draw added meaning from the existing family relationships. Old themes of intimacy, dependency, rivalry, trust, and fairness in the sibling relationship reappear in the business relationship. Business themes of power, control, responsibility, and succession in the business all depend on harmonious sibling relationships for successful resolution.

Siblings as Friends

In everyday language and in literature, friends are often regarded as "like a brother" or "like a sister," implying considerable similarity between the two types of relationship. According to Connidis (1989), there are many parallels between siblings and friends that suggest that close sibling relationships serve as friendships in later life. Siblings and friends are typically age peers (at least in childhood and adolescence); they both play a broad range of roles and have ready access to one another; the relationship is characterized by egalitarianism, equal power, and emphasis on sociability, with limited obligation. However, sibling relationships differ from friendships in that the sibling bond is ascribed while the friendship bond is voluntary, and siblings compete for parental attention while friends do not. Overall, 77% of the 294 older adults studied by Connidis considered at least one sibling to be a close friend, with these "friendship" relationships typified by mutual confiding and closeness of feelings. The larger the family of orientation, the more likelihood there is that an older individual will differentiate between siblings according to whether they are considered close friends. Among smaller sibships with from one to four siblings, more than two-thirds of all siblings are viewed as friends; among larger sibships, the percentage of all siblings seen as friends ranges from 11 to 53%. Sibling friendship is more likely when at least one sibling is a sister, is not married, and lives nearby. In a subsequent study of the availability of confidants and companions for the elderly (Connidis and Davies, 1990), friends were more prominent in the companion network than in the confidant network, while siblings were more prominent in the confidant network than in the companion network. These findings suggest that not all siblings can be regarded as friends, and that friends and siblings occupy subtly different roles in the elder's support system.

Communication

When siblings no longer live together, they communicate and presumably share experiences either by talking directly to each other in face-to-face meetings or on the telephone, by mail, or by communicating indirectly through a third person (Adams, 1968). Parents often serve as conduits of information from one sibling to another.

However, what goes on during sibling communication has been little studied. Shared family history and common language experiences should enable adult siblings to practice an intimate communication style, with many shortcuts and implied meanings, but there has been no study of sibling discourse to support such a hypothesis. Topics of sibling communication have been examined, however. When elderly interviewees were asked what topics they talked about with their siblings (Cicirelli, 1985a), most communication centered around the discussion of family events and concerns and around old times. Older people discussed old times more frequently with their siblings than with their adult children. The fewer the remaining siblings in the family, the greater the extent of such reminiscing. As the surviving members of their families of origin, siblings can use reminiscences of old times together and clarify events and relationships that took place in earlier years and to place them in mature perspective.

In addition to the above, an examination of the communication network in a single large family of siblings is included in Chapter 7.

Typologies

In earlier work, Cicirelli (1985b) discussed sibling relationships in terms of three orthogonal basic dimensions: affectional closeness, rivalry, and involvement. Other dimensions frequently used to describe the sibling relationship are value consensus, compatibility, and emotional support, but these have not been incorporated into a coherent scheme.

Although the use of a set or profile of dimensions may be used to describe the sibling relationship, some researchers prefer the use of typologies. Bank and Kahn (1982b) identified several types or patterns of sibling relationships based on a clinical interpretation of the degree of the individual's identification with the sibling: fused, blurred, hero worship (idealization), mutually dependent (loyal), dynamic independent, hostile dependent, rigidly differentiated, and disowned.

In work with the elderly, Gold (1989b) identified five types of sibling relationships based on patterns of psychological involvement, closeness, acceptance-approval, emotional support, instrumental support, contact, envy, and resentment: the intimate, the congenial, the loyal, the apathetic, and the hostile. Siblings of the intimate type are characterized by unusually high devotion and psychological closeness (affection, empathy, self-disclosure); they place the sibling relationship above all others. Congenial siblings are close and affectionate, but are characterized by friendship and caring; they place greater value on marital and parent–child relationships than on the sibling relationship. Loyal siblings are characterized by allegiance based on shared family background, basing their relationship on adherence to cultural norms; they support each other at special family events and crises and have regular but not frequent contact. Siblings of the apathetic type are characterized by indifference; they have mutual disinterest and see each other little, but are not rivalrous or hostile; their lives have simply gone in different directions. Finally, siblings of the hostile type have strong negative feelings toward each other, with considerable negative psychological involvement or preoccupation with the relationship. Their relationship is characterized by resentment, anger, and enmity. The intimate (14%), loyal (30%), and congenial (34%) types accounted for some 78% of all sibling relationships studied by Gold, while the remainder were divided into the apathetic (11%) and hostile (11%) types. This typology was essentially upheld by data reanalysis using a "fuzzy set" clustering methodology (Gold, Woodbury, & George, 1990), as well as in a separate study of sibling relationships among blacks (Gold, 1990). Gold's typology was given partial support in an independent replication by Scott (1990), although 95% of her sample fell into the first three types (23% intimate, 42% loyal, and 30% congenial), with the remaining 5% apathetic; there were no hostile sibling relationships in Scott's sample.

Other researchers (Matthews, Werkner, & Delaney, 1989) also have attempted to group sibling relationships in adulthood and old age into a few distinct types. They classified the relationships between the middle-aged brothers they studied into four groups: the closely affiliated (very close to extremely close), the lukewarm (somewhat close to close), the disaffiliated (little or no closeness), and the disparate (disagreed about their level of affiliation).

Although they are not identical, the typologies identified by the various researchers (Bank and Kahn, 1982b; Gold, 1989b; Matthews et al., 1989) bear some resemblance to one another and to the dimensions identified by Cicirelli (1985b). To the extent that the existence of such types has some generality, they may prove useful for describing sibling relationships. However, they share the problems common to all typologies: difficulty in classifying all cases, and use of nominal measurement which does not allow for degrees of variation within a type.

CHANGES IN SIBLING RELATIONSHIPS

For most people, sibling relationships continue in some form throughout life. However, there is a question as to whether relationships continue unchanged during adulthood and old age, once siblings leave their childhood home to establish their own households. Evidence bearing on this question comes from several sources.

Cross-sectional studies of sibling relationships for various age groups over adulthood and old age are one source of information. In an early study of nine subgroups of adults at various stages of the family life span, Leigh (1982) found some evidence for a decrease in the frequency of interaction with siblings during the middle portion of the life span followed by an increase in the later stages. Reviewing this and other existing data, Bedford (1990) postulated an hourglass effect in sibling involvement, in which sibling closeness as well as interaction gradually decrease in early adulthood, are low in the middle adult years, and rise again in late adulthood and old age. Somewhat different findings were obtained in a recent study. White and Riedmann (1992a) found that in their large national sample, frequency of contact declined with age over young adulthood, remained nearly stable in middle adulthood, and declined more steeply in later adulthood. However, affection (operationally defined as viewing the sibling as a close friend) did not vary with age. When cross-sectional age trends from late adolescence through adulthood and into old age were examined (Cicirelli, 1985b), mean feelings of closeness to siblings increased as age of the cohort increased; sibling rivalry declined over the same period. Rather than an hourglass effect, White and Riedmann's findings support overall decline in amount of contact and no change in affectional closeness, and Cicirelli's findings support a general increase in closeness. Differences in measures and sampling methods may account for the differences. Further, observed cross-sectional differences in sibling contact and closeness for the various age groups may reflect cohort differences in experiences and cultural expectations for sibling relationships rather than any intrinsic change in the sibling relationship over time.

Unfortunately, longitudinal studies of the sibling relationship over the adult age range have not been carried out to provide a basis for comparison with the cross-sectional results. However, retrospective data can be obtained from older individuals, revealing their own perceptions of how the relationship with a particular sibling may have changed over time. Cicirelli (1994b) asked adult sibling dyad members aged 35 to 65 to rate various aspects of their relationship at different portions of the life span: childhood, adolescence, early adulthood, middle adulthood, and (expected) old age. For sisters, positive qualities of the relationship (such as similarity of values, trust, enjoyment of each other's company) dipped sharply in adolescence, then increased through adulthood and were expected to remain constant in old age. For brothers, the trajectories were essentially flat. For both sisters and brothers, negative qualities of the relationship (such as argument, rivalry, and competitiveness) peaked in adolescence, then declined steadily to very low values in later life.

Apart from general trends in the sibling relationship over the life span, relationships between specific sibling pairs appear to wax and wane with individual life circumstances. Both Connidis (1992) and Bedford (1990) explored such changes.

In Connidis' (1992) study, changes in sibling relationships accompanying three types of major life events were investigated for 120 respondents aged 25 to 89: marriage and having children, divorce and widowhood, and death and poor health of family members. Both positive and negative changes following their own or a sibling's marriage were reported by approximately 40% of respondents, although the percentages reporting more positive relationships were greater than those reporting poorer relationships. Reasons given for closer relationships involved maturing, sharing marriage experiences, and closeness of spouse and siblings; reasons for poorer relationships included moving away from the family home, different family background of a spouse, and conflict with a sibling's spouse. Overall, having children produced positive changes in the emotional closeness of the sibling relationship for most respondents, although there was a tendency toward decreased contact as respondents became busier with their child-rearing responsibilities. For those respondents who reported their own or a sibling's divorce or widowhood, most changes were toward increased emotional closeness, contact, and support. It was clear that siblings responded positively toward one another's losses. Finally, a parent's illness or death, death of a sibling, or poor health of other family members drew siblings closer together in the great majority of cases reported.

Bedford (1990, July) studied longitudinal changes in sibling relationships of 54 same-sex sibling pairs aged 30 to 69 over a 4-year period in relation to the life events experienced in the interim. Critical events reported by these siblings as influencing the sibling relationship during this period involved marriage or divorce, changing interests, employment change, relocation to a new area, illness and death, behavior and achievement of children, family arguments, changing frequency of contact, and so on. About two-thirds of the respondents reported a change in feelings toward the sibling over time, with positive change as likely as negative change. However, there was deterioration of the relationship when the event indicated a change in the sibling's interests. In relation to a given life event, changes were positive for some sibling dyads and negative for others, depending on the circumstances and on the interpretations and interactions of the siblings in reaction to the event. A sibling's marriage resulted in a less close relationship for a third of the sibling pairs studied by Bedford (either the new spouse was not liked by the other sibling or the marriage disrupted the flow of a formerly close sibling relationship); for others, marriage to a spouse who was well liked brought siblings closer together.

It is not clear whether differences in the findings of the two studies could be accounted for by the fact that Connidis' (1992) study was retrospective whereas Bedford's (1990, July) was longitudinal, or by the fact that Connidis investigated only a few major life events whereas Bedford's subjects reported a wider variety of life events as responsible for changes in their affective relationship. What is clear is that sibling relationships are not static, but are influenced by ongoing events in the siblings' lives. Crisis events can act as turning points bringing change, yet the change may be only one of many ups and downs in the long-term course of the relationship. These studies illustrate the dynamic nature of family relationships while at the same time attesting to their continuity.

EFFECTS OF SIBLINGS ON WELL-BEING

Since sibling relationships continue to exist throughout adulthood, there is an opportunity for continued influence of siblings on one another. One question that has been more extensively investigated is whether sibling relationships lead to greater well-being in old age, although this question was unresolved until recent years. An early study (Cumming & Henry, 1961) found that older people with living siblings had higher morale. In another early study (Cicirelli, 1977), elderly men with sisters were found to have a greater sense of emotional security than those who did not have sisters, whereas women with sisters were stimulated and challenged in their social roles. However, a large sample study carried out by Lee and Ihinger-Tallman (1980) failed to find a significant relationship between the frequency of interaction with the sibling seen most often and a measure of morale, when a large number of control variables were accounted for. McGhee (1985) separated the effects of frequency of sibling interaction from the mere existence of a sibling and found that frequency of interaction was unrelated to the well-being of older people but that the existence and potential availability of a sister was related to greater life satisfaction. This finding offered support for the findings of Lee and Ihinger-Tallman with regard to the relationship between frequency of interaction and life satisfaction, as well as support for Cicirelli's findings relating the existence of sisters to aspects of well-being.

In further work, older people who had greater contact, closeness, and values agreement with their siblings had a more internal locus of control than those who did not. The number of brothers was associated with greater externality, whereas there was a tendency for the number of sisters (controlling for the number of brothers) to be related to greater internality (Cicirelli, 1980a). O'Bryant (1988) examined sibling social support and older widows' well-being and found that interaction with married sisters predicted higher positive effect among older widows. However, those widows who received support from sisters when nearby children did not provide support perceived the sibling support negatively. Cicirelli (1989a) found that the perception of a close bond to sisters by either men or women was related to well-being, as indicated by fewer symptoms of depression, while a close bond to brothers seemed to have little relevance for well-being. In a study of the elders' feelings toward dead siblings, not only did feelings of closeness and rivalry persist, but persisting rivalrous feelings were related to greater symptoms of depression among women with dead sisters (Cicirelli, 1989b).

Because siblings share a long and unique history, reminiscing about their earlier times together is an activity in which they engage at many points in the life span, although it seems to become more frequent in old age. In later life, reminiscence becomes part of the life review process (Butler, 1963), in which past experiences are analyzed, evaluated, and reintegrated in relation to present events, values, and attitudes. Prompted by the realization of biological decline in later years, the life review allows the individual to resolve old conflicts and to achieve integrity in the latter portion of life. Butler's hypothesis that spontaneous reminiscence in the life review led to better adjustment in old age has been supported by a number of studies, at least for those elders who engaged in reminiscence because they valued the activity (Coleman, 1986; Molinari & Reichlin, 1985; Osgood, 1985). There is little research regarding reminiscence of specific sibling experiences. Ross and Milgram (1982) observed that sharing recollections of childhood experiences appeared to be a source of comfort and pride for the elderly, evoking the warmth of early family life and contributing to a sense of integrity that life had been lived in harmony with the family. Cicirelli (1985a, 1988) found that old people reminisced about old times more frequently with their siblings than with their adult children. Gold's (1986) elderly subjects reported that reminiscing about sibling relationships during the course of the interview helped them to put their current relationships with siblings into a meaningful context, helped them to understand present events, and helped them to appreciate the significance of sibling relationships in their lives.

Over all the areas of research reviewed thus far, relationships with sisters appear to be particularly important in old age, whether it is a sister–sister or a brother–sister bond. One could attribute this to women's greater interest in initiating and maintaining family relationships; however, Gold (1989a) found that brothers initiated sibling contacts with sisters about as often as sisters contacted brothers. What seems more likely is that women's emotional expressiveness and their traditional roles as nurturers account for the importance of relationships with sisters (Cicirelli, 1989a).

One other aspect of sibling influence that has received little research attention is the effect of siblings on an individual's educational achievement and economic well-being in adulthood. Although the negative relationship between family size and educational attainment has long been known (Walberg & Marjoribanks, 1976), effects of sibling composition are less clear. A recent study (Butcher & Case, 1994) examined the effects of sibling sex composition on women's overall educational attainment and subsequent income in adulthood. Using data on men and women born in the United States between 1920 and 1965 obtained from three large national surveys, the authors used regression analysis to test various theoretical hypotheses about the effects of siblings on education and income. To control for family size, data for two-, three-, four-, and five-child families were analyzed separately, with quite similar results in all cases. Men showed no significant difference in educational attainment based on sibling sex composition. However, women who had brothers only received significantly more education than those who had at least one sister; the difference ranged from a half-year to a fifth-year of additional education, depending on the sample. Having more than one sister as compared to having any sister did not change the educational outcome. For those women currently working, having any sister also reduced log hourly earnings by at least 9% as compared to having only brothers; results were the same for single and married women. The effect of having a sister on income appeared to be an indirect effect of its effect on educational attainment.

Butcher and Case (1994) investigated a number of theoretical hypotheses ranging from economic decision making of the family to psychological spillover of sex roles in an effort to explain their puzzling findings. The best explanation was based on reference group theory, which suggests that the presence of a second daughter in the family changes the reference group for the first. If the family has only one daughter among sons, parents measure her achievements on the same scale as sons and tend to provide her with an equal share of the household's educational resources. Thus, in the absence of sisters, a daughter is forced to compete with sons and learn skills that sons typically learn. When a second daughter enters the household, parents group the daughters together and apply a different standard for achievement. Just how a reference group explanation of this sort is reflected in the day-to-day operation of the family system is a matter for further research. Within the context of sibling relationships in adulthood, it is important to remember that having a sister may have beneficial effects on family relationships for both men and women, but not having a sister may have beneficial effects on women's educational and economic outcomes.

THEORETICAL EXPLANATIONS FOR ADULT SIBLING RELATIONSHIPS

Most research on sibling relationships in adulthood thus far has been atheoretical in nature, or one or another existing psychology theory is cited in an ad hoc explanation. Yet there is a need to explain the origin of bonds between siblings and the persistence of such bonds over time and distance into old age.

Family Solidarity

Solidarity is a multidimensional construct involving a group's structure (number and proximity of members), contact, affection, consensus (of values, attitudes, and opinions), exchange of services, and adherence to norms of behavior (Bengtson & Mangen, 1988). Although there has been some use of generational solidarity theory from a sociological perspective (e. g., Gold, 1987) to explain sibling connections, it is largely a descriptive concept. However, the notion of early socialization of siblings within the family to norms of appropriate sibling behavior offers some explanation for their continuing relationship in adulthood. Such normative prescriptions as "one should love one's siblings," "one should keep in touch with them," and "one should help them when needed" appear to be more widely endorsed than such norms as "one should live close," or "siblings should agree on values." Thus, some adult sibling behaviors are governed by norms (e.g., presence at family ritual events such as weddings or deaths), and other behaviors (such as visiting) are regarded as voluntary. Just which norms are endorsed is a function of the cultural heritage of the family. According to Johnson (1982, 1985), norms of sibling solidarity are stronger in Italian-American families than they are in Anglo-Saxon Protestant families. Adherence to norms may also be a function of gender. Adams (1968) found that sibling contact by brothers in early adulthood seemed largely motivated by duty, whereas such contact by sisters seemed motivated by affection.

Adult Attachment

To attempt to explain adult sibling relationships, an adaptation of adult attachment theory can be used. Life span attachment theory (Bowlby 1979, 1980; Cicirelli, 1983, 1991) implies that the child's early attachments to the mother or primary caregiver and to other family members not only continue through the adult years but are the basis for the adult child's continued relationship with family members as well as helping behavior. To explain the maintenance of the sibling bond over extended separations in space and time, it is argued that the need for closeness and contact with the sibling is satisfied on a symbolic level through the process of identification. Attachment is an ethological–adaptational theory rooted in evolutionary biology, incorporating such concepts as biologically determined development of social attachments and the adaptational value for survival of family members sharing a common gene pool (Lamb, 1988; Nash, 1988; Scarr & Grajek, 1982).

Although few would deny that the adult individual has an affectional bond to a parent or sibling, for an affectional bond to be considered an attachment, it must fill several criteria: a need for proximity or contact with the attachment figure, distress or anxiety over separation or threatened separation, pleasure or joy upon reunion, grief at loss of the attachment figure, and feelings of security or comfort in the relationship with the attachment figure. While not all adult sibling relationships would meet these criteria, it is clear that many of them do. As indicated earlier in this chapter, most adult siblings do remain in contact, seek periodic visits, and find a sense of well being in the sibling relationship.

An implication of an attachment relationship is that the attached individual seeks to protect the attachment figure, seeking to maintain the survival of the attachment figure and protect the emotional bond (Cicirelli, 1983, 1985a). This is evidenced by findings regarding elders' desire for sibling help and sibling psychological support in a crisis. A recent study (Cicirelli, 1989a) found that sibling psychological support was related to an indicator of the strength of the attachment bond, with a stronger relationship when attachment to a sister was involved.

CHAPTER 6

Sibling Relationships in Cross-Cultural Perspective

UNIVERSALITY OF SIBLING RELATIONSHIPS

Because the existence of siblings is in itself an almost unavoidable part of family life, some sort of relationship between siblings also exists. Just how universally particular aspects of sibling relationships are found is an important question, however, in view of the great variety in cultural practices around the world. Examining sibling relationships across many cultures leads to an appreciation of the importance of siblings to human family life. Siblings' lives are closely intertwined throughout life in many non-industrialized societies, with carefully defined duties and responsibilities. In contrast, more aspects of sibling relationships in industrialized societies are voluntary, yet sibling relationships remain of significance throughout life for most individuals.

The research findings examined thus far have all come from studies carried out in the United States, the United Kingdom, or some other modern industrialized society. Considering all the differing nations and cultures existing in today's world, the question of whether existing findings about sibling and family relationships in Western societies apply universally is indeed an important one.

Two broad categories of societies will be contrasted here. The first consists of the modern urban industrialized technologically advanced societies of such "western" nations as the United States, Canada, the United Kingdom, and other countries of Western Europe, Australia, and so on. The second consists of nonindustrialized, technologically backward agrarian or pastoral societies found in more remote rural areas or villages of Asia, Oceania, Africa, and Central and South America. For brevity, these two types will be referred to simply as "industrialized" and "non-industrialized." Although it is recognized that there are variations in sibling relationships within each of the two broad types of cultures (Weisner, 1982, 1989a), details of these variations will not be emphasized here. Rather, we will attempt to make contrasts between modal industrialized and nonindustrialized societies.

To make comparisons with the existing literature on siblings in industrialized societies, more than 50 studies were reviewed which dealt with sibling relationships in nonindustrialized cultures of the South Pacific islands, India, Sri Lanka, Malaysia, Singapore, China, Japan, South and Central America, Mexico, and Africa. In addition, several review chapters (Ervin-Tripp, 1989; M. Marshall, 1983a; Schneider, 1983; Weisner, 1982, 1987, 1989a, 1993a, 1993b; Zukow, 1989) cite additional sources of information about siblings. With the notable omission of the Arab cultures of the Middle East, these studies cover a sufficient sampling of the nonindustrialized nations to allow some broad comparisons to be drawn.

A more difficult problem in making cross-cultural comparisons involves the differing types of questions investigated, methods of data collection and analysis used, and theoretical orientations presented in the various studies. The focus of studies carried out by researchers representing different disciplines, perspectives, and interests can vary so greatly as to make comparisons impossible in some areas (Weisner, 1982; Zukow, 1989). Nearly all the sibling studies in the industrialized nations have been carried out by psychologists and sociologists using such tools as survey methods, standardized interview materials, tests, systematic observations of behavior, and experiments. In contrast, nearly all the studies in the nonindustrialized societies have been carried out by anthropologists using ethnographic methods involving holistic qualitative fieldwork with direct observation and interviewing in natural settings over extended periods of time.

Interpretation of aspects of sibling relationships in different cultures is made more difficult because certain ideas and behaviors may not have the same meaning when different languages and cultural nuances are involved. Similarly, it is hard to obtain comparable representative samples or to establish appropriate units and measures for comparison when carrying out cross-cultural studies (Lonner, 1979).

Finally, achieving a complete understanding of sibling relationships should involve cross-cultural comparisons made over the total life span. However, neither systematic cross-sectional studies nor longitudinal studies of sibling relationships over the life span in any culture have been carried out thus far, although some limited longitudinal studies have been carried out.

IDENTIFICATION OF SIBLINGS

Various cultures differ in the way the term *sibling* is used and who is identified as a sibling. In industrialized societies, siblings are identified by genealogical or biological criteria, where full siblings have two biological parents in common and half-siblings share only one biological parent. Siblings may also be identified by legal criteria, as in the case of step- or adoptive siblings, or by affectional or behavioral criteria, as in the case of fictive siblings. Whether half-, step-, adoptive, or fictive siblings are accepted as full members in the sibling network seems to be a choice of the particular family involved. In some families, all are accepted as siblings without making any distinctions. In other families, half-, step-, or adoptive siblings are carefully distinguished as such and given only a partial or token membership in the network of full siblings. There may be little or no contact between full siblings and their half-, step-, or adoptive siblings. Fictive siblings may be referred to as if they were siblings, but their treatment, rights, and privileges may not be the same.

In nonindustrialized societies, siblings may be defined by extension of the term to certain types of blood kin, or by classification on the basis of other criteria than genealogical criteria alone. Depending on the particular society involved, the rules for identification as a sibling may become quite complex. To illustrate the variation in who is considered to be a sibling, in the Marquesas culture of Oceania only full biological siblings are identified (Kirkpatrick, 1983); in the Pukapuka culture of the Cook Islands in Oceania, "siblings" include the children of both parents' biological siblings (Hecht, 1983); in the Kwara'ae culture of the Solomon Islands, "siblings" include the children of the parents' cross-sex siblings (Watson-Gegeo & Gegeo, 1989). In the Malo culture of New Hebrides in Oceania an individual's "siblings" include cousins of the same sex, the parent's siblings of the same sex, and even grandparents of the same sex (Rubenstein, 1983). In the Abaluyia culture of Kenya "siblings" include children who were fostered in the same household (Weisner, 1989b); and in the Giriama culture of Kenya "siblings" include children of the same village or tribe who are of the same age range (Wenger, 1989). Such siblings are taken seriously as true siblings (Marshall, 1983a); demonstration of the expected behaviors and feelings toward other siblings is sufficient for identification as a true sibling, regardless of blood relationship. Such siblings are expected to fulfill all obligations required of siblings in that particular culture.

An even more extreme example of use of the term *sibling* is found in the culture of the Vaupés Indians of northwest Amazon region of eastern Columbia, where the term is extended variously to all members of the several nuclear families occupying the same longhouse, to all members occupying several longhouses in a given geographic area, to all members of the same language group or tribe, or to all members of related language groups (Jackson, 1984). The Vaupés, however, distinguish "real" biological siblings from other uses of the term.

In making comparisons across cultures, it is important to be aware of how the term *sibling* is defined in the particular cultures involved in the comparisons.

DIFFERENCES IN SIBLING STRUCTURE

Sibling structure refers to a hierarchical network of positions which identifies the status of each sibling relative to other siblings in the family. The positions in the network are defined in terms of the number of siblings (or size of the network), their birth order, gender, age level (chronological age), and the age spacing between one sibling and another. The concept of sibling structure overlaps with the concepts of sibling constellation variables and biosocial structure (Buhrmester, 1992; Cicirelli, 1982, 1985b).

In industrialized societies, sibling structure variables have been found to bear a relationship to sibling behavior and level of performance (Buhrmester, 1992; Cicirelli, 1982, 1985b). However, such relationships tend to involve interactions between the sibling structure variables, and vary with the overall family context.

In nonindustrialized societies, by contrast, sibling structure variables tend to be used to institutionalize sibling behaviors. That is, societal norms exist such that siblings in various sibling structure positions are expected to show certain role behaviors peculiar to that position.

Number of Siblings

In industrialized societies, the number of siblings born into a family has been declining over the last half of the 20th century (Bahr, 1989). At the present time, most traditional families rarely have more than three siblings, and usually only one or two. Various factors have been responsible for this decline, including the rising cost of rearing children, the entry of women into the work force, and the availability of effective birth control methods. (However, if one considers families that have been reconstituted through remarriage following divorce or widowhood, the overall number of siblings including half- and stepsiblings may be somewhat larger. Unfortunately, sibling subsets comprised of half- and stepsiblings have rarely been included in studies in the United States.)

Families in nonindustrialized societies tend to have a greater number of siblings than found in the industrialized nations. The number of children born into a family tends to be larger because more children are needed for work to help maintain daily family functioning and survival. Additionally, the inclusion of other individuals (cousins or nonfamily age mates) into the set of siblings increases the apparent size of the sibling subsystem.

There are various implications of the differences in the number of siblings. In nonindustrialized societies, the larger sibling group offers a greater support system for parents in old age as well as for members of the sibling group themselves. On the other hand, the larger sibling group would seem to offer greater potential for conflicts between siblings to arise.

Age Spacing

The smaller number of siblings in industrialized societies tends to have a greater age spacing between siblings than is found in families where the number of siblings is larger (Sutton-Smith & Rosenberg, 1970; Zajonc & Markus, 1975). Research has indicated that an age spacing of 2 to 4 years between siblings may be optimal for greater mental stimulation from one another while minimizing conflict. When both parents are working, spacing siblings still further apart may provide the parents with greater opportunity for career development and enhancement of the family's economic status.

With the greater number of siblings found in nonindustrialized societies, age spacing is usually reduced. In less industrial or technologically advanced societies, it is advantageous to have more siblings to share the family work load.

Sibling Gender

In industrialized societies, the relationship between siblings varies according to the gender of the siblings involved. The relationship between sisters appears to be the closest, with brother–sister pairs intermediate in closeness, and brother-brother pairs least close (Adams, 1968; Cicirelli, 1982). During childhood, sisters are more likely to have a caretaking role in relation to younger siblings than are brothers, although their relationship becomes more egalitarian in adulthood. Pairs of sisters may have their arguments, conflicts, and jealousies, but in the long run they maintain closer and more affectionate relationships than do brothers. This close relationship is important to their morale and general well being even into old age (Cicirelli, 1989a). When the relationship is disrupted, sisters show signs of depression and efforts are made to restore the relationship. Close bonds between brothers have less relevance for their morale or well being. Sisters who have a close relationship support each other through all the major tasks and events of adult life: marriage, childrearing, divorce, widowhood, aging, and even dying. In later adulthood, sisters seem to challenge or stimulate one another to continue to develop social skills for dealing with others, whereas brothers do not have this effect on one another (Cicirelli, 1977).

Sisters not only keep in touch more often than brothers but they provide greater help to one another if needed, both in tangible services and psychological support. They have an additional impact on the total family as well, by taking responsibility for coordinating family activities and bringing family members together for various occasions. If there is any norm for sibling role behaviors in industrialized countries, it may be for these responsibilities to maintain family relationships. Sisters tend to work together as a team to accomplish these things within the family.

Sisters seem to be very important for the emotional security of their brothers in later life. For example, elderly brothers who have more sisters report greater feelings of happiness in life and fewer concerns or threats in areas affecting their basic security, such as lack of money, loss of job role, loss of spouse or other important family relationships, and dealing with younger people (Cicirelli, 1977). The mere existence or availability of sisters appears to be important for their brothers' morale, apart from any specific interactions or helping behaviors (Cicirelli, 1989a; Gold, 1989a).

In short, sisters in industrialized societies assume a unique and important role throughout the entire life span that is not matched by relationships between brothers or brother–sister relationships. They are not only more important for promoting a higher quality of relationships between the siblings in the family, but they play major roles in preserving family relationships, providing care to elderly parents, and giving emotional support to brothers late in life. Sisters not only enrich one another's lives but are the glue which helps maintain the continuity of the family.

By contrast, at least in terms of normative behavior, the adult sister–sister relationship is of lesser importance in nonindustrialized societies; the brother–sister relationship tends to be of central importance in marital arrangements, and the brother–brother relationship is of major importance in social and economic activities (Mandelbaum, 1970; Nuckolls, 1993; Weisner, 1982, 1993b).

These differences in close relationships are related to the differing cultural context in the two types of societies. In industrialized societies, there is a greater tendency for discretionary motives to determine the nature and extent of sibling relationships, whereas the closeness of the sibling relationship in nonindustrialized societies appears to be mandated by normative rules.

Birth Order

Siblings in different birth order positions may have different opportunities, such as a difference in availability of family resources, availability of parental time, energy, and attention, quality of the relationship with parents, and influence on younger siblings (Wallden, 1990). In industrialized societies, older siblings have a considerable influence on younger siblings' cognitive, social, and emotional development. They may serve as models, teachers, counselors, and confidantes, although there are no norms or obligations that they do so. Similarly, older siblings may assume voluntarily a position of leadership in the family as adults, without any obligation to do so. Although inheritance customs favored transfer of the family wealth to the oldest son in earlier times, more recent trends favor equal division of wealth among all siblings or inheritance patterns idiosyncratic to the family concerned.

In nonindustrialized societies, cultural norms establish certain roles for older siblings. An older brother has the greatest seniority or status in the family, after which comes the oldest sister, and finally the younger siblings. Younger siblings are taught to respect older siblings and to obey them as they would a parent, with this authority continuing into adulthood. In many cases, the older sister has an important mediating role between the older brother and the younger siblings when inevitable conflicts develop. Although inheritance customs vary, the older brother or older sister is often in charge of distributing the wealth to other siblings.

Age Level

In industrialized societies, the siblings are not generally expected to assume adult responsibilities at an early age, although parents may delegate limited responsibilities in some cases.

In nonindustrialized societies, siblings assume certain adult responsibilities at a much earlier age. Older siblings may take on responsibility for child care, household tasks, food production, and so on, with a chain reaction as some tasks are delegated in turn to younger siblings (Weisner, 1982).

SIBLING CARETAKING IN CHILDHOOD

In both industrialized and nonindustrialized societies, older siblings are often delegated responsibilities for the care of their younger siblings. However, in industrialized societies, such delegation tends to be carried out informally by parents, primarily to give the parent freedom to pursue other activities. Bryant (1989) studied 168 American families of 7- and 10-year-old children, each with a sibling 2 or 3 years older, using observations, interviews, and various test instruments. She found that sibling caretaking involves little training of the caretaking sibling by parents; it tends to be episodic rather than continuous; and it is primarily custodial in nature. By custodial is meant such things as caring for the younger siblings' basic needs, supervising their activities to achieve socially acceptable behavior (e.g., preventing aggression, destruction of surroundings, harm to self or others), protecting them from the environment or from others, and sometimes entertaining them to prevent boredom or restlessness.

In the interactions between older and younger siblings during sibling caretaking, younger siblings learn various values, knowledge, and skills from their sibling caretaker at the same time as cognitive, emotional, and social aspects of their personality development are being influenced. Younger siblings might learn about various games, taboo topics (such as sex), confidential information pertaining to friends or parents, and so on. Older siblings may serve as models for the younger to imitate, although there is usually no expectancy for them to do so. The teaching and learning experiences provided by older siblings are informal, with no conscious intent to produce long-range effects. Sibling caretaking may result in long-term changes in cognitive, emotional, and social development of both the older and younger siblings, but there is no conscious intent to prepare the children for domestic chores, occupational work, or adult roles in the community (Bryant, 1989, 1992; Dunn, 1989). Teti, Gibbs, and Bond (1989) reported that in 44 infant–sibling dyads they studied, interaction with older siblings provided both an intellectually and socially stimulating environment for the younger child, particularly at wider age spacings between the siblings.

Zajonc and Markus (1975) demonstrated that older siblings in a family had greater intellectual ability than the younger, which they attributed to the experience of teaching a younger sibling. In a series of studies investigating the effects of sibling caretaking on school achievement, using large samples of preadolescent and adolescent school children in the United States, T. E. Smith (1984, 1990a, 1993) found that reading and language achievement of children were enhanced when they had a moderate degree of responsibility for younger siblings, but that there was a u-shaped curve such that higher amounts of sibling teaching appeared to be associated with no further gains in achievement compared to more moderate responsibilities. In other studies, T. E. Smith (1990b, 1992) found that time spent on household chores was related to lowered academic achievement. To the extent that time devoted to heavier sibling caregiving loads may be considered to be distracting from academic pursuits in the same sense as household chores, extensive sibling caregiving may be regarded as incompatible with the achievement demands of technologically advanced, industrialized societies.

On the social–emotional level, Dunn (Dunn, Beardsall, & Slomkowski, 1993; Dunn, Slomkowski, & Beardsall, 1994; Dunn, Slomkowski, Beardsall, & Rende, 1994) found in studies of 39 families in England from childhood to early adolescence that a warm and supportive relationship with an older sibling was associated with higher perceived self-competence and better adjustment of the younger sibling, while negative behavior from an older sibling was associated with the younger sibling's poorer perceived self-competence and poorer adjustment. When there was a warm relationship between the siblings, older siblings helped the younger deal with both minor difficulties and major life problems, resulting in a closer relationship between the two. Moreover, longitudinal analyses over a 7- to 8-year period revealed considerable stability in both the nature of the relationship and the outcome measures. Furman, Jones, Buhrmester, and Adler (1989) found substantial correspondence between the perspectives of both older and younger school aged siblings on the warmth-closeness, conflict, and relative status dimensions of their social–emotional relationship, lending support to Dunn's findings.

In nonindustrialized societies, a much greater degree of importance is attached to older siblings' role as caretakers of younger siblings and it appears to be an institutionalized function. Sibling caretaking may be delegated by parents with older children taking heavy responsibility for the younger, although the parents maintain ultimate control, as in the Abaluyia (Weisner, 1982, 1989b) or the Giriama (Wenger, 1989) societies of Kenya in Africa or in the Mandinka society (Whittemore & Beverly, 1989) of Senegal in west Africa. In these societies age groups of children (siblings and peers) may be supervised for extended periods of time by older siblings while the parents are busy elsewhere. In the island societies of Oceania, sibling caretaking tends to be more of a shared function with the parents, with older girls helping mothers with the women's tasks including the care of younger siblings; for example, Kirkpatrick's (1983) study of the Marquesans, Lambert's (1983) analysis of the Gilbertese, or Watson-Gegeo and Gegeo's (1989) study of the Kwara'ae in the Solomons, which provides a very detailed description of sibling caregiving activities. Older siblings feed and comfort babies, keep younger siblings out of mischief and discipline them, assign various household and gardening chores to them, and generally supervise their behavior. Younger children are taught to respect their older siblings and to be cooperative, thus fostering a highly interdependent sibling group. Sibling caretaking is also typical of South

Asian societies (Seymour, 1993), where boys as well as girls contribute to care of younger siblings.

In nonindustrialized societies, the objective of sibling caregiving is more than just to give the mother free time for other activities; it allows the parents to fulfill necessary work roles for family survival and maintenance. In addition, sibling caregiving serves as a backup system in the event the parents do not survive some catastrophe. Caretaking under such circumstances is more than merely custodial; custodial activities are combined with an educative mission to socialize and train younger siblings to become functioning members of society. Older siblings are trained by parents to teach their younger siblings some aspects of personal self-care, skills for doing household or domestic work (such as cleaning house, getting firewood or water), and skills for occupational or outside work essential for the survival or maintenance of the family (such as gardening, tending animals, cultivating crops). Thus, children not only learn activities that contribute to their survival, but practice parental roles and learn the values and activities of their society (Ervin-Tripp, 1989).

As sibling caretakers and younger siblings interact, various beneficial outcomes ensue. Younger siblings learn values, knowledge, and skills that help them to develop cognitively, emotionally, and socially, as well as values and knowledge about the larger society (such as respect for elders) that prepare them for future living. In addition, solidarity of the sibling group develops which carries over into adult life, as siblings learn cooperativeness, sharing, caring, and involvement in one another's lives, and placing the group above the individual.

Parents, for their part, train older siblings to be caretakers and younger siblings to be obedient to older siblings. The sibling caretaking system forms a hierarchy where an older sibling may care for a middle sibling, who in turn cares for a younger sibling (Weisner, 1982, 1989b). Depending on the task involved, a sibling may become a caretaker or a care recipient. Sibling caretaking is part of a larger childhood experience that stresses interdependence between siblings and leads to normative expectations and responsibilities governing sibling relationships throughout life (Dunn, 1993; Weisner, 1993b).

Weisner (1982, 1989a) has pointed out that there is considerable variation across families within a society in the extent to which the cultural norms are enacted in practice. Also, an established hierarchy of sibling caretakers can lead to tyranny of older siblings over the younger as well as de facto tyranny of the younger over the older as the caretaker tries to appease younger siblings to keep parents from being upset. Sibling fights, conflicts, and rivalries occur in nonindustrialized as well as industrialized societies, instead of the ideal cooperation, sharing, and love.

The age at which an older sibling assumes the caretaker role varies. In the Kwara'ae society of Melanesia (Watson-Gegeo & Gegeo, 1989), although a few caretaking tasks begin as early as age 3, fuller caretaking responsibilities begin at 7 or 8. In Samoa, more extensive care of infants is delegated at an earlier age (Ochs, 1982).

Methods of sibling teaching are informal but apparently effective. Older siblings' methods include probing, demonstration, providing feedback, repetition, speaking louder, paraphrasing, abbreviation of information, and so on, while younger sibling behaviors include questioning, soliciting repetition, use of intonation, and explaining (Ervin-Tripp, 1989). When there is no time to develop effective communication through dialogue in situations involving work, health, shame, or survival, the older sibling may physically grab or coerce the younger. Other methods involve teasing, challenging, or using others to transmit messages or rebukes (Watson-Gegeo & Gegeo, 1989).

In general, industrialized societies have underrated the degree to which siblings are socializing agents of other siblings (younger and older) and have never seriously formalized or institutionalized the use of older siblings in helping to care for their younger siblings. According to Weisner (1993a), parents in industrialized societies feel that their children should be treated as equally as possible, and that older siblings should not be burdened with too many caretaking and other domestic tasks. Thus whatever sibling socialization occurs seems to be a result of incidental and voluntary interactions.

MARRIAGE ARRANGEMENTS OF SIBLINGS

The predominance of cross-sibling relationships in connection with marital arrangements is a widespread feature of nonindustrialized societies. Among the lowland Indians of the Amazon region of South America (Basso, 1984; Crocker, 1984; Dole, 1984; Jackson, 1984; Kaplan, 1984; Kensinger, 1984; Kracke, 1984; Lyon, 1984; Shapiro, 1984; Sorensen, 1984; Whitten & Whitten, 1984), the ideal marriage involves an alliance of sibling sets involving brother–sister exchange such that a brother and sister marry a brother and sister from another socially distant family. The particular social rules involving such exchanges are complex and vary from group to group; they need not concern us here. The continued exchange of material wealth and assistance between the sibling sets, as well as the stronger interpersonal relationships, is considered to be important for the marriage as well as for the families as a whole. Despite the importance of brother–sister exchanges in marriage, most social interactions in these societies are within same-sex groups, so that brothers and sisters do not have close personal relationships.

Brother–sister exchanges are typical of marriages in the island societies of Oceania as well, although in Oceania the brother–sister relationship may be a very close one (Marshall, 1983a; Schneider, 1983). Families consider it important, therefore, to have a balanced number of sons and daughters. If the numbers of natural sons and daughters is unequal, or the total number of children is too small, one of the parent's siblings or cousins may give a child for adoption to achieve balance, as in Huntsman's (1983) study in Tokelau. Once the siblings attain adolescence, most of these societies practice some sort of cross-sibling avoidance; this ranges from very mild prohibitions against discussing sexual topics with the cross-sib or being alone with the cross-sib, as in the Solomon Islands or the Gilberts (Feinberg, 1983; Lambert, 1983), to actual avoidance of contact involving living in separate dwellings, as in Truk (Marshall, 1983b). Nevertheless, a brother and sister are often treated as a special unit for exchange marriages, with closely linked personal and economic interests throughout life.

In some nonindustrialized cultures, such as traditional India and Sri Lanka (Beals & Eason, 1993; Dean-Oswald, 1985; de Munck, 1990, 1993; Derné, 1993; Kolenda, 1993; Nuckolls, 1993; Seymour, 1993; Trawick, 1990; Weisner, 1982, 1993b), close sibling relationships are fostered, since a brother and sister will depend on each other to a great extent in negotiating marital arrangements. Brothers play an important role in increasing a sister's dowry through their labor and sharing their earnings, particularly if the father has insufficient income to increase the dowry to a level acceptable to the potential bridegroom's family (in some areas, a bride-price rather than a dowry is the custom). The brother may have to defer his own marriage until he helps provide dowries for sisters to get married first. In the meantime, he may attempt to influence his future wife's brother to contribute toward her dowry so as to expedite his own marriage. When he marries, he manages his wife's dowry and can use some of this wealth to contribute to the dowries of any still unmarried sisters. Ideal forms of marriage are those between cross-cousins or those in which there is an exchange of brothers and sisters from two different families (as in South America and Oceania), thus keeping the wealth within the combined families. Sisters and brothers are obligated by social norms to depend on each other to achieve successful marriages and get ahead in life.

There are variations on this theme in other nonindustrialized cultures, such as those of east Africa (Weisner, 1982). Again sister–brother relationships play a major role in marriage negotiations as they depend on one another to generate the wealth necessary for marriage, but in this case it is the prospective husband's family who provides the bride-price payment to the prospective wife's family. Although the wealth so gained goes to the father of the bride, it in turn may help to generate the brideprice for the bride's brother's own marriage. Funds paid for the younger sisters of the father may also help to provide for the son's marriage. Or a brother may depend directly upon a sister to obtain the bride-price from her prospective husband; he can then make use of this money to increase the wealth that he must pay to his future wife's family.

Thus, in nonindustrialized cultures, sister–brother relationships play a major role in the economic negotiations required for marriage and in marital decisions. Such marital customs increase the bonds of closeness between sisters and brothers throughout the life span.

SIBLING RELATIONSHIPS IN ADULTHOOD

In industrialized societies, adult siblings usually live independently of each other and the relationship between them is largely volitional, although there seems to be a weak norm that siblings should remain in touch (Adams, 1968). Most adult siblings do continue to see each other from time to time throughout their lives, but the frequency with which they interact depends on the closeness of the relationship between a particular pair as well their proximity and competing commitments and responsibilities (Cicirelli, 1985b; Gold, 1989a). In general, sister–sister relationships are particularly close, with cross-sex siblings intermediate in closeness and brother–brother relationships least close.

In industrialized nations such as the United States and Australia which have been populated by various groups of immigrants, there are ethnic group differences in sibling relationships. For example, Johnson (1985) compared Italian-American and white Protestants of northern European ancestry in the United States, finding closer relationships and much greater frequencies of contact with siblings among the Italian-Americans than among the Protestants, with sister–sister relationships particularly strong.

In many nonindustrialized societies, the sibling relationship assumes great importance throughout life, with siblings sharing scarce resources and thus maximizing the strength of the family. According to Weisner (1993b), sibling interdependence is necessary to attain economic, marital, or other benefits.

In Oceania, a brother and sister often have closely linked personal and economic interests throughout life. If a sister is separated from her husband she may go to stay with her brother and his wife. Sisters and brothers are regarded as complementary. Brothers are expected to protect their sisters, while the sisters are expected to be the spiritual mentors for their brothers (M. Marshall, 1983a). In New Guinea, sisters are valued over wives, with the feeling that men can replace their wives but not their sisters (Reay, 1975–76).

Whereas husbands and wives may have competitive interests, siblings are expected to cooperate for their own mutual benefit and that of their offspring. The relationship between sisters in adulthood is typically close. However, the relationship between brothers may involve considerable competition, rivalry, jealousy, and conflict (Goodale, 1983; Lambert, 1983). One problem in the relationship between brothers is that the siblings are supposed to respect the oldest brother's right to make certain decisions for the group; if the older brother becomes too officious or demanding, there will be a conflict with the male egos of the younger brothers.

In traditional cultures of India and Sri Lanka (Beals & Eason, 1993; Dean-Oswald, 1985; de Munck, 1990, 1993; Derné, 1993; Kolenda, 1993; Nuckolls, 1993; Seymour, 1993; Trawick, 1990; Weisner, 1982, 1993b), social norms for siblings lead to a close cooperative relationship throughout life. After marriage, brothers feel obligated to check on the welfare of their married sisters and their children, while married brothers typically live together with their parents in large joint households until their parents die and their own children are married.

In nonindustrialized cultures where sister–brother relationships play a major role in the economic negotiations required for marriage and in marital decisions, such customs appear to increase the bonds of closeness between sisters and brothers throughout the life span. In fact, the relationship between sister and brother is the focal point of social and cultural life in many of these nonindustrialized societies (M. Marshall, 1983a; Schneider, 1983; Weisner, 1982). In others, once the sisters are married and move out of the community, the relationship between brothers is the most important one in adult life (Nuckolls, 1993; Weisner, 1993b).

EFFECTS OF CULTURAL CHANGE ON SIBLING RELATIONSHIPS

The culture of a people is rarely static, but evolves in response to local, national, and international conditions. An abrupt change in cultural milieu, as found when members of one society emigrate to another, or a more gradual change in response to processes of modernization and cultural diffusion from the industrialized countries to a nonindustrialized society can affect the relationships among siblings as well as a wide range of cultural characteristics of a people.

Modernization can bring large changes in a society. For example, change from a subsistence farming and gathering economy to a wage-earning economy, increased contact with outsiders, occurrence of disease epidemics, and central government regulations and programs may be accompanied by loss of population, lowered birth rates, marriage outside the group, and migration to urban areas (Crocker, 1984; Lyon, 1984). The result may be a loosening of the authority of the elders in the society over the younger members, increasing deviation from traditional cultural norms, and ultimately erosion or replacement of the norms themselves.

Among the primitive Wachipaeri Indians in South America studied by Lyon (1984), a smallpox epidemic reduced the population to a third of its former size, the construction of missions introduced new ideas, and road construction brought an increase in the presence of outsiders, resulting in frequent marriage of the women to outsiders for economic gain and the disruption of traditional sibling exchange marriage patterns. Among the Giriama of Africa, migration of families to urban areas for jobs has interfered with traditional sibling caretaking groups, with a transition to at least some formal schooling (Wenger, 1989). In India, prolonged education and employment of women in the workplace have led to delayed marriages and much stronger relationships between sisters (Seymour, 1993). In Malaysia (Chee, 1979; Wong, 1979; Wong & Kuo, 1979), the earlier patterns of extended families with sibling caretaking and sibling interdependence are giving way to small nuclear families with pressures for self-reliance and achievement. Among native Hawaiians in the Honolulu area (Weisner, Gallimore, & Jordan, 1988), exposure to the wider culture has led to considerable variability in traditional Hawaiian patterns of sibling and age peer support, with increasing numbers of mothers feeling unsure about the validity of traditional values.

Similarly, changes are also found among those who emigrate to a new culture. Following the emigration of a group of Japanese to the Seattle area (Yanagisako, 1985), cultural values regarding inheritance rules and sibling relationships were found to shift toward an idealized American model in a generation. Another example is the change observed by Johnson (1985) among Italian-Americans who married non-Italians. As compared to those who had Italian-American spouses, sibling relationships were weakened as indicated by greatly reduced visiting patterns.

A large variety of ethnic groups is represented in the multicultural American society of today as a result of recent major emigrations from Mexico, Latin America, the Caribbean, southeast Asia, and so on. In most cases, these groups are characterized by very cohesive sibling groups with considerable authority for child caretaking delegated to the older siblings in childhood and continued close relationships between siblings in adulthood. It is to be expected that in ensuing generations, the pattern of sibling relationships will gradually move toward that of the dominant culture as these groups assimilate.

CONCLUSION

Perhaps the major difference in the sibling relationships found in the two types of cultures is the discretionary nature of the sibling relationships in industrialized societies as compared to the obligatory nature of sibling relationships in nonindustrialized societies. Discretionary sibling relationships are based on the siblings' desire to behave in certain ways toward one other or remain involved in one another's lives throughout the life course, whereas in obligatory sibling relationships the siblings are constrained by cultural norms to behave in certain ways toward each other. In nonindustrialized societies as compared to industrialized societies, sibling relationships are of fundamental importance in determining family functioning and the family's adaptation to the larger society, with sibling cooperation essential to attain marital and economic goals (Weisner, 1993b).

Siblings in industrialized societies tend to be identified primarily by biological or genealogical criteria, whereas in nonindustrialized societies, the term *sibling* is enlarged through extension to other kin members or through classification. As a result, individuals in nonindustrialized societies tend to have a greater number of siblings than those in industrialized societies. However, the growing prevalence of stepfamilies in high-divorce societies such as the United States may lead toward increasing acceptance of an enlarged conception of the term *sibling*.

The two types of societies also differ greatly in the nature and extent of sibling caretaking. In industrialized societies, parents have primary control over child caretaking with only occasional and incidental sibling caretaking, whereas in nonindustrialized societies, caregiving by older siblings is institutionalized and made part of the larger culture (Weisner, 1993b).

In industrialized societies, sibling structure has an influence on sibling relationships, but in nonindustrialized societies sibling structure variables are the criteria for establishing normative relationships between siblings, with roles established by birth order and gender. Typically, sister–sister relationships are the closest in industrialized societies while sister–brother and brother–brother relationships are the closest in nonindustrialized societies.

Variability in the quality of sibling relationships is found in both types of societies. In industrialized societies, sibling relationships can range from extreme closeness to rivalry to indifference at the discretion of the individuals involved. In nonindustrialized societies variation in sibling relationship quality also exists as a result of tensions, conflicts, and rivalries. However, control mechanisms exist in the society to attempt to deal with such problems, such as an emphasis on authority of older over younger members, ritualized avoidance, projections of witchcraft and sorcery, and so on (Weisner, 1982). When resources are limited, sibling cooperation is essential to accomplish the tasks necessary to maintain both the family and the larger community, and cultural norms limit sibling conflicts that could threaten such cooperation. Overall, the difference seems to be that variations are recognized as deviations from social norms in the nonindustrialized societies (Dunn, 1993; Weisner, 1989a).

It is difficult to make cross-cultural comparisons of sibling relationships between the two types of cultures because investigators have, for the most part, used different methods and asked different research questions. What is needed are more studies that provide a true basis for making comparisons. From a theoretical perspective, it would be important to study sibling attachment in the two types of cultures to determine whether attachment bonds are different in societies that make heavy use of sibling caregiving from those that do not. Also, if one could determine the proportion of sibling shared and nonshared environments for a continuum of cultures, it might help to account for commonalities and differences at the cultural level. In other words, understanding nonshared environments at the cultural level would contribute to the understanding of nonshared environments at the individual level.

CHAPTER 7

Understanding Sibling Relationships: A Hermeneutic Approach

This chapter summarizes an exploratory study of relationships between adult siblings in one large family. The study used a hermeneutic approach (Glaser, 1978; Glaser & Strauss, 1967; Strauss, 1987) in an attempt to determine how adult siblings perceived and interpreted their relationships within a family context. This exploratory approach allows insights, hypotheses, and tentative conclusions about family functioning to emerge; they can be tested more rigorously in further studies employing larger samples of smaller families more typical of present and future generations.

The subjects of the study were nine siblings, their parents, and their spouses, making 20 people in all. It was hoped that, by focusing on one family, new insights into adult sibling relationships would emerge. A family with many siblings was selected for study because it was felt that differences in the many dyadic relationships would be more likely to occur and be more easily detected. Spouses and parents were included in order to understand how the sibling relationships function within the total family context; that is, how the influence of siblings on each other may also depend upon their relationships with their spouses and their parents. For the most part, interpretations of the data are presented in a narrative form rather than attempting to present a quantitative data analysis.

STUDY PROCEDURE

Each family member living within a 65-mile radius was interviewed individually by the author for approximately 2½ hours. No other family members were present during the interview (except for babies or toddlers in a few cases), so that the interviewee was able to speak freely. The interview session was tape-recorded and then transcribed for further study. Those siblings and spouses who lived out of state were interviewed individually by telephone for 2 to 2½ hours, prearranging a time for the interview when they could be alone and speak freely. The author took copious notes of responses during these interviews.

During the interviews, certain questions were asked of all family members, other questions were directed only toward some of the family members. Some questions applied particularly to the siblings themselves, some to the spouses, and some to the parents. Follow-up questions to probe interviewees views more completely were used as needed. In addition, the content of some interview questions was modified as the study went on, after listening to and reflecting upon tapes of earlier interviews; some nonproductive questions were dropped, and a few new ones added.

The data were not statistically analyzed beyond determining some simple response frequencies. The author worked primarily like a detective, putting bit and pieces of information together from all the participants, and attempting to construct an overall account of how these siblings felt and dealt with each other, one another's spouses, and their parents.

At times, the narrative may seem to lack sufficient examples or quotations to support the statements made. This was a matter of the author's deliberate intent to protect the confidentiality of the family members' responses from acquaintances in the community as well as from each other. Also, rather than presenting comments of a particular sibling, the approach used was to summarize the comments from all the siblings as a group, or all the spouses, or the parents.

In every family, there are feelings or events that family members do not wish to divulge or make public, perhaps feeling that to do so might be socially unacceptable or painful to themselves or others. This seemed to be true in this case as some family members indicated that they did not wish to talk about certain areas. Others shared their thoughts to help the author understand the family but requested that the author not reveal this personal information; their confidence has been respected.

Like any study of this type, the interviews revealed only a snapshot of family members' perceptions and views at a given moment in time. Perhaps a different picture would have emerged if the family members had been interviewed at a later date and under different circumstances.

Overall, these family members were open and willing to share their perceptions of how their family functions. Without them, this chapter could not have been written, and the author is exceeding grateful for their cooperation.

BACKGROUND CHARACTERISTICS OF FAMILY MEMBERS

The seven sisters and two brothers in this family ranged in age from 26 to 47 years, a period encompassing young and middle adulthood. The age spacing between oldest and youngest was 21 years. The youngest five siblings, their spouses, and their parents lived within a 65-mile radius of one another; the oldest four siblings and their spouses lived at various locations out of state (three in neighboring states and one on the east coast). This lack of close proximity is typical of modern families where some members migrate to different areas rather than remaining near their parents in the same area. However, distances were not too far to prevent periodic visits.

Five of the sisters had occupations in the nursing field and were currently working outside the home. Two were housewives, one of whom was a home day care provider. One brother was in construction work and the other was a chemist. One sibling was currently attending university classes for purposes of career advancement. Occupational titles of the siblings' spouses varied considerably and included marketing, clinical counseling, mechanic, chemist, housewife, computer specialist, veterinary student, food inspector, and chiropractor. The majority of siblings and spouses had dual career families and were interested in upward mobility in their occupations. Apparently they were influenced by their father's expectations for achievement, whether they were conscious of it or not.

All of the siblings had children of their own, with families of from 1 to 7 children ranging in age from early childhood to young adulthood (a total of 28 children in the third generation of the family). The oldest siblings have completed their families and are beginning the child launching phase, while the youngest siblings are still in the early stages of childrearing. However, the children and relationships involving the children are not a major focus of this study.

As for the parents, the father was 72 years of age and retired from an executive position in a manufacturing concern; the mother was aged 68 and a housewife. The parents appeared to be well off financially, and in a position to help the children if they needed such help.

The number of siblings, their age span, and their various occupations indicates that the family is a diverse group whose members experienced differing family and extrafamilial contexts over their life history. These nonshared experiences certainly contribute to their individual differences.

FAMILY CLIMATE

The overall climate of the family during the siblings' childhood and adolescence appeared to be that of the traditional authoritarian family, with the father being the breadwinner and ultimate authority in the family and the mother managing the household and nurturing the children (Nye & Berardo, 1973). This family climate appears to persist at the present time.

The father was and still is head of the family, acting as the center of authority and power and setting the standards for the family. The mother and the siblings attempt to comply by carrying out his wishes, insofar as they can while meeting their own responsibilities. Most of the siblings felt that the mother did not have a favorite child when they were growing up, but they felt that the father did have favorites. However, the identity of the favorite child varied, depending upon which of the siblings was achieving the most at a particular period in time. Most of the siblings felt no resentment about whether or not they were the favorite. In fact, most seemed to feel relieved if they were not the favorite, because this position carried with it considerable pressure to maintain high standards of achievement. On the other hand, some of the siblings felt that certain other siblings constantly strove to achieve in order to win the father's approval and be the favorite child; this was somewhat resented.

To most of the siblings, the father appeared to be somewhat cold and distant, rather critical and difficult to talk to, and one with whom they didn't dare to disagree. This picture seems to be rather typical of the traditional authoritarian father, who has rather formal relationships with his children. On the other hand, a few of the siblings felt close to the father, sharing topics of common interest in long discussions with him.

The mother was regarded by all as warm and friendly, and the go-between linking father and children. Through her communication skills and persuasiveness, she was able to influence both the father and the children, persuading them to do things together, coordinating their views and activities, and clarifying any misunderstandings between them. She was able to relate to the siblings to give them warmth, understanding, advice, suggestions, and appreciation of their points of view. Many of the siblings expressed the view that they could talk to their mother and exchange views with her about anything, but they were not able to do this with the father. If they didn't want to do things his way, it was better to say nothing than to defy him.

Most of the siblings shared the above view of the family during the years when they were growing up. At present, however, siblings have somewhat varied views. Some siblings felt that others had succeeded in meeting their father's expectations, earning them a special status in which they could talk more freely with the father, exchange views, and influence him. However, there also seemed to be some degree of jealousy and resentment toward these particular siblings.

The family climate appeared to be dominated by three basic values held by the parents: career achievement, religion, and importance of family. Although both parents seemed to believe strongly in all three values, the father played a greater role in motivating and evaluating his children's achievement while the mother seemed more influential in the religious and family areas.

At the beginning of the parents' marriage, the couple had few financial resources but they worked hard, and succeeded on their own in attaining a relatively high standard of living. The philosophy of self-reliance and achievement motivated the father and probably became more important to him as he continued to experience his own career success. He extended his same concern for achievement to his children, expecting them to meet certain standards of school and career achievement; it was unacceptable if the children made no effort to develop their potential to make something of themselves. On the other hand, it was excusable if they did not succeed but had at least tried.

The father was able to easily categorize his children according to their levels of achievement. He made a strong point that he did not reject his children as individuals if they did not meet his standards, but was saddened by the disappointment. Apparently, however, such disappointment was communicated to the children who may have interpreted it as involving some degree of rejection. There was resentment and rebellion on the part of some of the siblings against the father's preoccupation with achievement. Some expressed the view that they just wanted to have jobs they liked, accomplish just enough to feel a degree of financial security, and then enjoy other things in life; they were not interested in higher levels of achievement or the associated financial rewards. This view was echoed by some spouses who felt that the family in general was too materialistic, and too concerned with using achievement as a vehicle to gain money, material goods, and status. They felt that this emphasis stemmed from the father and led to an unnecessary degree of rivalry between the siblings.

The mother was much concerned with religion, and with her children's continued adherence to religious practices, such as regular church attendance. She seem disturbed and frustrated that many of the children no longer followed various practices of the Catholic church. Her disapproval was communicated to the children, and she was further frustrated that they did not necessarily follow her wishes.

Both parents had strong family values. They felt that marriages should last, that parents should spend the necessary time and be responsible for raising their children properly, and that there should be great concern for family solidarity. Interestingly, these family values seemed to be the ones most accepted by the siblings. Yet, in actual practice, they may have been somewhat difficult to live up to. Some fundamental conflicts between certain family members remain unresolved. Also, many siblings criticized other siblings regarding such topics as the way they related to their spouses, their failure to assume sufficient responsibility for raising their children properly, placing their career ahead of family, paying insufficient attention to their parents, and letting their own rivalries interfere with better sibling relationships.

There was a general feeling that although the siblings were strong willed and independent, and were ready to criticize, argue, assert their superiority, or be competitive with one another, at the same time a strong underlying bond existed between them so that if there were a crisis or common threat from the outside, or a problem facing one sibling, they would come together as a group to help and protect one another. The relationships between these siblings reflected a typical ambivalence between disliking many things about the other and simultaneously caring deeply for the other. Obviously, feelings vary from sibling to sibling, but it seemed clear that an underlying group solidarity existed.

INFLUENCE OF SIBLING STRUCTURE

The sibling structure of a family at any given time is defined by the number of siblings, their genders and gender ratio, their birth order, their ages, and the age spacing between them. A consideration of the sibling structure of this family led to the exploration of some interesting hypotheses.

In terms of age and age spacing, it was possible to view the nine siblings as forming three subgroups, each containing three siblings. The siblings in the oldest subgroup ranged in age from 45 to 47 and were all born in the 1940s. Those in the middle subgroup ranged in age from 36 to 41 and were all born in the 1950s. Finally those in the youngest subgroup ranged in age from 26 to 32 and were all born in the 1960s.

The historical periods during which each of the three groups went through similar stages of childhood and adolescence were associated with different contextual experiences. For example, the decade of the 1950s is known for the conclusion of the Korean war, readjustment of veterans into society, national television, McCarthyism, school desegregation, formation of the transcontinental expressway system, and so on. The decade of the 1960s is known for the Vietnam war, the antiwar protest movement, the Cuban crisis, first Americans in space, the Watts riot, the hippie movement, growth of the drug subculture, the assassinations of the Kennedys and King, and so on. The decade of the 1970s is known for changing relations with China, the Supreme Court decision in favor of abortion, the Watergate scandal, the Iranian hostage crisis, and so on. During each decade, world and national affairs changed dramatically, accompanied by changing values, beliefs, and norms. Overall, the trend has been one of declining family values and reduced work ethic.

Given such sweeping changes in society over the period when the three sibling subgroups were reared, one might expect the siblings in the older group to be more traditional, conforming, achievement oriented; the middle group to be somewhat more adventurous and less concerned with getting ahead; and the younger group the least concerned with achievement and the problems of society and more self-absorbed.

Time did not permit a study in depth of the siblings' social views or life-styles. However, based on interview materials, the older three siblings were seen as more serious and responsible, and the youngest three were seen as the most rebellious against family values, most adventurous, most concerned with enjoying life at the moment. The siblings in the middle group were perceived as somewhat of a transition group between the more distinctly different older and younger sets.

How can such age differences between siblings be accounted for? The consensus view among the siblings was that the older three were raised in a more strict environment, with the parents holding them to a particular regimen of duties, that is, keeping up with their studies and doing household chores. If they deviated from their duties, they were punished (including being spanked). Also, the parents were strict in a religious sense, and expected the children to observe Catholic duties and traditions. Finally, the oldest three siblings were reared during a period when the parents were struggling to make ends meet. The father was still finishing his college degree, and everyone had to pull their weight to keep the family going.

When the middle group was being reared, the family was better off financially, there were fewer chores to do, and more children to share them, and the three siblings had more time for themselves. They had more opportunities to play and participate in social activities outside the home (e.g., scouting), and more such activities were available during this decade. Finally, the parents delegated some child care tasks to the older siblings, who were seen as being less strict than the parents.

By the time the younger group was being reared, more money was available to the family as the father was now well established and successful in his career. This led to the siblings participating in more diverse activities, and having more opportunities to have new experiences. Now some caretaking duties were passed down from the older group to the middle group of siblings, which perhaps was more tolerant of divergent behavior than the older siblings and which was certainly more tolerant than the parents. As a result, during their adolescence, the younger siblings were more adventurous, enjoyed partying more, and broke the family rules to a greater extent than had their older siblings at similar ages. Also, by this time, the parents may have experienced some "burnout" from years of raising children, and consequently accepted more divergent behavior than they had previously done.

However, and perhaps most interesting, none of the siblings viewed the age differences in siblings' behavior and values as due primarily to changes in society and different experiences of the three subgroups outside the family. They felt that the differences in the subgroups of siblings were more related to the changes or "stages of development" of the family. Although one spouse felt that direct participation in the larger society was very significant and another spouse felt that differences between siblings resulted from a combination of social changes and changing parents, the siblings themselves perceived the parents to be mediators of the changing society.

In effect, the siblings never escaped the influence of the family, no matter how much the wider society changed. Regardless of whether some siblings were more influenced by the environment beyond the family than others, most of the siblings felt that the parents were the mediators of that environment. The majority felt that interactions with changing parents (parents in different stages of life) and their other siblings had a more immediate impact on them than the changing and dramatic events beyond the family. The influence of outside events was determined by how the parents interpreted them, allowed children exposure to them, and how the children interacted with other siblings.

The gender ratio of the sibling structure of this family was also interesting, with seven sisters and only two brothers, suggesting a preponderance of feminine influence. The younger of the two brothers, one of the siblings in the youngest group, complained about having so many "mothers" caring for him as he grew up, as well as having to shoulder more than his share of the traditionally masculine chores. There seemed to be some division of parenting along gender lines as well, with the mother assuming major responsibility for rearing the daughters and the father assuming a larger share of responsibility for rearing the sons. As a result, the oldest of the brothers (the firstborn of the family) largely escaped the feminized environment and was in a better position to be more directly influenced by the father's values. Again, such observations present an interesting hypothesis for future studies with smaller families. The recent study of the effect of sibling sex composition on women's education and earnings (Butcher & Case, 1994) indicated that having a sister was disadvantageous for a woman but not for a man. However, this topic needs further investigation.

Finally, one might expect that the siblings within each of the three subgroups of siblings would feel closer to each other than to siblings from other subgroups because they had shared more experiences. However, this did not appear to be true, as feelings of closeness cut across age groups. Thus, it seems that shared experiences alone do not produce closeness and similarity, nor do nonshared experiences alone make for distance and individuality. One must consider how the personality of individual siblings interacts with shared experiences to lead to feelings of closeness. An additional factor is that the older siblings' caretaking duties may have brought them into closer contact with younger siblings than one might otherwise expect.

SIBLING PERCEPTIONS OF ONE ANOTHER

In interviewing the siblings, several strategies were used to determine how they felt about one another. First, each of the nine children was asked to rank each of his or her eight siblings according to closeness of feeling toward them. Next, each was asked to indicate what characteristics of each sibling were best liked and least liked. Then, each was asked to name the sibling with whom he or she had most in common, as well as the sibling who had the greatest impact on his or her life.

The siblings were exceedingly candid in these appraisals of one another. Out of consideration for the sensitivities and feelings of family members, and because particular combinations of characteristics would make individual siblings (both the appraiser and the one appraised) highly recognizable, this topic is discussed in general terms only without referring to specific siblings.

Mutual or Mismatched Feelings

Within a sibling dyad, the two siblings' views of each may be mutually positive (each likes the other) or mutually negative (each dislikes the other). On the other hand, frequently there is a mismatch of feelings, so that A likes B, but B dislikes A. First, the siblings' rankings of closeness of feelings were examined for mutuality of feelings within the 36 sibling dyads formed by the combinations of the nine siblings. Feelings were highly mutual in 39% of the pairs, with both siblings not differing in their rankings of the other or differing by only a point. Feelings were moderately mutual in 47% of the pairs, with the siblings' rankings differing by 2 or 3 points. A moderate degree of mismatched feelings was found for 14% of the pairs, whose rankings of each other differed by 4 or 5 points. No pairs exhibited a severe degree of mismatch.

Often people go through the motions of a relationship without revealing their deeper feelings, so the extent to which any mismatch in feelings influences the quality of the sibling relationship is not clear.

Closeness to Siblings

An average closeness of feelings ranking assigned by other members of the sibling group was calculated for each sibling. The mean rankings for the nine siblings ranged from 2.50 for the highest ranked sibling to 7.75 for the lowest ranked sibling, indicating considerable consensus among the siblings' feelings toward particular members of the sibling group.

In general, the mean closeness ranking did not appear to depend on age; that is, the siblings from no single age subgroup (young, middle, or oldest) were ranked as closest or least close. Additionally, although a preliminary hypothesis was that average closeness of feelings would be greatest for the siblings in the group who lived closest to one another and saw each other most frequently, closeness of feelings did not seem to depend on a sibling's proximity. Distant siblings received both high and low rankings, as did nearby siblings.

Overall, siblings' closeness of feelings for one another did not appear to be related to either age difference or geographic proximity, although it clearly was a factor in some individual rankings. Feelings of closeness seem to depend more on the perceived characteristics of siblings and the way that siblings behaved toward each other. When asked for their criteria used in assessing closeness of feelings toward a sibling, the group consensus was that they felt closest toward a sibling who was a good listener to their problems and concerns, who showed interest and cared about them as individuals, and who was nonjudgmental regarding their views or behavior.

Best and Least Liked Characteristics

Feelings of closeness to siblings were associated with perceived characteristics of the siblings' personalities. The siblings were all asked what they liked most and least about each of their siblings. Again, the results will only be presented in general terms and not connected with birth order to avoid any direct identification of the siblings. However, what was liked the most and least about each sibling seemed to follow a consensus, at least in the most predominant characteristics. Combining comments of the other eight siblings, the characteristics most liked about each of the nine siblings (presented with the siblings in random order) are as follows:

- Easy to talk to, easygoing, friendly, a confidante, empathic, understanding.
- Helpful, good businessperson, very organized, generous, easy to talk to, enjoyable conversationalist, enjoyable companion, nonjudgmental.
- Would do anything to help others, lots of fun, nonjudgmental, sense of humor, happy-go-lucky, enjoyable companion.
- A role model, responsible, dependable, brilliant, very helpful, hard worker.
- Willing to help, dependable, assertive, clear perspective, someone you can bounce ideas off, drive, ambition, intelligent, sets goals and achieves them.
- A role model to get things done, lots of fun, has ambition, cares for others, go-getter, achieves, fun to be with, hard worker, emotionally stable, always in a good mood.
- Open, fair-minded, nonjudgmental, accepting, very nice person, confidante, good listener, well-organized, gives advice, sense of humor.
- Easygoing, laid back, flexible, adaptable, fun to be with, good company, sincere, very organized, ambitious, caring, faces adversity with courage.
- Outgoing, gentle, relaxed, easy to get along with, brilliant, can discuss intellectual things, very perceptive of the environment, understanding, listens, helps one to resolve problems, shows loyalties, responsible, caring.

Counterbalancing the qualities that the siblings most liked about one another were the characteristics that they liked least. These *least liked* characteristics of each sibling (with the nine siblings again in random order) are:

- Too opinionated, undependable, adores money too much, judgmental, never on time, temper, too ambitious, tries to impress father, exploits others, attains goals at expense of others.
- Lacks confidence, can't confront or face things, can't think for self, spoiled.

- Very disorganized, never admits being wrong, abrupt, blunt, wants material goods without making effort.
- Makes no real effort to communicate, abrasive, too blunt, too concerned about money, workaholic, too formal, too stuffy, too materialistic.
- Puts on false front, disorganized personal life, always has to be right, temper, thinks he or she is better than others, ignores feelings and needs of others, sacrifices family to get ahead, competitive, argues too much, wants to impress everyone, wants to be in control.
- Won't reveal self, immature, lacks confidence, irresponsible.
- Complains too much, overbearing, authoritarian, highly emotional, highly sensitive, too self-centered, too dependent on other family members, not trustworthy, disrupts family.
- Too critical, tactless, too high-strung, too restless, too rigid, inconsistent, too influenced by others, temper, a little too ambitious, not sensitive about when not to talk.
- Puts on a false front, tries to impress everyone, whines, exaggerates everything, not honest, not trustworthy.

One can see from examining the most and least liked characteristics for the nine siblings that certain attributes tend to recur for various siblings. These patterns suggest that the siblings as a group tend to have certain values or standards in common which they used to judge one another and which influence their interactions with one another. Valued attributes seem to be clustered in a few areas: (1) intelligence, ambition, hard work, and achievement; (2) being a good companion and conversationalist, having a sense of humor, enjoying life; (3) being a confidante, trustworthy, accepting, caring, having empathy, understanding; and (4) confidence without arrogance, organization without rigidity, assertiveness without being controlling. Similarly, as a group the siblings tend to have values which lead them to dislike certain attributes: being overambitious, overmaterialistic, and overconcerned with impressing others.

In other words, what siblings like most and least about each other seems to reflect general family values or standards of what people should be like.

Impact and Common Interests

Finally, each individual was asked to identify the siblings who had the most and least impact on their lives, and the siblings with whom they had the most and least in common. Four siblings were named as having the most impact on the others, and five were named as having the least impact. Again, it appeared that personality characteristics were a dominant reason for these nominations; the older and younger groups each were represented on the most impact and least impact lists, as were distant and nearby siblings.

Regarding those with whom the other siblings had most and least in common, four siblings were named to each list. There was no clear pattern behind these nominations, although similarity of occupation played a part in some choices.

SPOUSES' PERCEPTIONS OF THE SIBLINGS

As noted earlier, all the siblings were married and established in their own homes. There has been little empirical investigation of the effect of siblings' spouses on the sibling relationship. However, in their investigations of the effects of various life events on the sibling relationship, both Bedford (1990, July) and Connidis (1992) found that a sibling's marriage could either bring siblings closer together or drive them apart, depending on how well the siblings and the new spouse got along.

Here, we examined how each of the nine spouses viewed the siblings. An underlying assumption was that if a spouse regarded a certain sibling negatively, the relationship between the sibling and the spouse's mate might be weakened.

Spouses' Closeness of Feeling to Various Siblings

First, the siblings' spouses were asked to rank the siblings (other than their mates) as to their closeness of feeling toward each sibling. An average degree of closeness was calculated in regard to each sibling.

The average ranking of feelings of closeness to siblings by the nine spouses ranged from a high of 3.12 to a low of 5.62, indicating that there was less consensus of feelings about the siblings among the spouses than among the siblings themselves. That is, each spouse was able to rank his or her feelings of closeness toward particular siblings, but as a group the spouses had no clear preferences.

Best and Least Liked Characteristics

The *most liked* characteristics of the siblings as viewed by the various spouses (presented in random order) were as follows:

- Friendly, open, fair, trustworthy, patient in dealing with demands of parents, accepting, down to earth.

- Very organized, good with children, down to earth, thoughtful, very friendly, similar beliefs.
- Always willing to help others, hard worker, good natured, likes a good time, very friendly.
- Successful, has initiative, intelligent, dependable, generous, organizational skills, willing to help others considerate, friendly.
- Aggressive, assertive, hospitable, thoughtful, ambitious, decisive, good intentions, good heart, knowledgeable in her occupation.
- Can have serious intellectual discussions with him or her, occupationally successful, very accomplished, brilliant, hard worker.
- Good parent, survivor, good person at heart, fun to be with, friendly, gives help when needed, considerate, sense of humor, down to earth.
- Gives good advice, brilliant, actively involved in life, makes a commitment and sticks to it, shows concern for others, hard worker.
- Easy to relate to, fair, trustworthy, concern for others, well organized, nonjudgmental, listens, gives advice, sense of humor.

Similarly, the *least liked* characteristics of the siblings as seen by the spouses are presented in random order below:

- Takes too much from others, gives in too much, can't think for self.
- Doesn't distinguish when to be loyal to family or spouse, tries to impress others, gossips, not truthful, has temper.
- Not motivated, sexist, lets people take advantage, impulsive, acts without plans, too easily influenced by others.
- Too pushy, wants to control others, authoritarian, shows off material wealth, hypocritical.
- Presumptuous, assumes own goals are family goals, pushes own goals at the expense of family, money hungry, insensitive, takes advantage of others, pushy, brags, tries to do too much, wants to impress everyone.
- Betrays confidences, depressed, gossips, inappropriate social behavior.
- Not a good parent, wants to control everyone, selfish, self-centered, doesn't complete tasks, disorganized, doesn't do fair share of work, too blunt, insensitive to others' feelings.
- Too overbearing, authoritarian, lacks self-confidence, overorganized, rigid schedule, always feels he or she is right, can't admit mistakes or weaknesses.
- Distant, cold, can't get close, too judgmental, conceited, preoccupied with money.

As a group, the spouses are able to see positive as well as negative characteristics of the siblings. One cluster of positive attributes that stands out is being open, friendly, and accepting; all are qualities that would make a spouse feel a welcome part of the family. One cluster of negative qualities that shows through many of the spouses' perceptions of the siblings is being pushy, overbearing, or controlling; clearly, the spouses don't want a mate's siblings to push them around.

SIBLING COMMUNICATION AND CONTACT

A second area of interest in this investigation of family functioning was the extent of interaction between the various siblings, and how such interactions came about.

Existence of Sibling Contact and Communication

If there was no contact or communication between siblings, then they could not be said to have an ongoing relationship at present but only set feelings and perceptions built up from the past. During the interviews, the siblings were asked about the frequencies of face-to-face contact with each sibling, as well as the frequency and amount of time spent in telephone conversations with each sibling. (These family members did not write letters to one another, so communication by letter was not a factor.)

Interview data indicates that the siblings did communicate with one another by telephone and have face-to-face visits, but the frequency of visiting and the amount of telephone time varied with the particular dyad involved. For most dyads, the amount of telephone communication per month was in a range from 5 minutes to an hour. (This same range was also the case for siblings' telephone communication with their parents.) However, some sibling pairs spent up to 5 hours a month on the telephone with each other. (Telephone time with the mother ranged up to 15 hours per month for a few siblings.)

The face-to-face contact for some sibling pairs was limited to a few times a year at annual family gatherings or special occasions such as relatives' marriages, a niece's or nephew's graduation, and so on. Other sibling pairs had more frequent contact, ranging up to more than once a week.

In general, both contact and telephone communication were determined by geographical distance, cost of telephoning or traveling, degree of common occupational interests, shared tasks or projects, competing demands (of spouses, children, work, etc.), and existence of personality differences. Whether at a low level or high, contact and communication did exist between these family members; they were involved with each other's lives. Indirect communication also took place through a very active family grapevine.

Spouses usually saw the siblings and each other only as they accompanied their mates on family visits or when certain siblings and their spouses got together. In regard to telephone communication with other siblings' spouses, such direct communication was relatively rare; direct communication between the spouses themselves was practically nonexistent. Thus, the spouses' contacts with and information about other siblings took place via linkage through their mates and in a sense was filtered through their mates.

Sibling Task Communication System

In an effort to understand how the communication system of the family functioned, the siblings were questioned about the occasions and reasons for contacts between them (either in person or by telephone) and about who initiated the contact. A study of the interview data suggested the existence of three different and overlapping family communication networks.

One communication network, a task-oriented network, appeared to be used primarily to solve problems, make decisions, or coordinate and mobilize family members to participate in common tasks or activities. This network operated primarily among the siblings. When a decision or activity involved the parents, things were settled between the siblings first and then the parents were involved at the final stages. (There was also some attempt to screen information from the father to keep him from criticizing or getting upset; some siblings felt that he was not an effective communicator. The father himself seemingly did not care to talk very long over the telephone to children, so telephone communication from the sibling task network typically went to the mother and only indirectly to the father.)

Communication within the task network was usually initiated by a sibling who had an idea for a family activity or was concerned about some family problem. If the topic involved a simple invitation to an activity, the initiating sibling might call the rest directly. More often, the communication went to one or two of the sisters who seemed to be focal points or nodes in the system. They acted as informal leaders and would call others or delegate a chain of calls.

Sibling Social Communication System

A second sibling communication system appeared to exist apart from the sibling task system. In this system, calls were initiated at random from one sibling to another in no particular pattern or chain. Calls were initiated for social reasons (to exchange information and gossip, to check on a family member's welfare, to arrange activities involving just two or three siblings), or to seek or give help or advice.

Indirect Parental Switchboard System

There appeared to be a third communication system in the family which was used to exchange social information, gossip, or check on everyone's welfare. In this case, a sibling called or visited the parents, usually the mother, who became a central switchboard relaying information to the other siblings. Some siblings felt that this indirect social network fostered the vicarious sharing of other siblings' experiences.

The siblings differed somewhat in their views about this indirect social communication system. Some felt that it was the major communication system in the family, whereas others felt that it was of minor importance or denied its existence.

Overall, socially oriented communication appeared either to follow a random sequence involving dyads or subgroups of siblings or proceeded indirectly through the parents (the family grapevine appeared to function in both systems). However, most task-oriented communication tended to follow a specific sequence from the sibling who initiated the task to certain leaders who ensured the acceptance and implementation of the task.

It must be mentioned that some conflicts, as well as cliques or coalitions of certain siblings, did exist, and these limited or disrupted communication between certain siblings.

Reasons for Communication

Various siblings indicated that most communication was not initiated basically for social reasons or just to talk. Competing responsibilities of work, spouse, and children limited the amount of time available for purely social purposes. For telephone calls involving siblings at greater distances, cost also became a limiting factor. As a result, most calls were those needed to accomplish specific tasks. Sibling communication was initiated to mobilize participation in an event, to promote activities initiated by one sibling, to help deal with a task or family crisis, or to obtain expert information from various siblings. Each sibling was perceived as an expert in a certain area, and the siblings depended on one another for instrumental help in those areas (such as recommendations about business, stocks, taxes, health problems, home repairs, mechanical difficulties, and so on).

Effectively, they perceived a division of labor in the family on these matters. Overall, most contacts were initiated primarily for various task purposes, with exchange of family social information a side effect.

Influence of Spouses on the Communication System

One particularly interesting question was just how the siblings' spouses functioned in relation to the family communication network. As noted before, there was little direct communication from one sibling's spouse to other siblings or their mates. Yet, spouses participated in family functions and were affected by decisions made within the sibling task network.

The majority of siblings indicated that the siblings made most family decisions independently of their spouses. This was true particularly when siblings were dealing with an immediate family problem, or something very specific that siblings themselves wanted to do. For their part, most spouses indicated that they did not interfere, feeling that the siblings had a right to make their own family decisions.

However, the spouses did influence the sibling decision making in certain ways. First, and most typically, spouses exerted influence on the siblings' family decisions through their mates, discussing family problems and expressing their own views. Potentially, this could be a powerful influence, but it was not clear just how important it was. Second, a spouse might be asked for direct input if he or she had expertise in a particular area. Third, if a spouse felt that a family decision under consideration would have an undesirable impact on their own family life, and they felt their mate didn't exert sufficient influence on the other siblings or would be unduly upset by the decision, then the spouse would interact directly with the siblings on the matter. (Only a few spouses took this course.) Finally, if a spouse had been a family friend for many years (before marrying one of the siblings), that spouse sometimes voiced his or her views directly to the siblings.

From another perspective, certain spouses' attempts to exert an influence were perceived negatively by the majority of siblings and their influence was resisted. The consensus among most siblings was that spouses did and should influence the siblings indirectly through dialogue with their own mates rather than by direct participation in sibling issues or problems. Most of the sisters felt sufficiently independent of their husbands that they could make their own decisions regarding family matters, but some felt that their brothers' decisions were dominated by their wives.

CONCLUSION

The siblings in this large family still maintain live and vital relationships in adulthood. This is a relatively healthy sibship composed of intelligent, strong-willed, independent, and ambitious people who seem to reflect the family's basic values of strong ties and caring between family members and striving for achievement goals. There are special feelings of closeness among certain siblings who share common interests and personality characteristics; these appear to be independent of age or distance. Athough sibling coalitions and cliques exist to some degree, they do not appear to be divisive to the family.

The interactions and relationships between the adult siblings in this family are still influenced greatly by their parents, either directly or indirectly, with the parents' core values setting the tone for the family. Parents are still the focus of much talk and concern; some siblings seem more attached than others. For some siblings, much energy seems to be directed into seeking the father's approval and interacting in ways that circumvented his disapproval.

There appears to be a three-tiered sibling communication system in this family. One is a task-oriented network of the siblings, one is a random social network of the siblings, and the third is an indirect network operating through the parents.

One would expect that interactions in a large family would involve a certain degree of conflict and tension, and indeed this is the case. Both overt and subtle conflicts exist between certain siblings, between siblings and parents, and between siblings and certain spouses. There are some indications of moderate rivalry between certain siblings, evidenced by ambivalence of feeling toward a sibling, criticism of a sibling to other family members, resentments when other siblings flaunt achievements or material goods, and sometimes a lessening or avoidance of communication with a particular sibling. Some siblings acknowledged that rivalries existed; others felt that there were none.

In any event, these siblings seem ready to close ranks to give help in the event of a crisis or outside threat, as well as to cooperate on family tasks or projects. Basically, there is an underlying caring for each other and solidarity that seem to transcend ordinary conflicts and rivalries. These siblings provide help to each other when needed, both instrumentally and emotionally. However, requests for help seem to be selective relative to the helper's particular resources, skills, or expertise. There is a division of labor among siblings in which each has a role which uses his or her particular expertise to help the others.

For the most part, the influence of the spouses on sibling relationships is indirect and exerted through their mates (although a few spouses with personal concerns and strong personalities attempt more direct influence). Despite this, most spouses participate in family activities and many are astute observers of the way the family functions. Some spouses feel resentful that a mate devotes too much time to sibling and family of origin concerns because it limits the time that could be spent as a couple or with their own children.

Although all of the siblings have children of their own, it doesn't appear that the children influence the siblings' relationships greatly, other than limiting the amount of time available for sibling interactions.

Topics for Further Research

Many of the observations concerning the functioning of this group of adult siblings need to be tested with larger samples as well as samples involving smaller sibships. The existence and use of different communication systems for different purposes is one example. Which sort of communication system predominates in various types of family? Does this depend on socioeconomic status level, that is, is a task communication system predominant in high socioeconomic status families and a social communication system predominant in low socioeconomic status families? How does this depend on structural characteristics of the family (e.g., gender ratio), sibling personality, and the history of earlier relationships? In this family, the organization of the sibling task communication system around two sisters suggests that the family "kinkeeper" role does not belong exclusively to the matriarch, but that auxiliary kinkeepers may emerge among the sibling group much earlier in life. How general is this phenomenon?

A deeper understanding of the role of core values in an adult family is needed. To what extent are parents' values reflected in the lives of the adult children and their spouses? If present, how do these values operate to regulate the interactions and relationships between adult siblings and other family members?

Further research is needed into the way siblings handle conflicts in adulthood. To what extent do they negotiate differences, simply leave conflicts unresolved, avoid one another and become estranged, and so on? What is the parents' role in sibling conflicts?

Finally, much more attention needs to be paid to the role of spouses in adult sibling relationships. Under what conditions (spouse's and mate's personalities, family boundaries, vested interests) do they become direct participants in family matters between siblings? How do they act indirectly to foster or erode relationships between siblings?

These and many other questions about sibling relationships in adulthood remain to be answered. It is hoped that this chapter will stimulate interest in further investigations.

Sibling Helping Relationships

Over the life span and in most cultures, siblings carry out a great variety of helping and supportive acts for one another. Such acts range from caregiving and teaching in childhood to exchange of goods and services in adulthood to social support and caregiving in old age (Weisner, 1989b).

Goetting (1986) has outlined the developmental tasks of siblings across the life span. In childhood and adolescence, the developmental tasks include the provision of companionship and emotional support, caretaking for younger siblings, and the provision of aid and direct services (e.g., the forming of sibling coalitions to deal with parents or to compensate for parents' inefficacy, and such miscellaneous services as money lending, physical protection, teaching of skills, helping with homework, and sharing of friends). In early and middle adulthood, the tasks include the provision of companionship and emotional support, cooperation in caring for elderly parents, and the provision of occasional aid and services (e.g., help during illness, baby-sitting, sharing possessions, and lending money). In old age, developmental tasks include the provision of companionship and social support (increasing social support to compensate for losses), the sharing of reminiscences for perceptual validation, the resolution of sibling rivalry, and the provision of aid and direct services to siblings when called upon (e.g., help when ill, and help with decisions, business dealings, homemaking, home maintenance, transportation, shopping, and the like). In Goetting's analysis of these tasks, providing emotional support as well as providing aid and direct services are important at each stage of life, although the contact and form of these helping behaviors may differ somewhat at each stage. She regards sibling helping activities in adulthood and old age as having a firm foundation in childhood and adolescence.

In this chapter, findings supporting the existence of siblings' help to one another will be considered at each stage of life.

SIBLING HELP IN CHILDHOOD AND ADOLESCENCE

Sibling help during the years of childhood and adolescence usually occurs within the context of the home. It can involve a direct act intended to benefit another sibling in some way, as in the case of sibling helping interactions or sibling teaching; on the other hand, it can be more indirect, as in the case of sibling modeling and sibling socialization. One might also consider whether the helping activity is spontaneous in nature (such as attempts to comfort) or whether it is directed by a parent (such as caretaking).

Sibling Helping Interactions

An important aspect of the sibling relationship is the direct help and support siblings can provide for each other. Even in early childhood, there is evidence of some altruistic behavior toward siblings (Dunn, 1989; Dunn & Kendrick, 1982b), with siblings responding to the other's distress with attempts at comforting, giving toys, and so on. Similarly, Stewart and Marvin (1984) found that 94% of preschool siblings responded to a distressed infant with attempts at giving comfort; half responded within the first 10 seconds. Abramovitch, Pepler, and Corter (1982) also reported that helping behavior toward a sibling exists in early childhood, most frequently between pairs of sisters.

It may be that empathy for the distress of another is innate. The work of Howe (Howe, 1991; Howe & Ross, 1990) supports such a view. When younger siblings aged 3 to 5 were observed with a 14-month-old sibling, the older child made numerous remarks about the emotions and needs of the infant; such comments were more likely during the mother's absence and during sibling conflict and play. Sibling play in early childhood appears to provide practice in perceiving and interpreting feelings of others, so that the young child learns when another is distressed and some form of comfort is needed. Brown and Dunn (1992), in a longitudinal study where the youngest child was a preschooler, found that the talk about one another's feelings in sibling pairs increased over time whereas mother–child talk about feelings decreased.

In middle childhood and adolescence, too, siblings help each other in terms of shared tasks and activities (Bank & Kahn, 1982b), sharing and lending possessions, and helping each other in avoiding parental displeasure and otherwise dealing with parents. In some cases, an older sibling will function as a substitute parent when a parent is unresponsive or is ineffective in meeting the child's needs (as in the case of alcoholic, drug-addicted, or mentally unstable parents.

In a recent study (East & Rook, 1992), social support provided by sibling relationships was examined. The researchers identified sixth-grade children who were isolated or who had difficult and aggressive relationships with peers at school and compared these children with those who had normal school peer relationships. Isolated children found their sibling relationships to be more supportive than either school or nonschool peer relationships; those who experienced high support from a favorite sibling were better adjusted than those who had less sibling support.

Often sibling help is strongly resisted by younger siblings, who perceive it as an attempt to assert dominance and control rather than as a well-intentioned desire to help. From this perspective, an offer of help from an older sibling may be only a veiled power maneuver and is responded to as such (Bryant, 1982). Whether help is accepted, then, seems to be a function of the overall relationship between the siblings concerned. Some empirical data bears this out. In longitudinal studies (Dunn, Beardsall, & Slomkowski, 1993; Dunn, Slomkowski, & Beardsall, 1994; Dunn, Slomkowski, Beardsall, & Rende, 1994), when a warm and supportive relationship existed between siblings, the older siblings helped the younger with minor difficulties as well as major problems, which resulted in a still closer relationship between the two and better adjustment of the younger siblings.

Sibling Caretaking

Usually sibling caretaking activities are delegated by a parent, although sometimes an older sibling will spontaneously undertake care of a younger sibling.

The use of older siblings as caretakers for younger ones is very widespread, especially in less advanced cultures (Weisner, 1982; Weisner & Gallimore, 1977; see also Chapter 6). In the United States, sibling caretaking is more prevalent in lower socioeconomic status groups, among children of working mothers, and in families with a child who has an illness or mental disability. The style and extensiveness of sibling care varies widely. In many cases, there is mimicry of adult caregiving patterns, often resulting in excessive authoritarianism, with older children tending to tyrannize, harass, and threaten younger siblings. In other cases, neglect or overindulgence by older siblings occurs, with younger children becoming overdemanding. In most cases, sibling care takes place within an area where the mother or other adults are available to oversee activities or for emergency help, but differs in terms of the responsibility placed upon the siblings. Most sibling caretaking is delegated to older sisters, with boys freed for play or other tasks. Thus, in the area of sibling interaction as in many other areas, sisters play a special role.

Bryant (1989) studied caretaking of young siblings by older siblings who were preadolescent as well as adolescent. Few older siblings were delegated full responsibility for a young child by a parent, but both older and younger siblings perceived the older sibling to have a caregiving function that was distinct from the caregiving by the parent. Further, sibling caregiving tended to be modeled after parent caregiving, but was found to have a significant independent influence on the social–emotional development of the younger child. Ervin-Tripp (1989) concurs that older siblings not only provide caregiving functions per se but also contribute to educating younger siblings to the value and activities of the society (didactically and in play activities).

In a series of studies on the effects of sibling caretaking in preadolescent and adolescent school children (T. E. Smith, 1984, 1990a, 1993), school achievement of sibling caretakers was enhanced when they had a moderate amount of caretaking responsibility but suffered when large amounts of caretaking were involved.

When sibling caretaking takes place without a parent or other adult nearby, the authority delegated to the older sibling may be used to take advantage of the younger one in a number of ways. Conflicts sometimes escalate into violence or abuse or a younger sibling may be sexually abused by the older one (see Chapters 11 and 12). Although serious abuse is relatively rare, the relationship between the siblings is likely to suffer in all such cases.

Siblings Teaching Siblings

A major function of the sibling relationship is the teaching–learning process that goes on when one sibling serves as the teacher and the other serves as learner. Siblings who serve as teachers profit as much as, if not more than, their younger siblings. According to the Zajonc confluence model of intellectual development (Zajonc & Markus, 1975), the experience of teaching a younger sibling is a factor adding to the intellectual development of all but the youngest child in the family.

In laboratory studies of sibling teaching-learning on a concept teaching task in middle childhood (Cicirelli, 1972, 1973, 1975), girls teaching their siblings tended to use a deductive teaching method, whereas boys used an inductive method; both sexes taught differently with nonsiblings. Girls were also more effective as teachers. Younger siblings were more ready to accept direction from an older sister than from an older brother, perhaps attributable to greater rivalry with brothers. Bryant (1982) views sibling teaching and caretaking as another means of asserting power over a younger sibling; thus, resisting sibling teaching may be a way of resisting domination. Yet, older siblings at wide age spacings were found to be more effective teachers than those at close age spacings, although those at wide age spacing should clearly be perceived as more powerful.

Ervin-Tripp (1989) indicates that older siblings do a great deal of teaching work within the family when they communicate with a young sibling and try to understand the child's communications. Older siblings show a considerable amount of accommodation to the young child's low level of language competence, including speaking in a special register (baby talk), gesturing and demonstrating, repeating, speaking louder, paraphrasing in simpler terms, eliciting imitation, and reducing information speed and density. Older siblings as listeners also use such means as soliciting repetition by the young child, asking clarification questions, and offering expansions that guess what was said. According to Ervin-Tripp, siblings seemed to be more ready than adults to carry out such communication tasks. Hoff-Ginsberg and Krueger (1991) videotaped toddlers' interactions with 4- and 5-year-old siblings as well as with 7- and 8-year-old siblings. Behavior which promoted the toddlers' language development was found to increase with age.

In a study in which 7-year-old children were taught to build a model by either a 9-year-old sibling or a familiar 9-year-old peer (Azmitia & Hesser, 1993), those children taught by older siblings were more active in a building task and had higher posttest scores than those taught by older peers. The older siblings gave more spontaneous guidance on the task, more explanations, more positive feedback, and gave the learners more control of the task than did the older peers. These results support Cicirelli's (1972, 1973, 1975) earlier findings. Although the older siblings' teaching took place on a laboratory task, the findings suggest that older siblings would be able to make use of the same kinds of teaching skills in home situations for the benefit of their younger siblings.

Siblings as Models

As might be expected, older siblings can serve as models for their younger siblings in regard to a wide variety of behaviors. Even in infancy, children as young as 6 months showed significant improvement on cognitive tasks after sibling modeling, provided the infant was already at the stage of development needed for such learning (Wishart, 1986).

In infancy and early childhood, imitation of the older siblings occurs with some frequency. Dunn and Kendrick (1982c) observed imitation of an older sibling's behaviors by a 14-month-old child, with both verbal imitation and imitation of actions occurring. The frequency of imitation was about twice as great among same-sex than among opposite-sex pairs. Curiously, the older child imitated the baby to about the same degree as the baby imitated the older sibling. Abramovitch et al. (1982) concurred only in part with the findings of Dunn and Kendrick, reporting much more imitation of the older sibling by the younger than vice versa. Lamb (1978a,b) also found evidence of imitation of the older sibling in infancy.

In adolescence, too, older siblings have been found to have a significant influence on younger siblings' sexual behavior (Rodgers & Rowe, 1988), although the mechanism for such a transmission from older to younger siblings remains somewhat unclear. Younger siblings were found to have consistently higher levels of sexual activity at a given age than their older siblings, with sibling influence greater than that found among friends. Modeling was regarded as the only influence when siblings had a wide age spacing, while direct interaction between siblings was also involved when the siblings were close in age.

Socialization for Adult Roles

Sibling relationships can also be viewed as socializing the sibling pair for adult roles (Essman, 1977). Through play in childhood, siblings practice roles they will later assume. Also, older siblings model school behaviors, dating behaviors, employment behaviors, marriage and parent behaviors, and responses to life crises throughout their lifetime. Siblings directly instruct each other in many skills, as well as give advice on many topics. In addition, there is mutual regulation (Schvaneveldt & Ihinger, 1979) of role behaviors as siblings interact to shape each other's behaviors according to common family or community values.

SIBLING HELPING RELATIONSHIPS IN ADULTHOOD

Once siblings leave the family home, helping behaviors continue to some extent. Adams (1968) found mutual aid between young adult siblings to be relatively infrequent, occurring most often between pairs of sisters and pairs of brothers. It is clear that the greater similarity of roles leads to greater help from the same-sex siblings. Also, help was more frequent among those siblings who felt affectionally close.

In middle age, siblings are seen as a source of aid in time of crisis (Troll, 1975), caring for children, sharing household responsibilities, and even making funeral arrangements when this becomes necessary. More important, they provide companionship and support to each other in time of crisis or serious family problems. This is an area in which much further study is needed.

SIBLING HELPING RELATIONSHIPS IN OLD AGE

Sibling helping activities in old age have been more extensively studied than those in young and middle adulthood. The help from elderly siblings is often overlooked, on the assumption that spouses and adult children are the major caregivers of the frail elderly person or that the elderly siblings are themselves too frail to help. However, at times, siblings can take on important helping and caregiving functions.

Among the elderly, siblings sometimes provide a great deal of help. After the death of their mother, older sisters may assume the mother's earlier role in looking after the brothers in the family (Townsend, 1957). Also, a sister may assume many of a deceased wife's duties for her brother, or a brother may take on some of the deceased husband's roles for a widowed sister. Such role substitution helps to explain the growth in closeness to cross-sex siblings that has been observed in later life.

In a survey of family relationships of the elderly (Cicirelli, 1979), siblings were seen as a primary source of help in the area of psychological support for some 7% of all elderly. Smaller percentages regarded siblings as primary helpers with business dealings, protections, and homemaking and as a source of reading materials and social and recreational activities. Surprisingly, siblings became more important among the oldest age groups. If occasional and supplementary help had been considered in the study, the contribution of siblings would surely have been much greater.

Despite the fact that most older people say that they want to give tangible help to their siblings in time of need, and also regard their siblings as a resource to be called upon in their own need (Cicirelli, 1979, 1989a; Goetting, 1986), relatively few actually rely on a sibling for help. On the other hand, psychological support is a type of support for which siblings may be uniquely suited by virtue of their common values and perceptions (Avioli, 1989; Dunn, 1985; Cicirelli, 1988), and it appears to be freely exchanged. Tangible sibling help was regarded as most important when a brother or sister was ill, needed transportation, needed household repairs, or lost a spouse (Cicirelli, 1979; Goetting, 1986; Kivett, 1985; Lopata, 1973; Scott, 1983).

Those who never married or who were widowed tended to receive more help from siblings (Johnson & Catalano, 1981). In addition, sisters were found to both give and receive more help (Gold, 1989a), while blacks and whites tended to give different types of help (Suggs, 1989). When half-siblings and stepsiblings were involved, there was less help to one another in old age than occurred among full siblings (White & Riedmann, 1992b).

In a survey study (Cicirelli, 1979), relatively few elderly depended on siblings as a primary source of support. Most help in families is exchanged in a vertical direction, with children (after the spouse) viewed as the primary source of support in old age. If the need for help becomes too great for the spouse or children to handle or if the normal scheme of family obligations is disturbed, siblings then tend to step in to give help. Indeed, some 60% of the elderly respondents indicated that they would give help in a crisis, although only 7% (or fewer, depending on the type of help involved) regarded a sibling as a primary source of help. Surprisingly, sibling help became more important among the oldest age groups. This age trend was also noted by Hoyt and Babchuk (1983). If occasional and supplementary help had been considered in the study, the contribution of siblings would surely have been much greater. Sibling help was regarded as most important when the brother or sister was ill, needed transportation, needed household repairs, or lost a spouse (Cicirelli, 1979; Goetting, 1986; Kivett, 1985; Lopata, 1973; Scott, 1983). In addition, those who had never married tended to receive more help from siblings (Johnson & Catalano, 1981).

Siblings' general readiness to give help was illustrated in a recent study of support by family members to hospitalized elders (Cicirelli, 1990), where support from siblings was second only to support from spouses in certain areas of tangible aid (such as bringing needed items to the hospital or helping in posthospital care). Only about 20% of the elders reported receiving any kind of tangible sibling help while in the hospital, and only about 6% wanted or expected instrumental help from siblings once they had returned home. In contrast, about half of the elderly patients interviewed wanted psychological support from their siblings, which they received in the form of visits and telephone calls.

In a study of sibling helping among elderly blacks and whites, Suggs (1989) found that siblings in both racial groups exchanged help in the areas of illness, housekeeping, and transportation. Gold (1986, 1989a) carried out a 2-year longitudinal study of elderly sibling helping patterns, finding that instrumental help appeared to go to those siblings with greater needs for help, that is, those who were older and who were widowed. Although instrumental help declined over the 2-year period, in every case it was because the helper's own needs or declining health prevented them from continuing to give help to the sibling. A decline in help was generally accompanied by great regret. When recent widows were interviewed about the extent of help from siblings since their husband's death (O'Bryant, 1988), sibling help was found to be greatest when the sibling lived nearby and there was no adult child in the vicinity. While both sisters and brothers provided help, the help tended to be gender-stereotypic in nature.

Bedford (1989b) reported somewhat differing findings in a study of adults representing a wide age range. In her sample, instances of sustained sibling help in old age were rare, although siblings did help in crisis situations.

In an analysis of longitudinal data from the National Long Term Care Survey (Cicirelli, Coward, & Dwyer, 1992), only about 7% of impaired elders received help from siblings on a given measurement occasion. The provision of sibling help was associated with the number of the elder's impairments of instrumental functions and not impairments in basic activities of daily living, indicating that sibling help tended to be given in such areas as housekeeping, transportation, financial matters, and so on, rather than in areas involving direct personal care. Further, sibling help tended to go to those elders who had neither spouse nor children, supporting the concept of a substitution hierarchy of family helpers. The majority of sibling helpers continued to help over the 2-year period; those who ceased helping appeared to do so either because the elder's health had improved or because they themselves were older and perhaps in poor health. Gender and race were not associated with receiving help from siblings, failing to support earlier findings of Gold (1989a) and Suggs (1989). One source of explanation is the differences in methodology between the studies. The National Long Term Care Study determined only the presence or absence of help received from siblings, whereas Gold obtained a quantitative measure and Suggs determined frequency of help. Also, the former study focused on recipients of long-term care whereas Gold and Suggs studied elders who were comparatively well. As a result, sibling help may have been more a matter of volition in the Gold and Suggs studies whereas in the long-term care study, siblings may have felt compelled to give aid (regardless of the gender of the recipient) in a situation where no other family member was available. An additional finding was that those elders receiving help from siblings were younger on the average than those who did not receive such help. However, the maritally disrupted and the never married may experience impairment at a younger age than those who are married (Kasl and Berkman, 1981). Also the siblings who provide help to impaired elders are themselves elderly and may have health problems of their own; thus, siblings may not be able to give help to those elders in the upper part of the age range regardless of how much they might wish to do so. Both factors may play a part in accounting for the younger age of elders receiving help. Those elders who were older were more likely to report the cessation of sibling help over time; this is consonant with Gold's (1989a) finding that older siblings stopped providing help because their own health had declined. Unfortunately, the study did not provide data about the elderly caregiver's health that would have allowed researchers to determine whether such might be the case. The findings support the generalization that help from siblings comes when an elder has functional impairments that require help and when support from a spouse or adult children is unavailable for one reason or another. Gold found that when elders stopped providing help to siblings, it was because their own health had declined. Bedford (1989b) suggested, however, that cessation of help to a sibling occurred when there had been no history of reciprocation of help from that sibling; this was particularly likely when the sibling was a brother. Again, the study did not include any data about the prior exchange of help. Overall, the findings support the generalization that help from siblings comes when the elder has functional impairments that required help and when support from a spouse or adult children is unavailable for one reason or another.

However, when elders were asked whether they would consider living with a sibling if they could no longer live alone, more than half said that they would or might consider it; reciprocity did not seem to be an issue for them (Borland, 1989). Apart from need for help, willingness to live with a sibling was related to increasing age, higher level of education, fewer children, greater closeness of feelings in middle age, and greater congeniality and commonality of values and interests.

In a recent study using a Canadian sample of 678 persons aged 55 and over (Connidis, 1994), two measures of sibling support in old age were obtained: instrumental support actually received from siblings and perceived availability of instrumental support if needed in the future. Received support was examined separately for help during illness and help other than with illness and finances; perceived support was examined separately for help during a crisis, help during longer term illness, and the possibility of coresidence. Overall findings supported earlier conclusions about sibling help. Only a minority (about one-fourth) of respondents had received sibling help, and that was "other" help. A majority would turn to a sibling for help in a crisis and would share their homes with the sibling (only a fourth indicated that they would live in the sibling's home, however); up to one-third would turn to a sibling for longer term help when ill. Further, both perceived and received help were associated with close proximity to siblings. As compared to those respondents who had only one sibling, both perceived and received help were greater for those respondents who had two or more siblings; help tended to be dispersed over the sibling network rather then involving only one of the siblings. Further, effects of gender and marital status for either the respondent or the sibling differed somewhat for the two sibling size groups. Findings did confirm the greater role of sisters in helping behavior, and the greater role of sibling support in regard to single, widowed, and divorced siblings as well as those who are childless.

Motivations for Helping Behavior

Three basic theoretical explanations have been advanced for sibling helping behavior in old age: attachment theory, normative obligation, and exchange theory. According to attachment theory (Cicirelli, 1989a), attachment to siblings develops in childhood subsequent to the child's development of attachment to the mother. It would be expected that the attachment bond would be stronger toward a sibling who is viewed as stronger and wiser and who offers security, comfort, and support in time of stress. However, attachment between sibling can be mutual since a younger sibling can provide some degree of comfort and support to an older one. When the health or well-being of a sibling is perceived as being threatened in some way, the attached sibling will respond with help and support to preserve or promote the existence of the attachment figure. Cicirelli (1989a) investigated the general hypothesis that the strength of the attachment bond between siblings is related to psychological support in later life. A measure of sibling psychological support was related to an indicator of the strength of the attachment bond; the relationship was stronger when the ties involved a sister. In earlier work, a modification of the adult attachment model (Cicirelli, 1983, 1987) was tested in relation to such indicators of sibling psychological support in old age as offers to help, talking over problems, emotional support in a crisis, boosting morale, and adjustment to aging. Results of path analysis indicated that an indicator of attachment had a strong direct effect on psychological support, with a much weaker indirect effect through effects of attachment on visiting and telephoning.

Most adults have been socialized to accept such norms of proper sibling behavior as maintaining contact, helping when sick, and so on, and throughout life feel an obligation to behave according to such norms. However, norms pertaining to siblings are usually not as strong as those pertaining to parents, so some sibling support functions are viewed as optional. Lee, Mancini, and Maxwell (1990) found that those adults with stronger sibling responsibility expectations also reported more contact with siblings and stronger obligatory and discretionary contact motivations.

In actual practice, the obligation to help a sibling in adulthood and old age is usually seen as conditional on the balanced reciprocity predicted by exchange theory. That is, an individual is obligated to help a sibling only if the sibling has provided help to that individual in the past. Most siblings' helping relationships tend to be characterized by balanced reciprocity in the exchange of help (Johnson, 1988). Such mutual helping behavior by elderly siblings has been reported by several researchers (Avioli, 1989; Bedford, 1989b; Gold, 1989a; Suggs, 1989) In time of need or in situations where reciprocity is not possible, an elderly person may extend help to a sibling based on a shared history of reciprocal aid; but such help is usually temporary unless some reciprocation occurs (Brady & Noberini, 1987; Stoller, 1985). Unilateral or unreciprocated help seems to be troublesome both to the sibling help giver (who tends to feel burdened and distressed) and the sibling help receiver (who is distressed by feelings of weakness and incompetence in comparison to the sibling). Elderly siblings who have never married or who are childless are thought to have built up a store-house of social credits with other siblings which then qualifies them for reciprocal support in old age (Avioli, 1989).

Avioli (1989) regards the motivation for the social support given to siblings in later adulthood to be some combination of attachment and obligation, with the actual provision of help a function of such factors as proximity, health and functional status, developmental stage (certain role functions decline with age), gender composition of the dyad, ethnicity, and network structure. The author concurs with Avioli's view; when a close attachment to a sibling exists, help is likely to be forthcoming above and beyond that prescribed by norms of family obligation. However, when attachment is disturbed, norms of reciprocity and family obligation are likely to result in at least a minimal amount of help in time of need.

Models of Support

In adulthood, people live in a network or convoy of close relation-ships which includes spouses, adult children, siblings, grandchildren, in-laws, friends, neighbors, and so on (Antonucci, 1994). It is difficult to predict which member of an older person's convoy will give help in a particular case, whether helping as a primary caregiver, as a secondary caregiver, or as an occasional helper. In addition, when several people help, it is difficult to explain which person gives particular kinds of help. Three theoretical models have been proposed to account for existing data, a hierarchical substitution model, a task-specificity model, and a func-tional specificity of relationships model.

The first model proposed to explain which convoy member helps in later life is the principal of hierarchical substitution (Cantor, 1979). When help is needed by a family member, a hierarchy of substitution exists such that help is given first by a spouse. If there is no spouse or the spouse is unavailable, help from adult children usually comes next, followed by help from siblings or grandchildren (or a parent, if living), and so on. Social norms determine this hierarchy to some extent, but for a given individual the closeness of affectional relationships as well as the prior history of mutual exchange of help also help determine who will help. Various studies (e.g., Cicirelli et al., 1992) provide support for this model in regard to the identification of a primary caregiver; however, the model does not account for the dispersal of helping activities among other helpers. Another problem is that the substitution hierarchy does not specifically account for gender differences in helping unless each position in the hierarchy is specified by gender. The gender problem is particularly troubling in explaining sibling data where the gender composition of the sibship is also important. Further, as Connidis (1994) correctly points out, in the case of the single and the childless, a sibling cannot be said to substitute for a lost relationship that never existed; instead, the single and childless are likely to have negotiated supportive ties with their siblings over a lifetime.

The task-specificity model proposed by Litwak (1985) suggests that the function required by a particular helping task determines who will help. That is, the needs of the task are matched with the abilities of the individuals in the support network. (The adult family described in Chapter 7 appears to be an example of the task-specificity model.) This model has difficulty in explaining why some helpers perform multiple functions when others with greater ability to perform specific functions do not emerge as helpers.

The third model, the functional specificity of relationships model (Simons, 1983–84), hypothesizes that some relationships in a convoy (e.g., spouse, sibling) are most likely to perform a given helping task function, but functions are not tied to particular relationships. That is, one helper can perform several functions, and a given function can be dispersed over several helpers. This model would seem to be well-suited to explain the dispersal of help over several siblings in larger families, but does not really predict which relationship (e.g., sibling, adult child) is most likely to be the major helper.

Each of the three models plays some part in explaining existing phenomena, but each has certain deficiencies. Analysis of actual cases indicates that which family members help and which ones give particular types of help often involves complex negotiations and contingencies.

However, the models do help in the depiction of broad trends in family helping behavior.

CONCLUSION

Perhaps the most important feature of sibling help in adulthood and old age is that most siblings indicate that they are ready to help one another if needed, and they perceive other siblings as resources they can call upon for help if needed. In actual practice, siblings are called upon for tangible help infrequently in old age. However, the fact that siblings are in readiness to help is a source of comfort and security leading to a sense of well-being in old age (Avioli, 1989; Bedford, 1989b; Cicirelli, 1989a, 1992b; Gold, 1989a). The fact that this readiness is translated into reality in a variety of cases, including the assumption of primary caregiver responsibilities in some cases (Cicirelli et al., 1992) is a testament to the seriousness with which the promise of sibling readiness is extended and perceived.

One cannot help being struck by the continuity of help and support between siblings over the entire life span. Evidence of helping behavior on the part of older siblings exists as early as infancy and often continues until near the end of life. It has its roots in attachment relationships and early childhood socialization, and is fostered by the development of a close relationship between siblings. Those siblings who fail to achieve a good relationship with one another also miss the sense of security and comfort that help from a sibling (either real or in reserve) can provide.

Siblings as Caregivers of Elderly Parents

One of the developmental tasks of a sibling group in midlife is the care of aging parents during the parents' decline and death (Goetting, 1986). The usual trajectory involving an aging parent is that the spouse provides needed help for as long as possible, with occasional help from adult children and others. With increasing frailty, illness, or death of the spouse, one or more adult children provide added help needed to maintain the parent in his or her own home. As the parent continues to decline, a pattern of regular caregiving by adult children is established. When the parent's care needs become too great to be met in this manner, one of the adult children takes the parent into his or her home for care or the parent enters some kind of formal long-term care facility.

The traditional stereotype in the caregiving literature is that one adult daughter assumes or is propelled by family and social forces into the principal caregiver role (Aldous, 1987; Brody, 1990), taking on the burden of providing help to elderly parents with only occasional help from other family members. In the past, few studies examined the caregiving contribution of other siblings in a systematic way. However, the extent to which each sibling in the family participates in this developmental task, the factors influencing participation, and the effect of such participation on sibling relationships have been subjects of considerable recent research.

WHICH SIBLINGS IN THE FAMILY HELP AND HOW MUCH?

Most existing knowledge in this area has been gained from interview studies in which the adult child identified as the principal caregiver (the one providing the most help to the elder, or the one turned to first for help) is interviewed regarding the amounts of help of various types he or she provides to the parent as well as the amounts of help provided by siblings and other family members. Alternatively, the elderly parent is interviewed regarding the help provided by the adult children and other family members.

Studies of the contributions of siblings of caregiving daughters (Brody, 1990; Brody, Hoffman, Kleban, & Schoonover, 1989; Brody, Kleban, Hoffman, & Schoonover, 1988) have yielded considerable support for the "daughter as principle caregiver" model. Daughters serving as principal caregivers reported that they provided an average of 24 hours of help weekly to the elderly parent (this included daughters sharing a residence with the parent), whereas their sisters who lived nearby provided 8 hours of help weekly. In contrast, brothers who lived nearby provided only 4 hours of help.

However, in a recent study using data from the National Long-Term Care Survey (Dwyer, Henretta, Coward, & Barton, 1992), a given adult child's initiation or cessation of help to an impaired elderly parent was found to depend on the helping behaviors of that child's siblings, suggesting that the sibling group acted in concert and not as isolated individuals.

Cicirelli (1984) investigated the contributions made by siblings of the adult child who was considered by the elderly parent to be "closest" and the one turned to first for help. Two groups of adult children were studied, those who had intact marriages and those who had experienced some form of marital disruption (i.e., divorce, widowhood, or remarriage). Adult children with intact marriages reported giving significantly more help to their elderly parents than their siblings, while those with disrupted marriages reported giving about the same amount of help as did their siblings. In both cases, however, there were gender differences in the type of help provided, with sisters named more frequently as helpers with homemaking, personal care, home health care, transportation, and psychological support, and brothers named more frequently as helpers with maintenance, bureaucratic mediation, and protection.

In a more recent study of adult sibling helping networks (Cicirelli, 1992a), four patterns of sibling help were identified, depending on the portion of the caregiving load assumed by the various siblings. The patterns and the percentages of families manifesting each pattern were: principal caregiver provides all care while siblings provide none, 5%; principal caregiver provides over half the caregiving load while siblings share the remainder, 55%; respondent provides more care than siblings but no one provides over half of the caregiving load, 19%; and approximately equal division of caregiving load between all siblings, 21%. It must be remembered, of course, that respondents' egocentric bias will lead them to over-estimate their own contributions in relation to those of their siblings (Lerner, Somer, Reid, Chiriboga, & Tierney, 1991). In about half of the families, all siblings coordinated their efforts in providing care to parents, while in about fourth of the families there was partial coordination of sibling efforts, and in the remaining fourth of the families each sibling helped with care as he or she wished and independently of the others.

Matthews' studies (Matthews, 1987, 1988; Matthews, Delaney, & Adamek, 1989; Matthews & Rosner, 1988; Matthews & Sprey, 1989) have focused on the contribution of the entire middle-aged sibling subsystem to the care of elderly parents. In looking first at the sharing of responsibility by pairs of sisters in a two-child family, Matthews and Rosner (1988) found that pairs of adult sisters tended to share responsibility for tangible help as well as moral support to parents, with the division becoming more equal when both sisters were employed.

In larger families, support was less likely to be shared by all, especially in those families including one or more brothers (Matthews & Rosner, 1988). For larger families, five types of sibling participation in parent care were identified: routine help, where regular assistance to the parent was incorporated into the child's ongoing schedule of activities; backup help, where a sibling not routinely involved in care could be counted on for special emotional support or tangible aid when requested by the siblings giving routine help; circumscribed help, where the help provided to the parent was carefully limited by amount or type; sporadic help, where occasional assistance to the parent was provided at the child's own convenience; and dissociation, where the adult child abdicated from any responsibility to help the parent. The relative frequencies of these types of help were quite different. In most cases, help from one or more adult siblings in these larger families was either circumscribed in nature, sporadic, or nonexistent.

However, styles of caregiving participation within the adult child sibship tended to be associated with gender (Matthews & Rosner, 1988). Sisters were more likely to use routine or backup styles of participation, while brothers' help tended to be sporadic or circumscribed, usually limited to typically male areas of expertise. Brothers spent fewer hours in helping tasks for their elderly parents than did their sisters, and took on fewer caregiving tasks involving personal care and household chores. Yet, when families consisting only of brothers were examined (Matthews, Delaney, & Adamek, 1989), the brothers appeared willing to cooperate to meet parents' needs for care and to fulfill their filial obligations. Perhaps brothers can and do take over traditionally female caregiving tasks when there are no sisters in the family.

Recent work by Coward and Dwyer (1990) shed further light on the caregiving contributions of brothers. Information regarding adult children of dependent elders was based on interviews with 683 caregiving sons and daughters obtained in a large national survey. Subjects' sibling networks were subdivided into single gender networks, mixed-gender networks, and only children to determine the effects of the gender composition of the sibship. Sons from all three types of sibling networks were less likely than were daughters to participate in parent care or to become principal care-givers. However, participating sons from networks where there were no sisters provided essentially as many hours of care as daughters from networks where there were no brothers (whether these sons provided the same types of care as did daughter is not reported). Only in the mixed-gender network did daughters provide significantly more hours of care than did sons. Since mixed-gender sibships are far more prevalent than the other types, these findings are not at odds with those of other studies (Brody, 1990; Matthews, Delaney, & Adamek, 1989; Matthews & Rosner 1988).

Overall, one can conclude that an adult child's helping behavior to an elderly parent is influenced, at least in part, by the participation of the sibling network. Depending on the size and gender composition of the network, adult children in a sibling network may respond to an impaired parent with a cooperative group effort or the responsibility for helping may be left to only one or two of the siblings.

The findings of the various studies of the siblings in the adult child generation show considerable convergence despite the different methods used (Cicirelli, 1992a). The data clearly indicate that there is a great deal more support from siblings than has been generally recognized, particularly in cases where a daughter has experienced marital disruption or is employed. Overall, sisters provide more help than brothers; sisters have a greater tendency to share help equally; and sisters and brothers tend to provide different types of help, structured according to traditional gender role norms.

Use of Formal Care Services

There are two ways in which the sibling group interacts with providers of formal care services regarding parent care: mediation on behalf of the parent with professionals and agencies to secure needed supplementary health and custodial care services when the parent resides at home, and providing family support to a parent who has entered a long-term care institution. With regard to mediation to obtain services, Cicirelli (1981) found that the adult child who was the parent's main source of overall help also carried out most mediation activities. Some 34% of these adult children reported that their siblings also provided some help with securing services, with brothers named most frequently. Brothers' mediation activities reflected such areas of traditional male expertise as legal and financial services and dealing with government agencies. Similarly, sisters who were nurses or who had other expertise in the health care field tended to mediate the use of formal health care services.

When a parent enters a nursing home or other type of long-term care facility, the adult children may take responsibility for making the care arrangements, monitoring the care provided by the staff, and providing incidental care as well as social support for the elderly parent. As with sibling participation in parent caregiving while the parent is still living at home, some sibling groups work cooperatively to accomplish these tasks whereas others let all supportive activity default to a principal caregiver. This is an area that needs to be further studied.

DECISION MAKING BY ADULT SIBLINGS

One important area of adult children's help to elderly parents is the making of decisions about the parent's care, especially when the parent is no longer able to make decisions autonomously. A recent study (Cicirelli, 1992a) investigated first how sibling decisions were currently made about the care to be provided to the parent and then how decisions would be made when parents could no longer decide on their own. For current care, in only 17% of families did all siblings discuss specific caregiving tasks together; in 45% of the families, one or two of the siblings would decide things; in 22% of the families, the sibling who had specific abilities in an area made caregiving decisions in that area; in 8% of the families, whichever sibling happened to be on the scene made the decision; finally, in only 8% of the families, the parent made the decision. Regarding future decisions in the event of the parent's incapacity, in 65% of the families all siblings would reach a consensus decision, while in the remainder of the families one or two siblings would make the decision.

In another portion of the same study (Cicirelli, 1992a), decision-making beliefs and caregiving decisions themselves were compared for two groups of caregiving daughters. The first group of daughters provided all or the majority of care needed by the parent, while the second group shared caregiving more equally with siblings. Beliefs about whether caregiving adult children should respect their parents' rights to make their own decisions autonomously and about whether adult children should make decisions paternalistically in the parents' behalf were measured. In addition, the daughters were asked about how decisions were made in 40 common caregiving areas. Although the two groups of caregiving daughters did not differ in their beliefs about autonomy and paternalism, they did differ on how the caregiving decisions were actually made. In the sibling-shared caregiving group, significantly more decisions were made autonomously by the parent than in the single caregiver group. Conversely, daughters in the single caregiver group made more paternalistic decisions for the parent than those in the sibling-shared caregiving group. It appears that siblings acting as a group to make caregiving decisions have more respect for an elderly parent's autonomy than does a single adult child deciding things independently. Somehow, when the siblings make decisions together, there seem to be checks and balances that insure that the parent's views are respected and represented.

FACTORS INFLUENCING SIBLING HELP

Several factors hypothesized to play a role in determining which siblings are likely to give care have been investigated in various studies of adult sibling helping behavior.

Gender

In the studies reviewed above, the patterning of sibling help by gender is clear. In mixed gender sibships, sisters are the ones providing most of the care, with brothers contributing occasional help at best. Only in sibships composed entirely of brothers or in mixed gender sibships where sisters are unavailable do brothers assume substantial caregiving roles (Coward & Dwyer, 1990; Stoller, Forster, & Daniho, 1992). Most studies indicate that sons caring for an elderly parent tend to provide different types of help, purchase more services, and abdicate the caregiving role sooner than do daughters (Brody, 1990; Montgomery & Kamo, 1989), although Stoller (1990) found no gender difference in the stability of help. It is possible, however, that existing studies fail to recognize the extent of sons' contributions because they measure only those kinds of help typically provided by daughters.

Helping and caregiving roles have traditionally been considered to be largely women's roles, with women taking on most of the expressive and instrumental aspects of care of the elderly (Brody, 1985; Cicirelli, 1981). When men have taken on caregiving tasks, the tasks tended to be stereotypically male ones, such as home maintenance, financial management, and transportation.

The demographic reality that elderly widows are the preponderant group requiring help from adult children may lead to the prevalence of daughters and sisters as caregivers. Also, it has been suggested that a sex-role taboo prevents sons from giving more intimate types of care to their mothers and the same taboo prevents mothers from asking (Coward & Dwyer, 1990; Matthews, 1988; Montgomery & Kamo, 1989), which contributes further to the prevalence of women as caregivers.

At present, studies do not exist that examine brothers' and sisters' contributions to the care of elderly fathers compared with the care of elderly mothers. It may be that gender differences follow a different course with respect to elderly fathers, depending on the degree of impairment and the range of caregiving tasks required.

Proximity

Brody found that sibling gender differences in helping disappeared when siblings were geographically distant from the parents, mainly because little help was provided by either brothers or sisters (Brody, 1990; Brody, Hoffman, Kleban, & Schoonover, 1989; Brody, Kleban, Hoffman, & Schoonover, 1988). Obviously, for regular help to occur, an adult child must live close enough so that the travel (time and cost) is feasible. Stoller et al. (1992) supported Brody's results, finding that the likelihood of help from more distant siblings was low, regardless of whether an elderly parent was functionally impaired or not married, or whether there were any nearby sibling.

However, existing studies have not examined occasional support from distant siblings. Anecdotal reports indicate that in some families, a distant sibling provides respite care to a dependent parent so that the sibling in a principal caregiver role can take vacations or carry out other activities. In other cases, a distant sibling provides financial support or tangible goods needed by the parent. More frequently, a distant sibling will provide psychological support to both the parent and caregiving sibling by long-distance telephone. Just knowing that a sibling is interested, appreciative of the principal caregiver's efforts, and available if needed can contribute to the caregiving sibling's well-being. Finally, in some families, parent care is rotated between the adult children, with the parent spending part of the year with each parent in turn.

Sibling Marital Status

Adult siblings without competing family responsibilities (i.e., those who are widowed, divorced, or never married) were more likely to assume parent caregiving responsibilities than those who were married or remarried, but were less likely to receive assistance from siblings (Brody, Litvin, Albert, & Hoffman, 1994).

Effects of Sibling Employment

Employment has been hypothesized to be a factor determining whether or not a member of the sibling group will help to provide care for an aging parent. The pressure of job responsibilities is a frequently given reason for brothers' lack of help to aging parents. With high percentages of women now in the workforce, the question of how their employment affects their contribution to care of an aging parent has been studied.

Overall, daughters who were employed did not differ from those who were not in the amount or types of care given an aging parent (Brody, 1990; Brody & Schoonover, 1986). However, in Brody's sample, 28% of the daughters who were not employed stated that they had given up a job to care for a parent. It is rare that a son does so.

Matthews, Werkner, and Delaney (1989) compared the relative contributions of help to their elderly parents by 50 pairs of sisters in the same family when one was employed and one was not. They found that when parent health was relatively better and care needs were less, both sisters contributed equivalent amounts of help. The employed sisters felt, however, that their jobs limited the amount of social time they could spend with their parents. On the other hand, when parent health status was relatively poor and care needs were greater, the nonemployed sisters contributed more tangible help than did the employed sisters. The employed sisters were not excused from responsibility as brothers might be, but contributed to parent care during evenings and weekends. The sisters worked cooperatively to manage the total caregiving task.

Coresidence with the Elderly Parent

When a caregiving adult child shares a residence with the parent, the remaining siblings provide less help than when the parent lives alone (Brody, 1990; Brody et al., 1994). In a coresidency situation, the major portion of caregiving responsibility falls to that child by virtue of the immediacy of many care needs and the inclusion of other caregiving tasks within the fabric of ongoing household duties. Thus, less help from the caregiver's siblings may be needed.

Another possibility, borne out by anecdotal material, is that siblings may be put off by changes in family relationships accompanying a parent's coresidence with one sibling. At the very least, siblings may be hesitant about intruding in the caregiver's family life and routines, whereas they would feel more free to help the parent in the parent's own residence. Jealousy of the sibling who now has a more intimate relationship with the parent may be a second factor. Another consideration is that other siblings are subject to the dominance of the coresident child when they attempt to help the parent (what kinds of help should be given, and when and how), and they don't want to be bossed. Such factors are intensified when the nonresident sibling does not have a close relationship with the caregiving child.

Sibling Status

Little is known about the contribution made by half-siblings and stepsiblings to the care of an elderly parent or stepparent. However, one study in this area (White & Riedmann, 1992b) indicates that less help is provided by halfsiblings and stepsiblings than by full siblings.

Level of Impairment

The effects of the care recipient's level of impairment on sibling helping relationships have received little attention. There seem to be three trends in the way the middle-aged sibship responds to an increasing level of parental impairment. First, adult children tend to provide more help as parents' need increase (Cicirelli, 1981). Second, as the parent's needs increase, one adult child (usually a daughter) tends assume a principal caregiver role (Aldous, 1987, Brody, 1990); if so, the care load for other siblings is lessened. Third, Matthews and Rosner (1988) indicated that when parents' needs increased, the siblings tended to hire supplementary caregiving services rather than increase their own caregiving involvement. However, the families studied by Matthews and Rosner were in comfortable financial circumstances. Hiring supplementary services is an alternative that may not be available to all families.

EFFECTS OF PARENT CAREGIVING ON ADULT SIBLINGS

Sibling Conflict and Issues of Fairness

Because the findings regarding task performance and hours of care indicate unequal distributions of parent caregiving among middle-aged siblings, the question arises as to just how equitable and fair these unequal contributions are perceived to be. As one might suspect, considerable sibling conflict can occur when the help provided to a parent by various siblings is viewed as inequitable. Up to half of all families report some kind of conflict (Brody, 1990; Cicirelli, 1992a, 1992b; Matthews & Rosner, 1988), with conflicts centered around whether siblings were doing their fair share and around criticisms of one another's actual helping behaviors.

Matthews and Rosner (1988) indicated that about half of the families they studied experienced conflict over caregiving arrangements, although much of this conflict could be attributed to events in family relationships that had occurred long before caregiving responsibilities became an issue. Nevertheless, current sources of conflict tended to be centered on the issue of whether or not a sibling had met filial responsibilities. One would think that criticism on this issue would be directed more toward brothers than toward sisters, in view of the finding that brothers' help is more likely to be sporadic or circumscribed. However, Matthews and Rosner did not present specific findings regarding gender differences in conflict over caregiving arrangements. It seems that just how a sibling's dissociation from caregiving responsibilities is interpreted depends upon a complex history of contingencies and loyalties within the family (Matthews & Sprey, 1989).

Brody (1990) also noted that 30% of principal caregivers, 40% of their sisters, and 6% of their brothers reported strain from sibling interactions regarding parent care. Difficulties arose when the principal caregiver regarded siblings as not doing their fair share, as well as over sibling criticisms of the caregiver's performance. The siblings in Brody's study reported frequent attempts by the principal caregiver to make them feel guilty or to make them assume greater responsibility. It is interesting that such attempts appeared to be directed toward sisters to a greater degree than toward brothers; the brothers' work responsibilities seemed to be regarded as legitimate excuses. Alternatively, the daughters giving care simply may not have expected their brothers to help with traditionally female tasks. As the caregiving load and the family strain increased, so did the caregiver's complaints to her siblings. Overall, the equitable sharing of responsibilities was regarded as a major problem by most of the siblings in this study.

In a study of 50 adult daughters providing at least 10 hours per week of caregiving help to their mothers (Cicirelli, 1992a), only 21% of respondents reported an approximately equal division of caregiving load between all the siblings. Yet, despite the apparent inequities in caregiving contributions, 63% of the daughters rated the division of responsibilities with their sibling networks to be fair or very fair, while only 37% rated it as unfair or very unfair. When classified into groups according to sibling gender, 33% of those with sisters only, 25% of those with brothers only, and 44% of those with both brothers and sisters regarded the division of responsibilities as unfair. Judgments of fairness or unfairness were not related to the perceived equality or inequality of caregiving contributions. Rather, they seemed to be based on complex considerations of a sibling's proximity, competing responsibilities, interest and willingness to help, gender role norms, and history of family relationships, all weighed in comparison with the caregiver's own situation. Most siblings were understanding of another sibling's situation; only 22% failed to understand why certain siblings could not contribute to the parents' care. However, when the caregiving sibling felt that another sibling had no valid excuse for failing to contribute to parent care, there were feelings of resentment and bitterness and the sibling relationship suffered.

If any conclusion can be drawn from the existing studies of gender differences in judgments of fairness regarding siblings' caregiving participation, it is that such judgments are directed toward sisters more than toward brothers. Brothers' lesser contributions appear to be legitimated by their work responsibilities as well as by established social norms.

Stress and Burden of Caregiving

Because care of an elderly parent tends to fall unequally on one daughter (or a few daughters), one would expect the burden and stress of caregiving also to fall unequally. This may be the case with regard to objective burden measured in terms of tasks or time, but since subjective feelings of burden depend more on how the caregiver perceives the situation than on actual caregiving load (Zarit, Reever, & Bach-Peterson, 1980), the extent of subjective burden experienced by middle-aged siblings may be quite different from what is expected. Unfortunately, there are few findings bearing on this question.

According to a study by Brody (1990), daughters who were the principal caregivers for an elderly parent experienced the most burden and strain; of their local siblings, the brothers experienced the least stress and burden, and the sisters experienced an intermediate amount. Among geographically distant siblings, sisters felt more stressed and burdened than brothers. Above and beyond the burden of trying to provide help to a parent over a distance and in addition to competing responsibilities, the siblings (especially sisters) were subject to complaints from the principal caregiver and feelings of guilt that they should be doing more. These findings have been supported in clinical work (Tonti, 1988).

Brody's (1990) findings are somewhat puzzling when compared with those from Montgomery and Kamo's (1989) study of caregiving sons and daughters. The latter authors found that although caregiving sons engaged in fewer and less intense caregiving tasks than did daughters, the amount of subjective and objective burden reported by the two groups did not differ. By way of explanation, one can speculate that gender norms do not lead sons to anticipate parent caregiving responsibilities (Spitze & Logan, 1990); when called upon to assume a principal caregiver role, sons may feel particularly burdened because they do not feel that it is a man's role. In a secondary caregiving role, as Brody (1990) observes, brothers feel little strain accompanying their more limited helping role and little guilt that they should be doing more. The work of Coward and Dwyer (1990) is also relevant here. For single-gender sibling networks and only children, caregiving sons and daughters did not differ in perceived stress or burden measured in terms of caregiving problems. However, caregiving daughters from mixed-gender networks had significantly more burden and stress than caregiving sons, paralleling the greater number of hours of care provided.

Overall, sisters experienced greater caregiving burden than do brothers. However, when brothers do assume a major caregiving role, their feelings of subjective burden may be disproportionately great in view of their objective burden.

Affection and Life Satisfaction

Just how effectively adult siblings accomplish the developmental task of helping an aging parent (Goetting, 1986) can have important implications for their affectional relationships with each other and for their general life satisfaction and sense of well-being.

Tonti (1988) has outlined several phases of change that many adult children undergo as they deal with their parents' aging. Most adult children undergo denial of a parent's aging process until some critical event forces them to reappraise the situation. In an initial phase, the siblings tend to move closer to one another emotionally, with increased communication about the parent's situation. In the second phase, the parent's needs increase to the point that the children need to provide some care; the role of a primary caregiver begins to emerge. In the third phase, the parent's needs increase to the point that coresidence with the child who is the principal caregiver becomes necessary. In the final phase, the intensity of the parent's care needs becomes so great that the parent is transferred to a long-term care facility.

How adult siblings handle these changes depends on the history of their relationship. According to Tonti (1988), there is a history of closeness and care in some families, and tasks are divided as equally as possible among the siblings. In other families, siblings tend to distance themselves emotionally from one another under the stress of caregiving. In still others, old patterns of sibling rivalry are reactivated, with active conflict arising among siblings. Parental favoritism, use of excessive or abusive control tactics, or the splitting of responsibility and authority among siblings can cause or exacerbate conflicts. Finally, in some instances, the relationship between the siblings and the parent is so dysfunctional that the siblings are unable to organize to provide care for the parent, leaving it up to formal agencies. The existing studies of relationships among middle-aged siblings in caregiving situations provide some support for Tonti's clinical observations. Matthews and Rosner (1988) found that conflicts among the siblings they studied stemmed from events in their past that were unrelated to their caregiving responsibilities. Unless conflicts were extreme, however, the siblings managed to maintain caregiving activities. This was true of caregiving brothers as well as sisters (Matthews, Delaney, & Adamek, 1989). Conversely, Brody (1990) reports increased conflicts among siblings as a result of caregiving. In Brody's study such conflicts were more characteristics of relationships between sisters, who assumed the major portion of care responsibilities, than for the other sibling gender combinations.

Findings from a study of caregiving daughters (Cicirelli, 1990) include information on whether the daughters felt that their relationships with siblings had grown closer, stayed the same, or grown less close as a result of their caregiving experiences. Some 65% of the daughters reported that their feelings toward their siblings had stayed the same, 23% said they had grown closer to their siblings, and 23% felt that their sibling relationships had grown less close. Daughters who felt that there was an unfair distribution of caregiving tasks among the siblings tended to be more likely to report that the relationship had grown less close (16% of those who claimed the distribution of tasks was unfair reported that they had grown less close, compared with 7% of those who regarded it as fair). With regard to gender, all of the daughters from sister-only networks reported that their relationships had grown closer or stayed the same, while the groups of daughters with brothers only and daughters with both sisters and brothers were as likely to report that their relationships had grown closer as to say that they had grown less close. Looking at the last two groups from another perspective, all the daughters who felt that their sibling relationships had grown less close as a result of caregiving had at least one brother.

CONCLUSION

Several conclusions can be drawn from existing findings regarding adult siblings' contributions to their parents' care. Overall, sisters provide greater caregiving help than do brothers. Sisters and brothers tend to fulfill caregiving tasks depending on how the tasks fit traditional conceptions of male and female roles. The present generation of adult siblings appear to be influenced by cultural gender role expectations that override the demands of individual caregiving situations. Within the adult sibling system of a family, sisters tend to share the parental caregiving burden more equally than do brothers. Further, they do so regardless of employment responsibilities, whereas brothers regard their work as a legitimate excuse to avoid such responsibilities. Siblings take many factors of one another's situations into account before reaching a judgment that a sibling is evading a fair share of parent caregiving responsibilities. However, once such a judgment is reached, the sibling relationship suffers. On the other hand, successful cooperation in parent caring can make sibling relationships closer.

One aspect of this topic that needs further research is how adult siblings' attachment to one another and to an aging parent are related to the relative contributions of different siblings in the family to parent caregiving.

In speculating about the future, one can predict that sibling participation in caregiving will increase by default. Increased longevity of elderly with chronic conditions, especially elderly widows, indicates increased demand for care. Yet economic realities in the foreseeable future point to a limited role for the formal care system. By default, family members (primarily spouses, adult children, and elderly siblings) will have little choice but to care for their elderly family members themselves. However, with smaller sibship sizes, larger numbers of women in the work force, and larger numbers of divorced and never-married adult children, the task will be too great for any one caregiver. The only way that most siblings will be able to cope with their elderly parents' needs for care is through increased cooperation. Thus, in the future, daughters propelled by gender role expectations into the role of principal caregiver must rely more than they have in the past on sibling assistance, including assistance from brothers.

Siblings with Mental Retardation, Illness, or Disability

When a child in the family is afflicted with mental retardation, chronic illness, or disability, the normal course of development is altered. The question that, in one form or another, has stimulated research over the past three or four decades is: What is the effect on the siblings of the afflicted child?

SOME PRELIMINARY CONSIDERATIONS

This area of inquiry is characterized by great variability and lack of standardization of the terms used to describe the afflicted child's condition, as well as lack of clarity in their definition. In general, terms for particular chronic illnesses and conditions (such as cerebral palsy and diabetes), are standard and clearly defined. However, the areas of physical disability and mental retardation each have problems with variability and definition of terms. Conditions of physical disability have been labeled as impairments, disabilities, and handicaps in the literature; some older studies refer to crippled children. An international classification scheme has been developed (S.C. Brown, 1991) which refers to (1) an *impairment* as a loss of psychological, physical, or anatomical structure or function; (2) a *disability* as a restriction due to an impairment in the ability to perform activities that are normal; and (3) a *handicap* as a social disadvantage imposed by the disability on the performance of social roles. Unfortunately, usage has varied in less recent literature. The international classification applies to mental retardation as well as physical conditions. However, the field of mental retardation has applied such terms as *mentally deficient, mentally handicapped, mentally disabled, special, exceptional, developmentally delayed, developmentally disabled,* and *learning disabled* to individuals whose mental impairment restricts their ability to perform normally on intellectual tasks. Following current usage (e.g., Stoneman & Berman, 1993) the term *mental retardation* will be used in this chapter to refer to individuals with a cognitive disability.

One group of studies has been concerned with the effects of a particular condition (e.g., Down's syndrome, cystic fibrosis, mental retardation) on siblings of the afflicted child, whereas another group of studies has been concerned with the effects of a disability or illness in general.

An example of the first type is a study by Craft, Lakin, Oppliger, Clancy, and Vanderlinden (1990) of siblings of children with cerebral palsy, in which siblings were used as agents of change in an intervention program. The study was restricted to siblings of children with a particular condition and is limited in generalizability.

An example of the second type is the recent study of the effects of a family member's disability on children's well-being (LeClere and Kowalewski, 1994). These researchers analyzed data from the National Health Interview Survey on Child Health for 11,248 children aged 5 to 17 who did not themselves have disabilities, to determine the relationship between the children's behavioral problems and living with a parent or sibling who was chronically ill or disabled. In this study, all kinds of illnesses and disabilities afflicting parents, siblings, and family members were represented, and although findings indicated that behavioral problems were more likely for those children who lived with a disabled person and more likely when the disabled person was a parent than a sibling, one doesn't know whether certain types of chronic illnesses or disabling conditions have greater effects than others.

Large age ranges of both afflicted children and their siblings are found in many studies, frequently with no analysis of age effects on sibling relationships. Admittedly, the age range often is dictated by considerations of expediency when researchers are confronted with the difficulties of finding a sample, particularly when relatively rare illnesses or handicaps are involved. Nevertheless, effects on siblings do change with age as cognitive understanding and emotional maturity develop.

Studies often include samples of afflicted children exhibiting great variability in the severity of their condition. For example, the difference in functional abilities between children with mild and severe cerebral palsy is great, placing different demands on siblings and having different effects on sibling relationships.

Finally, issues of methodology are important, and existing studies differ greatly in terms of their methodology (G. Brody & Stoneman, 1993; Stoneman & G. Brody, 1984). Although a few studies report on a single group consisting of siblings of an afflicted child, under most conditions comparison groups should be used. To insure that comparison groups are comparable in other ways to groups with a disabled or retarded sibling, most investigators use some form of matching. However, whether the groups should be matched on chronological age, mental age, some criterion of performance, demographic characteristics, or some combination of criteria is a matter that each researcher has to deal with. In addition, whether to use interview and self-report methods, various test instruments, or observational methods is a major decision. In some studies, the only source of data about sibling behaviors and adjustment is a parent interview. However, parent reports may be positively biased. A combination of methods may give the most complete picture of sibling relationships, but is somewhat more costly. Finally, questions of sample size and which sibling structure characteristics (age, age spacing, whether normal sibling is older or younger, sex of normal and afflicted sibling) should be specified in a study and which left free to vary must be settled.

The literature in this area is large, and no attempt will be made to review it here. Instead, selective use will be made of previous studies that illustrate major themes of sibling relationships in families with a disabled, chronically ill, or mentally retarded person as the siblings proceed through the life span.

SIBLINGS IN CHILDHOOD AND ADOLESCENCE

Childhood

The interests of researchers studying this stage of life have focused on two major areas of concern. The first concern is to determine how the well or normal siblings in a family adjust to having a sibling who is chronically ill, disabled, or mentally retarded. The second concern is to understand how the well and the afflicted sibling interact with each other in a family context and what factors influence their interaction.

According to Lobato (Lobato, 1983, 1990; Lobato, Faust, & Spirato, 1988), young children who have a sibling with disabilities or mental retardation tend to be unaware of the afflicted sibling's condition or to have only a limited understanding of it. In general, they are aware of only the most salient aspects of the condition. When they can't see particular symptoms they have difficulty understanding why the afflicted sibling can't do something or needs the parents' special attention. However, they are able to make comparisons between the afflicted sibling and their own health and development.

Normal siblings often feel concerned and confused about the reasons for the afflicted child's condition. In addition, they are exposed to the emotional distress of their parents and other family members, heightened parental attention to the afflicted child, frequent disruptions of family plans, and absences of the afflicted child and parents for special treatments or therapy (Lobato, 1983, 1990; Lobato et al., 1988). The way in which parents perceive and deal with the disability or mental retardation not only affects how the afflicted child will deal with his or her condition, but how the normal sibling will react. Open communication with the siblings is important if they are to gain an understanding of the disability or mental retardation. Often parents will project all their educational aspirations on their normal children, with their heightened expectations acting as a stressor on them.

According to Gamble and Woulbroun (1993), normal siblings of children with chronic illness or disability may feel stressed when parents expect them to accept the disabled child to the same degree that the parents do, and fail to recognize that the siblings may have different feelings. Normal siblings will feel similarly stressed when the parents assume that any accomplishment is possible for the ill or disabled child and expect the well siblings to interact normally; when the well siblings must follow different rules than the disabled sibling; and when parents assume that the well siblings are preoccupied with the needs of the disabled child and do not have interests and concerns of their own.

A number of factors relating to the adjustment of siblings of children with chronic illness, disability, or mental retardation have been isolated. Sibling gender is an important consideration. Sisters assume more caretaking responsibilities than brothers, and experience more negative interactions with the mother and afflicted sibling (McHale & Gamble, 1987, 1989), whereas brothers tend to engage in more peer group activities outside the home. The sibling's age influences his or her adjustment, with older children making a better adjustment than younger ones. The effect of age is not surprising, considering younger children's limited understanding of an afflicted sibling's condition; older children are better able to put the situation in perspective and to understand the problems involved in dealing with an ill, disabled, or retarded sibling. Relative birth order of the normal sibling with respect to the afflicted sibling is also important. If the normal sibling is younger, there may be problems associated with assuming a crossover leadership role; however, evidence on this point is mixed (Boyce & Barnett, 1993). The closer in age spacing the normal sibling is to the afflicted child, the greater the adjustment problems. Siblings at wider age spacings have less interests and needs in common and there is less likelihood of competition and rivalry. A normal sibling who is several years older will have experienced some years of normal family life before the afflicted child comes on the scene, and may even be in school. On the other hand, when the normal child is several years younger, the care of the afflicted sibling is likely to already be taken over by other family members (Dyson, 1989, Dyson, Edgar, & Crnic, 1989). Still another factor influencing adjustment is the number of children in the family, with adjustment better in larger families. If the normal child has at least one normal sibling, adjustment is better. The normal children can share caregiving responsibilities and also provide psychological support to one another (Dyson, 1989; Lobato, 1990). Finally, in the case of chronic illness or disability which has a later onset, the age of the well sibling at the time the condition is diagnosed can be an important factor. Both the normal and the afflicted sibling will have had the opportunity to develop a relationship before the onset of the condition; however, the normal child can suffer the effects of loss of parental attention and problems of the family's adjustment to the condition.

Characteristics of the afflicted sibling affecting the well sibling's adjustment include the afflicted child's competence level and the social acceptability of the child's appearance and behavior. In general, the higher the functional level of the afflicted child, the better the sibling's adjustment. Further, helplessness or behavior that is intrusive, socially objectionable, or embarrassing, or an appearance that is repulsive or bizarre can be associated with adjustment problems (Boyce & Barnett, 1993). Whether the afflicted child resides at home or in an institution obviously affects the normal sibling. Also, given the current practice of including ill, disabled, and retarded children within normal school populations, normal siblings attending the same school may have added responsibilities of looking after the afflicted child on the way to and from school and during recesses as well as possibly experiencing rejection and teasing from peers.

Finally, the parents' characteristics are important. Parents at a higher socioeconomic level can afford to hire additional help for the afflicted child, but they may also place more achievement pressures on the normal sibling. Parents at a lower socioeconomic level tend to place more caretaking responsibilities on the normal child. In the case of mental retardation, others are more likely to generalize the retardation to include the whole family. Probably the most important factors influencing the normal child's adjustment are the attitudes, acceptance, and adjustment of the parents (Dyson et al., 1989; McHale, Sloan, & Simeonsson, 1986). If the parent has difficulty accepting and coping with the afflicted child's condition, has a negative attitude toward life or is depressed, and has trouble communicating with the normal sibling, the siblings' adjustment will be poorer.

Nearly all studies concerned with sibling adjustment have considered only the adjustment of the well or normal sibling. Questions of how well the ill, disabled, or mentally retarded sibling was able to adjust to life with normal siblings, or how the sibling environment affected the general development of the afflicted child were not approached in these studies. Normal siblings who are jealous of the parental attention given the afflicted child, or resentful of their own caretaking responsibilities may reject or tease that child. Wiehe (1990) presented anecdotal evidence to indicate that retarded children were vulnerable to aggressive actions or abuse by their siblings.

Some of these questions have been approached in studies investigating dyadic interactions between normal children and their ill, disabled, or retarded siblings. In addition, studies of dyadic interactions provide evidence of the ongoing family processes and parental influence.

When interactions of siblings (aged 1–11) of children with Down's syndrome (aged 1–10) were compared with interactions of normal sibling pairs (Abramovitch, Stanhope, Pepler, & Corter, 1987), most aspects of the sibling interactions in the two groups were similar. However, siblings of the Down's syndrome children quickly assumed dominant leadership roles in the interaction, regardless of whether they were older or younger than the Down's child, and showed significantly more nurturing and affectionate behavior than did siblings in the other group.

A series of studies by G. Brody, Stoneman, and their associates (G. Brody, Stoneman, Davis, & Crapps, 1991; Stoneman, G. Brody, Davis, & Crapps, 1987, 1988) has added greatly to understanding the sibling relationship when one sibling has mental retardation. The studies made use of interviews of mother and siblings, use of measuring instruments, and direct home observation of the sibling dyad to obtain a multifaceted picture of the sibling relationship. Interactions of sibling dyads in a group where one sibling was retarded were contrasted to sibling interactions in a comparison group where neither sibling was retarded. Observations were used to code the various roles assumed by the siblings in the interaction (such as teacher, helper, playmate) and the affective tone of the interaction (instances of positive affect such as hugging, smiling, or laughing, and instances of negative affect such as hitting, quarreling, crying, or name-calling). The role relationships involving a retarded sibling were generally asymmetrical, with the normal sibling assuming the dominant role regardless of a younger relative age. In normal families, older siblings always assumed the dominant role. However, contrary to predictions, in dyads with a retarded child there was less conflict and negative behavior than in the normal dyads. The lowered amount of conflict may have been due to parental sanctions in the families with a retarded child. The normal child did not appear to have fewer peer friends or out-of-home social activities than the comparison group children. However, the retarded children had fewer friends and fewer out-of-home social activities than their age peers in the comparison group. Their restricted social experiences may have prevented them from learning the social skills needed to form friendships outside the home.

McHale and Gamble's (1989) study also used observations of sibling dyads at home supplemented by interview data. Their results were generally in agreement with those of the Brody and Stoneman group. They did find, however, that ratings of the sibling interactions made by mothers and nonretarded siblings were more positive (e.g., greater warmth and less aggression) than observational data showed them to be. This finding suggests that the actual experience of the retarded child may be somewhat different, and less positive than either the normal sibling or the parent perceives it to be.

Adolescence

By the adolescent years, the pattern of normal siblings' relationships with an afflicted sibling are fairly well established. However, the interaction of normal teenage concerns at this particular stage of life with certain aspects of the relationship with an afflicted sibling can lead to particular difficulties in adolescence. First, normal siblings have a dominance relationship with their afflicted siblings rather than the more egalitarian sibling relationships characteristic of normal adolescents. This situation can make peer relationships difficult if the normal sibling has not learned the give and take of egalitarian relationships. If the normal sibling has had heavy caretaking responsibilities throughout childhood, a lack of opportunity for normal peer relationships can lead to isolation and loneliness and interfere with the development of heterosexual relationships at this stage of life. If the normal sibling has developed greater maturity as a result of the sibling caretaking experiences, typical teenage concerns can seem trivial and the sibling may feel out-of-step with peers. Also, given the heightened emotionality and sensitivity typical of adolescents, some normal siblings feel a stigma associated with having a retarded or disabled sibling. They may feel rejected in certain friendships or dating relationships for this reason.

The evidence regarding the effects on the normal sibling in adolescence is mixed. Bagenholm and Gilbert (1991) studied siblings of autistic and mentally retarded children, finding these siblings to have more loneliness and peer problems, more behavior problems, and greater concern for their future than siblings of normal children. However, others (Auletta & DeRosa, 1991) found no differences in psychosocial adjustment for siblings of the mentally retarded. These inconsistencies may be resolved if one considers the findings of an early study by Grossman (1972), who compared the adjustment of college students with a mentally retarded brother or sister to students with normal siblings. There was no difference in the mean adjustment of the two groups (the siblings of retarded children actually had slightly higher college achievement averages), but the students with retarded siblings had a greater variation in responses when asked about their feelings regarding growing up with a retarded sibling and how they felt that their lives had been affected. Some students with positive responses indicated that the relationship with a retarded sibling had given them greater maturity, greater tolerance toward others less fortunate, more humanitarian concerns, greater sense of responsibility, greater feeling of altruism, greater self-confidence, greater appreciation of their own good health and intelligence, and a greater sense of closeness with the family. On the other hand, students at the negative end of the spectrum experienced greater feelings of being neglected by parents, extra home responsibilities and resulting restrictions on their own social activities, feelings of resentment toward parents and their retarded sibling, a sense of distance in the family, embarrassment and shame at the retarded sibling's appearance or behavior, feelings of guilt about their own good health and normal intelligence, and pressure resulting from their parents' expectations for their achievement. The findings of a study by McHale et al. (1986) supported Grossman's conclusion that normal siblings of retarded children had a greater range of variation of responses, both positive and negative in relation perceptions and feelings about their sibling.

SIBLINGS IN ADULTHOOD

The great bulk of sibling research in the area of disability, illness, and mental retardation has been concerned with childhood and adolescence. Much less is known about what happens to the sibling relationship during the adult years. One reason for this gap in knowledge is that in earlier decades, individuals with disability, illness, or mental retardation tended to have a short life span. Although some individuals survived to a greater age, this group was small and not considered sufficiently important to study. As a result of better medical treatment, the life span for such individuals has increased. Consequently, more studies of the effects on adult siblings have appeared in the literature, investigating such questions as the following: Do normal siblings maintain the relationship with an afflicted sibling in adulthood and continue to offer support, or do they withdraw from the relationship to live their own lives? If they maintain the relationship, what kind of a relationship do the siblings have? What are the effects on the normal sibling?

Recent studies have indicated that about 80% of individuals with mental retardation continue to live with or under the direct supervision of their families throughout adulthood (Krauss, Seltzer, & Goodman, 1992; Seltzer & Krauss, 1989). In most cases, they remain in the homes of their parents, who continue to care for them over 5 or 6 decades into old age. In an analysis of the social support networks of 418 mentally retarded adults living at home (aged 15–66), Krauss et al. found that social support networks were typically small (4 people, on the average) and composed mainly of parents (31%), siblings (27%), other kin (16%), and long-term friends (20%). Most of these same individuals were also members of the mothers' support networks. Siblings comprised a larger percentage of retarded brothers' support networks than sisters' networks, largely because the sisters' networks included more friends. It is clear that sibling relationships continue to be important for individuals with mental retardation in adulthood. (In comparison, mentally retarded persons living in group homes received the bulk of their social support from peer friends and professionals rather than from family.) One needs to ask what the relationship is like for the siblings involved.

In an early study, when nonretarded adult siblings of institutionalized mentally retarded adults were asked how having a mentally retarded sibling had influenced major aspects of their lives such as career, marriage, and family decisions (Cleveland & Miller, 1977), the majority of respondents reported no lasting effects. However, sisters who had assumed major caretaking responsibilities in childhood continued to maintain a close relationship with their retarded siblings in adulthood and tended to choose careers in the helping professions. On the other hand, brothers who had had little contact with their retarded siblings in childhood tended to be fearful of having a retarded child of their own in adulthood.

In a study of mentally retarded adults living in family care homes (Stoneman & Crapps, 1990), 62% received no visits from siblings from their family of origin and 21% were visited only yearly or less, although 86% had living siblings. Only 4% were visited by a sibling more than once a month. Only 43% of the retarded siblings ever left their family care homes to visit a sibling, and when they did it was to visit a sister, typically during the holidays. Nonretarded siblings were more likely to visit when they lived nearer, had participated in the placement decision, and the retarded adult was older. Siblings continued to visit after their parents' death, apparently assuming the parents' former support roles. Only 12% of the nonretarded siblings felt very close to their retarded siblings, whereas 45% felt not at all close. The sibling relationship was likely to be closer the older the retarded adult, the better the retarded adult's cognitive abilities, and when the nonretarded sibling lived nearer to the family care home.

To determine whether closer sibling relationships were maintained when adult retarded siblings lived in the parents' home, 411 such families were studied, of whom all but 28 had a nonretarded sibling (G. Seltzer, Begun, M. Seltzer, & Krauss, 1991). Only about a fifth of the retarded siblings received any instrumental support from siblings, and this help came mainly from nonretarded siblings who also coresided in the parents' home. In contrast, 80% received affective support from at least one sibling, with sisters and nearby siblings the most involved. The retarded siblings reciprocated with some affective support to nonsiblings; however, there was an overall imbalance with the nonretarded siblings providing more than twice the support. Families in which there was a high degree of sibling involvement with the retarded sibling were also more cohesive, expressive, achievement-oriented, and independent. Sibling involvement had an indirect effect on mothers' well-being, with less burden and stress and greater life satisfaction.

Begun (1989) studied the sibling relationships of 46 sisters of moderately to profoundly retarded and developmentally disabled individuals, ranging in age from middle childhood into old age. Comparing these relationships to those with their normal siblings, relationships with the disabled sibling were less intimate, more neutral affectively, less competitive, and less satisfying. The better the functional abilities of the afflicted sibling, the more normal the sibling relationships.

Whereas the above studies examined the sibling relationship from the perspective of the nonretarded siblings, Zetlin (1986) carried out extensive interviews with 35 mildly retarded adults living independently in the community, as well as participant observation over an 18-month period, to determine how they perceived relationships with 74 siblings. There was a great deal of variability in the quality of the sibling relationships. On the basis of judged warmth of feelings, amount of contact, and amount of sibling involvement, sibling relationships were assigned to one of five levels. The highest level on the relationship continuum involved very warm feelings, frequent contact, and extensive involvement, and the lowest level involved hostility, rare or no contact, and no involvement. A sibling relationship at the highest level was reported by 23% of the retarded adults; 29% reported one or more relationships at level 2; 57% at level 3; 34% at level 4; and 11% at level 5. For half of the eight sibling pairs on the highest relationship level, the nonretarded sibling acted as a surrogate for a deceased or aging parent, and provided a great deal of assistance to the retarded sibling. For the other half of the pairs, the nonretarded (although poorly functioning) and retarded siblings interacted on an equal peer basis as best friends, spending a great deal of time on shared activities. The second (12 pairs) and third (27 pairs) relationship levels were characterized by warm feelings but diminishing contact and involvement. On both levels, the nonretarded sibling provided some degree of assistance which the retarded sibling reciprocated, at least in part. The retarded adults regarded their siblings as important people in their lives. However, those at the third relationship level often had their invitations to visit or to share some activity turned down by their nonretarded siblings. They expressed a desire for a closer relationship, but made excuses for their normal siblings' limited involvement. At all three levels, there was an expectation that the nonretarded siblings would continue their involvement into the future and would look after the retarded sibling following the parents' death. The fourth relationship level (20 pairs) was characterized by resentful feelings and minimal contact and involvement. Limited indirect contact occurred through the parents or other siblings. The retarded siblings interpreted their nonretarded sibling's disinterest in a closer relationship as rejection, but nevertheless felt that they could count on that sibling in an emergency. The fifth and lowest relationship level (7 pairs) was characterized by hostile feelings and no contact or involvement. Relationships between the siblings at this level had apparently always been poor, with jealousy, fighting, name-calling, and so on during the years when they were growing up. Attempts by retarded siblings to make contact as adults were rebuffed, adding to the feelings of animosity. There was no expectation that these nonretarded siblings would be a resource if help were needed. Overall, relationships with retarded siblings were hierarchical rather than egalitarian in most cases, with nonretarded siblings providing help and support. Middle-aged siblings who had developed stable life-styles were viewed by their retarded siblings as their best and most reliable supporters. It was clear that the degree of nonretarded siblings' involvement at the five levels reflected the parents' expectations for the relationship as well as the kind of support given the retarded child by the parents. Further, it seemed to be a continuation of the kind of sibling relationship existing earlier in life.

Future Care when the Parents Die

The care of a mentally retarded child is frequently a life-long burden for the parents. The question of who will assume responsibility for the care of a retarded sibling when the parents die is one that concerns parents and adult children alike. The decline of institutions for the mentally retarded and the growth of various forms of community-based care have made the question of planning for future care a central one for family members. The existing studies of sibling relationships in adulthood reveal that in most families there is an expectation that one or more siblings will take over the parents' role when they die (Begun, 1989; G. Seltzer et al., 1991; M. Seltzer & Krauss, 1989, 1993; Zetlin, 1986). Such an expectation is congruent with the general concept of a substitution hierarchy in family caregiving, where a spouse assumes primary responsibility, followed by adult children, siblings, grandchildren, and other kin. If the highest person in the hierarchy is unavailable, the one next in line takes over. Once the parents of mentally retarded adults die, siblings are the next closest kin, as few retarded individuals marry and have children of their own.

In a recent study (Griffiths & Unger, 1994), 41 pairs of siblings and parents of mentally retarded adults participating in sheltered workshop programs were interviewed regarding plans for future care. Half the parents (51%) indicated that, when they were no longer able to provide care, they would arrange to place the retarded child in a group home or state-operated facility for the retarded. Only 22% expected a sibling to provide care, and all of these expected that sibling to be a daughter. (The remainder were uncertain, or indicated placements with other kin or friends.) For their part, 54% of the siblings indicated that they never wanted their retarded sibling to be placed outside the family, with 44% willing to take on the responsibility themselves. When factors related to sibling willingness to assume responsibility were investigated, the perceived stress arising from the retarded sibling's cognitive disability, pessimism about the situation, and family problems were important factors limiting sibling involvement. Siblings were more willing to give care when the retarded siblings' cognitive disabilities and physical incapacities were less, and when the sibling's spouse agreed with the plan to give care. Only about half the siblings reported that discussions with the parents about permanency planning for the retarded sibling had taken place; those who reported such communication were also more willing to assume care responsibilities. The Griffiths and Unger study may present a high estimate for the willingness of siblings to give care, because it sampled only siblings nominated by parents and was carried out with well-functioning middle-class white families. However, it supports other findings.

CONCLUSION

A few general themes have recurred throughout this chapter. First, the parents' views about their afflicted child and their expectations regarding sibling relationships are powerful forces influencing their normal children's relationships with the afflicted child from early childhood through middle and old age. Second, having an ill, disabled, or mentally retarded sibling may not affect the normal sibling's development on the average; however, some siblings may benefit greatly from the experience of helping to care for an afflicted sibling whereas others may suffer greatly from the experience. Third, a variety of characteristics of the afflicted child, the sibling, the family, and the situation can mediate the effects of having an afflicted sibling. Last, the kind of relationship developed with an afflicted sibling early in life tends to persist throughout life. A normal sibling who resents or rejects an ill, disabled, or retarded sibling in childhood will rarely maintain more than a cursory relationship in adulthood. By the same token, the disproportionate share of caretaking duties given sisters early in life is associated with sisters' continuing support to parent caregivers in adulthood and the eventual assumption of care responsibilities when the parents are no longer able to do so.

Existing studies provide no information about sibling relationships when a stepsibling, half-sibling, or adoptive sibling has a chronic illness, disability, or mental retardation. One would expect that, depending on how well the afflicted sibling is integrated into the family, the normal sibling would feel less responsibility for helping than if the afflicted child were a full sibling, and would be likely to have more resentment and other negative feelings if pressed to assume a helping role.

Sibling Conflict, Aggression, Violence, and Abuse

An idealistic conception of siblings is that they are always close, loving, and ready to care for one another. Unfortunately, this is only part of the portrait. Sibling conflict exists, and sometimes continues throughout life. In the absence of better means, aggression, violence, or abuse may be used to deal with it.

DEFINITIONS AND DISTINCTIONS

Definition of Conflict

Although both intrapersonal and interpersonal conflict exist, the present book is concerned only with the latter. Interpersonal conflicts may be defined as social events involving opposition and disagreement (Shantz, 1987; Vandell & Bailey 1992). According to Vandell and Bailey, conflict is marked behaviorally by actions such as quarreling, fighting, resisting, opposing, refusing, denying, objecting, and protesting; conflict occurs whenever two or more individuals engage in oppositional behavior.

Although this seems to be a reasonable definition, the following modification is proposed here in an attempt to better distinguish between related terms: Interpersonal conflict exists when two individuals disagree in their desires or ideas, when the disagreement is accompanied by some degree of emotion, and when the individuals have the expectation of actively opposing each other. If one person expects to oppose and the other expects to submit, then compliance rather than conflict exists. For interpersonal conflict to exist there has to be mutual opposition. Shantz and Hobart (1989) make this point by distinguishing between conflict and aggression. Aggression can be unidirectional, but conflicts involve mutual opposition. Verbal expressions as well as physical actions may be used to make clear the existence of a conflict, but when behavior goes beyond this point, it should be distinguished from conflict. More extreme verbal or physical behaviors then become ways of dealing with the conflict. The modified definition differs from that of Vandell and Bailey (1992) and Shantz (1987) on this point.

The content of disagreement can vary widely. For example, two people can disagree regarding what is true, what should be done, who should control a situation, who is the best person in a situation, who is the owner of a certain property or territory, who can succeed in inflicting damage on the other, who can outdo or humiliate the other in a situation, and so on. Individuals may verbally or physically express their disagreement by stating their positions, protesting or objecting to the views of the other, using gestures or facial expressions, or behaving in other ways that express their differences.

Disagreements between siblings in childhood and adolescence are similar in many ways. In both age groups, siblings may have disputes concerning control of resources and possessions (e.g., toys, clothes, television, or telephone), or concerning for rights and entitlements (Felson, 1983; Raffaelli, 1992). However, young adolescents have more conflicts dealing with territory or someone invading their space (e.g., someone sitting in their chair).

Management of Conflicts

Once conflicts begin, individuals use various means in an attempt to deal with or manage them. In general, conflicts may be dealt with in a socially acceptable manner, in a mildly or moderately unacceptable manner, or in a very unacceptable manner.

Acceptable modes of dealing with conflict include verbal discussion, give and take, problem solving, and negotiation. All of these are associated with a relatively low intensity of emotions. Unacceptable modes of dealing with conflict involve use of physical or verbal acts of aggression, violence, and abuse, and are associated with a more intense level of emotions. In the latter case, one sibling may be considered the perpetrator and the other the victim, or both siblings can enact these roles either alternatively or simultaneously.

Outcome of Conflicts

However a conflict is managed, at some point there is an outcome. The outcome may be temporary or permanent, depending upon the intensity and duration of the conflict, and it can be constructive or destructive.

A constructive outcome is a solution whereby the siblings agree to abide by a particular rule, or a resolution where there is a compromise in their viewpoints or actions. Such an outcome usually follows from discussion, problem solving, and negotiation. Another type of constructive outcome may occur when the conflict is unresolved but within a context of sibling acceptance of each other (as when there is an opposition of views and an expression of emotion, but the subject is dropped). There may be periodic flareups of an unresolved conflict; however, the duration of the conflict is short and there is a dissipation or reduction of emotional feelings of anger or hostility after each episode. Eventually the unresolved conflict may simply dissipate or be forgotten.

A destructive conflict outcome occurs when a solution is imposed by force (by the stronger sibling, a parent, etc.) and when there is no real solution or resolution. The conflict may continue to exist at a conscious level within a context of hostile emotions, and with the recurrent use of aggressive, violent, or abusive acts as ways of dealing with it. Destructive conflicts may become dormant, only to emerge again when a crisis occurs. However, the conflict itself may be consciously avoided, denied, or repressed as the siblings attempt to move on to other concerns.

Long-Range Consequences of Outcomes

The long range effects of constructive conflict outcomes are positive growth in the characteristics of the individuals concerned, improvement in their interpersonal relationships with each other (e.g., closer bonding), and improvement in their relationships with others as they transfer conflict management skills learned in the immediate conflict situation to conflicts with other family members and friends. More specifically, siblings with constructive conflict outcomes may learn to deal more effectively with conflict through improving problem solving and negotiating skills (G. Brody & Stoneman, 1987), and attain an increase in their social understanding and self-esteem (Bank & Kahn, 1982b; Dunn, 1988; Shantz & Hobart, 1989). Additionally, learning to deal constructively with conflict may facilitate deidentification (Schachter, 1985), and thereby strengthening siblings' self-identity. Relationships are undermined by destructive conflicts, especially if unresolved conflicts accumulate over time. In destructive outcomes of conflict, the long-range effects are usually negative; that is, siblings may become more anxious and depressed, and there is likely to be a disruption in the relationship itself.

Constructive conflicts also are believed to enhance social understanding and problem skills, whereas destructive conflicts are not associated with these developmental outcomes (Bank & Kahn, 1982b; Dunn, 1988; Shantz & Hobart, 1989).

Problems in Studying Sibling Conflict

Although the concept of conflict can be defined in an acceptable manner that is conceptually distinct from management of conflict, outcome, and long-range consequences, defining the negative ways of dealing with conflicts presents problems for researchers. No standardized definitions of aggression, violence, or abuse exist at present. As a result, there are no standard criteria for use in survey studies to determine the prevalence of aggression, violence, and abuse; comparison of results from different studies is difficult; finally, the formulation of adequate explanations of the phenomena for eventual use in intervention programs is hampered.

Additionally, physical and emotional forms of aggression, violence, and abuse need to be distinguished. Wiehe (1990) pointed out that physical and emotional aggression usually go together and also frequently overlap with sexual abuse. Emotional aggression, violence, or abuse may occur mainly on the verbal level, when the perpetrator teases, insults, ridicules, threatens, intimidates, and so on, with the intent of degrading, humiliating, or demeaning the victim. However, in this chapter the physical actions of aggression, violence, and abuse are emphasized, recognizing that emotional aspects may occur concomitantly.

Inconsistent definitions of aggression, violence, and abuse have been the rule in the literature, accompanied by inconsistent ways of operationalizing them. The same physical or verbal acts classified as aggression, violence, or abuse in one study may be classified differently in another study. Or, different physical or verbal acts may be assigned to the same term (e.g., *violence*) by different researchers. Specific acts that have been classified as violence in various studies include arguing, name calling, teasing, threatening, protesting, retaliating, slapping, pushing, shoving, spanking, punching, kicking, biting, choking, burning, attempted drowning, cutting, and so on.

A related problem is that, even if consistent distinctions between terms existed, some actions may be judged to be acceptable behavior by one particular subculture or culture and not by another. For example, everyone may agree that siblings' hitting one another is an example of aggressive behavior. Such aggressive behavior may be unacceptable in an Anglo-Saxon culture, whereas it may be viewed as normal in a Latin culture. Or, parents may consider sibling fighting as violent behavior but still accept such violence simply because it is so common among siblings. Also, a sibling's aggressive behavior may be accepted in a culture if it is considered a means of disciplining a younger sibling; that is, an older sibling may be given tacit approval to spank a young child if the latter has violated certain rules and deserves to be punished; the spanking may be carried out not only for the sake of discipline but as a way of modifying the child's behavior. Finally, a culture may accept aggressive behavior from a young sibling toward an older one but not from an older sibling to a younger one; similarly, it may be unacceptable for brothers to hit sisters, but not vice versa.

In short, even if appropriate distinctions are made between aggression, violence, and abuse, and agreement is reached about which physical and verbal acts are to be assigned to each term, the distinction between them may be blurred by the social norms regarding the acceptability of particular actions under various conditions. Thus, the problem of operationalizing the terms for research remains.

Potential Criteria for Distinguishing Aggression, Violence, and Abuse

One criterion that may be considered is the level of intensity of the physical or verbal act. For example, if a child pushes a sibling lightly in dealing with a conflict, one might consider this an aggressive act. If a child roughly pushes the sibling to the ground, this might be considered violence. If a child pushes the sibling down a flight of stairs, this might be considered abuse. One can envision a continuum beginning with mildly aggressive acts, with violence as an extreme aggression, and abuse as extreme violence; that is, with a quantitative increase in the intensity of the physical act.

Another criterion that can be considered is the impact of the physical or verbal act on the victim. One could possibly distinguish aggression, violence, and abuse on the degree of pain, injury, harm, or humiliation experienced by the victim. For example, abuse might occur when the pain or harm is so great as to require medical attention, or the humiliation so great as to require counseling.

Still another criterion is the degree to which the victim can or does defend himself or herself from the perpetrator's assault. If the victim fights back in self-defense, should this act be exempt from consideration as either aggression, violence, or abuse? Or should it be one of the three, depending upon the intensity level of the action taken? A related criterion is the degree to which the victim is unable to resist the perpetrator's assault, and must submit to the former.

It is suggested that physical aggression be defined as acts which are intended to cause pain or physical harm (minor scratches or cuts, bruises, etc.), and that emotional aggression be defined as verbal or physical acts intended to cause emotional distress. At times, they may be difficult to separate.

Similarly, physical violence or physically violent behavior may be defined as acts leading to injuries that require medical attention for healing, and that emotional violence be defined as verbal acts so devastating that the victim needs outside counseling. It is a matter of severity; that is, violence is an extreme form of aggression on a continuum.

Physical abuse involves coercion based on a recognized power difference between perpetrator and victim. Physical abuse involves physically coercing or forcing the victim to carry out certain acts to satisfy the desires of the perpetrator and also to humiliate the victim. The autonomy of the victim is submitted to the power of the perpetrator; the victim is unable to resist. Aggressive or violent behavior may be used to demonstrate the power or increase the pleasure of the perpetrator, but it is not essential to abuse. Abuse primarily involves subordinating the will of another who is unable to resist in order to do one's bidding and humiliate at the same time. In this case, it is difficult to separate physical and emotional abuse. There may be little or no overt violence by the more powerful sibling in a sibling abuse situation as there is little opposition. The perpetrator may simply be imposing his or her will to do little or serious harm to the sibling, and for various motives, such as sadistic pleasure, releasing frustrations, expressing feelings of anger, and so on. There may be no opposition but only submission to possibly severe physical harm or pain, or emotional distress that is demeaning and humiliating. In some cases, there may be severe or lethal harm to the victim.

Feld (1988) pointed out that the weak sibling who seems incapable of defense against a more powerful sibling may resort to occasional violent acts to achieve desired goals, or may commit anonymous violent acts against the property or person of the more powerful sibling. At times the weak sibling will retaliate in the presence of a parent, feeling sure of the parent's sympathy and support. It is clear that the interactions of family members in situations such as these may be quite complex.

However, the above definitions are merely advanced here for purposes of possible clarification; they do not represent a consensus among researchers in this area. Various researchers have used still different terms, such as sibling rivalry (Prochaska & Prochaska, 1985; Stocke 1992), sibling conflict and fighting (Felson, 1983; Felson & Furman & Buhrmester, 1982; Patterson, 1986; Shantz, 1987), between siblings (Furman & Buhrmester, 1985). It is not alwa what actions are implied by these terms or whether these res~~~ ~~~~s are thinking in terms of sibling aggression, violence, or abuse.

At the present time, most researchers in the area have given up any attempt to seek standardized definitions. Instead, they define and measure these terms within the context of their research studies, or they use the terms interchangeably as labels for one definition and measuring procedure.

Finally, there is the question of mild, moderate, and severe aggression, violence, or abuse. Many studies carried out with preschool children seem to involve mild or moderate conflicts, and mild or moderate degrees of aggression (Abramovitch, Corter, & Lando, 1979; Abramovitch, Corter, Pepler, & Stanhope, 1986; Abramovitch, Corter, & Pepler, 1980; Abramovitch, Pepler, & Corter, 1982). This may be attributed in part to the use of very young siblings as research subjects and in part to their high socioeconomic status level.

It should be noted that Straus and Gelles (1986) and Steinmetz (1987), prominent researchers in the field of family violence, define violence as an act carried out with the intention of causing physical pain or injury to another person. Also, they suggest that abuse might be a more extreme form of violence, indicated by the severity of the physical act carried out.

Because no consensus solution exists for the definition and measurement problems at the present time, an attempt will be made to follow a researcher's use of terms when surveying various existing studies in this chapter.

PREVALENCE OF CONFLICT, AGGRESSION, VIOLENCE, AND ABUSE

In an early study, Steinmetz (1977) investigated the frequency of physical violence between 88 pairs of siblings from 57 randomly selected families with two or more children between the ages of 3 and 17. Information about the occurrence of violent acts was obtained from a diary kept by one of the parents. Major findings were that 78% of the sibling pairs 8 years old or younger, 68% of the pairs aged 9 to 14, and 63% of those aged 15 or older used forms of physical violence as a means of resolving interpersonal conflict. For the youngest group, conflicts dealt mostly with possessions; for those aged 9 to 14, the conflicts centered around personal space boundaries, touching, or "looking funny" at each other. For the oldest group, the conflicts centered around responsibilities and obligations. Other early studies reported percentages of children using physical violence as ranging from 62 to 78% (Steinmetz, 1977, 1982; Straus, 1971, 1974). However, Steinmetz noted that when parents report sibling violence, they tend to lump conflicts together and attribute a single cause to them, they have difficulty deciding on the severity of the conflict, they record a series of incidents as one, they don't necessarily observe all the conflicts which have taken place, and they don't report the gender of the siblings in relation to specific violent actions.

Straus (1974) reported that 62% of a sample of college students had used physical force on a brother or sister during the previous year. Male siblings more frequently threw things, pushed, and hit than did female siblings. The highest use of physical violence occurred in brother–sister sibling pairs (67%); brother–brother sibling pairs were next (61%), and sister–sister sibling pairs used physical violence the least (22%). Regardless of gender, older siblings were less likely to use physical violence than were younger ones. However, Steinmetz (1977) reported that 72% of young adults between 18 and 30 years of age used physical violence to resolve conflicts, seeming to contradict the idea that older siblings used physical force less. Because Steinmetz' sample was not representative, this findings is somewhat in doubt.

Straus, Gelles, and Steinmetz (1980) carried out a national survey of 2,143 families to investigate all types of family violence occurring in 1975, including sibling violence. The sample included 1,224 pairs of siblings ranging in age between 3 and 17 years. The pairs used various methods of violence to resolve conflicts: pushing-shoving, 60%; slapping, 45%; throwing, 39%; kicking, biting, hitting with fist, 38%; hitting with an object, 36%; beating up, 14%; threatening to use a knife or gun, .8%, and actually using a knife or gun, .3%. When asked whether they had ever used any of the more violent methods, 18% of the sibling pairs reported having beaten up their sibling in the past, and 5% reported using a gun.

There are no national statistics on the prevalence of sibling homicide. However, Straus et al. (1980) reviewed earlier reports of sibling homicide in New York and Philadelphia and reported that sibling homicides comprised about 3% of all homicides in these large cities. These early statistics call attention to the potential seriousness of sibling violence, but do not give information about prevalence at the present time. Other more recent studies also have reported the existence of sibling homicide (Adam & Livingston, 1993; Nelson & Martin, 1985; Steinmetz, 1987).

Straus et al. (1980) drew several other conclusions from their national survey. Although occurrence of sibling homicide was less frequent than marital or filial homicide in the families studied, the prevalence of severe nonhomicidal violence (e.g., beating up, threatening use of a gun or knife, and using a gun or knife) was greater among siblings than among parents and children or between spouses. Also, less severe violence among siblings was more prevalent than other types of family violence, boys were more likely to physically abuse siblings than girls, and the highest levels of abuse occurred in families with male children.

Straus et al. (1980) felt that the amount of violence among siblings has been underestimated for various reasons. There is a normative acceptance of sibling violence in our society. Many parents feel that it is an inevitable part of growing up, and may even encourage it at times. Some parents feel that sibling violence is important training for dealing with aggressive behavior from others. Parents may not observe all the sibling violence that takes place.

DEVELOPMENTAL COURSE OF CONFLICT, AGGRESSION, VIOLENCE, AND ABUSE

Sibling conflict accompanied by heightened affect seems to be more frequent in infancy, childhood, and adolescence than in adulthood. The frequency of conflict declines during childhood (McHale & Gamble, 1989; Prochaska & Prochaska, 1985), even when the degree of sibling interaction is controlled (G. Brody, Stoneman, MacKinnon, & MacKinnon, 1985). Although conflicts with siblings continue to be part of children's everyday lives (Furman & Buhrmester, 1985), the nature of the conflicts becomes more sophisticated during childhood and on through adolescence. Sibling conflicts become more verbal, and children increasingly try to justify their actions (Vandell & Bailey, 1992). These justifications may be simple assertions rather than being logical (Phinney, 1985), they may be based on the children's own feelings and wishes, or they may be justified by social rules and material consequences.

Also, as children grow older, the rates of using violence to resolve conflicts between siblings decreases (Straus et al., 1980). For example, teenagers have a greater tendency to be verbally aggressive when there is a difference of opinion in conflict situations rather than being physically aggressive.

Conflicts between adolescents tend to involve intense affect (e.g., anger), reflecting the general lability of emotions at that stage of life. However, the conflicts tend to be brief. Young adolescents report that 42% of their arguments with siblings are resolved within 5 minutes and that an additional 46% are resolved within an hour (Raffaelli, 1992). By late adolescence, disagreements between siblings are relatively rare.

Such a decline is consistent from childhood through adolescence, and continues through adulthood and old age. However, there is some evidence that conflicts can continue to exist at a subconscious level in adulthood, or remain dormant until a crisis occurs (Bedford, 1989a; Cicirelli, 1988).

There are various reasons for the decline in siblings' conflicts and use of violence as children develop. Children increase in their social understanding and social problem solving and logical thinking, which helps them to deal more effectively with conflicts at the verbal level and even to negotiate compromises to settle disputes. Sometimes siblings tend to ignore or withdraw from each other following conflicts (Montemayor & Hanson, 1985; Raffaelli, 1992; Roscoe, Goodwin, & Kennedy, 1987). Withdrawing tends to reduce violence but also reduces the likelihood of a constructive resolution of the conflict (Straus et al., 1980). Another aspect of the situation is that, as they grow older, children spend more time with peers and less time with each other, reducing the potential for conflict.

FACTORS ASSOCIATED WITH SIBLING CONFLICT

Some siblings have minor disagreements; others have major disagreements accompanied by aggression or violence. Some siblings rarely argue or fight; others do so continually. The origins of conflicts, modes of dealing with them, their outcomes, and long-range consequences all are related to aspects of the larger family context. Some factors that have been associated with sibling conflict, aggression, violence, and abuse are the family climate, the relationship between spouses, the relationships between parents and children, the differential treatment of children by parents, and characteristics of the siblings themselves and their relationship.

Differential Treatment by Parents

Differential parental treatment of siblings in a family can be related to sibling conflict. In the most egregious cases, parents play favorites by pampering and praising one child and ignoring, depriving, or punishing the other. The resulting rivalry and resentment between the siblings can lead to aggression and violence. However, according to Vandell and Bailey (1992), there are times when differential treatment of siblings is appropriate and might even be necessary. When children are in different stages of growth, or there is a large age difference between them, or they have different temperaments and talents, parents may treat them differently to protect one from the other, to fulfill different expectations for each one, or to provide different entitlements to each one, all in the name of fairness. That is, parents may find it necessary to treat siblings differently to attain the same goals. In these cases, parents are trying to be fair, but the siblings perceive differential love and acceptance. Whether parental favoritism is real or perceived, sibling conflict is likely to increase.

Considerable empirical support exists for the role of differential parental treatment in sibling conflict. From childhood to adolescence, greater maternal responsiveness and affection were found to be related to both the favored and nonfavored siblings' disparagement of one another (Bryant & Crockenberg, 1980), competitiveness and attempts at control (Stocker, Dunn, & Plomin, 1989), and aggressiveness, rivalry, and lack of affection (Hetherington, 1988).

Differential parental treatment can come about as a parent attempts to prevent victimization of a younger child. If parental behavior toward the same child changes over time, as with a change in attention to the firstborn child after the birth of the second, the change may be reflected in negative interactions with siblings (Vandell & Bailey, 1992). Similarly, children who have negative interactions with a parent may behave negatively in interacting with a sibling (Kendrick & Dunn, 1983). School-aged children of mothers who used punitive disciplinary techniques were more hostile and antagonistic to siblings than children whose mothers did not (G. Brody & Stoneman, 1987; Hetherington, 1988). Alternatively, the frequency and intensity of mother–child conflicts are correlated with conflicts between siblings (Hetherington, 1988; Volling & Belsky, 1992).

Insufficient Parental Attention

Another source of sibling conflict is the parent's failure to devote adequate attention to the physical and emotional needs of the child. This may be a particular problem when one sibling is handicapped or ill, where children may perceive parental favoritism and inequitable treatment in favor of their handicapped sibling in addition to parental neglect of their own needs. In such cases, sibling conflict and negative behavior have been observed, as well as sibling empathy and helpfulness (Abramovitch, Stanhope, Pepler, & Corter, 1987; McHale & Gamble, 1987, 1989).

Emotional Climate of the Family

Parents influence their children's sibling relationships through the general emotional climate created within the family as a byproduct of the parents' psychological states and their relationship with each other. Generally, family conflict breeds sibling conflict, but it can increase sibling closeness, cooperation, and protectiveness (Bank & Kahn, 1982b; Hetherington, 1988).

The family stress involved when parents divorce and then remarry can be particularly trying for sibling relationships as all family members attempt to readjust to changed circumstances. High frequencies of sibling and parent–child conflict and aggressive behaviors are typical of the first 2 years after remarriage (Beer, 1989; Hetherington, 1988).

Parental Response to Sibling Conflict

The way in which parents respond to sibling conflicts and aggressive actions is an important factor in further conflicts and their outcomes. Some parents adopt a hands-off policy and leave siblings to settle things on their own. According to G. Brody and Stoneman (1987), parental intervention prevents children from acquiring conflict resolution skills. Felson and Russo (1988) suggest that, left on their own, siblings establish a balance of power and conflict decreases. When parents intervene, they tend to favor the weaker, younger sibling, with the result that conflicts increase and are prolonged (G. Brody, Stoneman, McCoy, & Forehand, 1992). Additionally, if they respond inconsistently to sibling conflicts, the frequency of conflicts is likely to increase.

On the other hand, some parents adopt a policy of intervention in sibling conflicts, feeling that they can play a constructive role. Mothers may attempt to explain their younger child's behavior to the older ones and suggest ways to conciliate conflicts, or they may instruct children in social and moral rules within the family. Mothers who mediated conflicts of 18-month-old siblings by referring to rules and to children's feelings had children who showed more mature conflict behaviors such as less teasing and more conciliating at 24 months of age (Dunn & Munn, 1986a). Bank and Kahn (1982b) observed that by adopting consistent moral principles and communicating them clearly to quarreling siblings, parents minimize the likelihood of one sibling victimizing or abusing the other.

Ross, Filyer, Lollis, Perlman, and Martin (1994) delineated various types of parental roles in intervening in their children's conflicts. One aspect of parental role behavior was the degree of partisanship they showed. Another aspect was the type of conflict settlement strategies they employed. Strategies at one end of a continuum were those of a friendly peacemaker attempting to distract or persuade the children to abandon their dispute. Intermediary strategies were those of a mediator or arbitrator, where the parent helps the siblings to resolve the conflict on their own.

At the other end of the continuum were strategies of a judge or repressive peacemaker, where the parent imposed a resolution of the conflict on the siblings. One can hypothesize that use of more repressive strategies would lead to increased conflict and poorer relationships between siblings instead of construction resolution of conflicts. Ross et al. studied parents' interventions in conflicts of their 2- and 4-year-old children. Although the parents generally expressed support for a number of rules for family interaction, violations of certain rules were generally overlooked and only a few rules (e.g., rules prohibiting aggression and promoting sharing) were strongly enforced. It appeared that only a few rules were observed by the children themselves in the absence of parental intervention. Unfortunately the study did not attempt to link particular parental intervention strategies to children's rule observance.

As yet, research findings provide no clear direction as to what parents' role in sibling conflicts should be. What is clear, however, is that parental inconsistency is likely to lead to increased conflict.

Characteristics of Siblings

To some extent, variations in sibling conflicts appear to be related to children's individual characteristics as well as to characteristics of the sibling dyad. Conflicts are related to factors such as the siblings' relative ages, age spacing, gender, and temperament.

Regardless of age or age spacing, the older of two siblings is more likely to be the aggressor, and the younger is more likely to be the victim of the older child's aggression. This occurs with preschoolers and toddlers (Abramovitch, Carter, & Lando, 1979; Lamb, 1978a, b; Pepler, Abramovitch & Corter, 1981), as well as with school-age children (Berndt & Bulleit, 1985: Sutton-Smith & Rosenberg, 1970). Interviews with adolescents and college students describe a similar pattern in which the older of two siblings initiates more conflicts than the younger one (Felson, 1983; Graham-Bermann, Cutler, Litzenberger, & Schwartz, 1994). However, younger siblings are not totally at the mercy of older brothers and sisters. Younger siblings develop their own strategies for controlling conflicts, such as crying, pouting or seeking parental interventions to get their way (Sutton-Smith & Rosenberg, 1970; Dunn and Munn, 1985).

The frequency of sibling conflicts also is greater when one or both of the siblings have highly active and emotionally intense temperaments (G. Brody, Stoneman, and McCoy, 1994; Munn & Dunn, 1988; Stocker et al., 1989; Volling & Belsky, 1992).

As noted earlier, sibling gender is also a factor, with boys involved in more sibling conflicts than girls, and more likely to use threats and physical aggression (G. Brody et al., 1985; Graham-Bermann et al., 1994; Volling & Belsky, 1992). Opposite-sex siblings actually have more conflicts than do same-sex ones (Dunn & Kendrick, 1981; Pepler et al., 1981). Conflicts are especially common among older brothers and their younger sisters, and are frequently provoked by younger sisters.

Evidence indicates that the quality and quantity of sibling conflicts are related to the difference in sibling ages, especially if sufficiently wide age spacings are contrasted. Closely spaced siblings (less than 2 years apart) have more quarrels than those who are more than 4 years apart. It should be noted, however, that sibling abuse is more likely at wider age spacings (Wiehe, 1990).

Other Factors

Sibling conflicts also reflect the children's prior interaction histories. In addition to reflecting ongoing social interactions, sibling conflicts can reflect long-term family histories involving unresolved conflicts, aggression and violence, and differential parental treatment.

Also, the quality and quantity of sibling conflicts vary as a function of the ongoing situational context. Conflicts are more common when siblings are in competitive situations such as board games or sports and less common when they are watching television or doing crafts (G. Brody & Stoneman, 1987). A common observation is that siblings on long trips with nothing to do have more conflicts (Prochaska & Prochaska, 1985).

FACTORS ASSOCIATED WITH SIBLINGS' CONFLICT MANAGEMENT MODES

Various researchers have attempted to identify the factors associated with sibling use of aggression, violence, and abuse in managing or dealing with conflicts. Age of the siblings is one factor. In middle childhood, most conflicts are verbal, but other tactics include physical force, bullying, harassing, and crying (Steinmetz, 1977; Sutton-Smith & Rosenberg, 1970). Seventh graders report yelling, threatening, teasing, and name calling as well as physical force (Roscoe, Goodwin, & Kennedy, 1987). Many sibling conflicts during early adolescence involve coercion.

Closely spaced siblings are more likely to use physical aggression, whereas verbal aggression is more common between widely spaced siblings (Vandell & Bailey, 1992).

Some researchers feel that sibling violence is a learned response. Straus et al. (1980) believe that siblings learn from their parents that physical punishment is an appropriate technique for resolving conflicts. They found that there was a significant relationship between parental physical punishment and sibling abuse; the more violent parents are to a child, the more violent that child is to his or her siblings. On the other hand, children raised in nonviolent environments may learn that there are a variety of nonviolent techniques available for resolving conflicts with brothers and sisters. Cornell-Pedrick and Gelles (1982) caution, however, that factors associated with violence as used by adolescents are not the same as those factors associated with child and spouse abuse. In other words, teenagers do not use violence for the same reasons that adults are violent to each other or children.

Graham-Bermann et al. (1994) first investigated the prevalence of sibling violence during childhood and adolescence reported by college students and then examined violence in high-conflict dyads more closely. They compared the experiences of four groups: those who were violence perpetrators, those who were violence victims, those who felt violence was reciprocal, and a low-conflict control group. Students in the three violence groups reported higher use of violence to deal with conflicts than did students in the control group; surprisingly, those in the control group reported lower use of problem solving to resolve conflicts as well. Results suggested that older brothers were more likely to be perpetrators (both in the amount and type of violence) whereas younger sisters were more likely to be the victims of violence. Sibling use of violence was found to be related to parental use of violence to resolve conflicts.

Those who have studied sibling murder often attribute the cause of such extreme aggression to aspects of family dynamics. Adelson (1972) concluded that preschoolers are capable of homicidal rage as a result of extreme jealousy when their sense of security in the family unit is threatened. Tooley (1977) observed that the young victims of sibling violence may sometimes be family scapegoats. Whether the same factors associated with fratricide are also related to less violent forms of sibling aggression has not yet been established.

FACTORS ASSOCIATED WITH OUTCOMES AND CONSEQUENCES OF CONFLICT

Many researchers hold that sibling conflict resolution becomes more constructive throughout childhood, leading to increased social understanding (Dunn, 1988; Lamb, 1978a,b; Stewart, Mobley, Van Tuyl, & Salvador, 1987; Vandell, 1987).

In a longitudinal investigation of 43 toddlers (18 to 36 months of age) interacting with preschool-aged siblings (Dunn, 1988; Dunn & Munn, 1985, 1986a, 1986b, 1987; Munn & Dunn, 1988), some sibling conflicts were characterized by distress and anger and others by use of constructive resolution techniques. Frequencies of negative emotions in conflicts were correlated negatively with cooperative interactions, and older siblings' helping and sharing behaviors. Dunn concluded that destructive conflict with intense negative affect undermines sibling relationships.

However, only one-quarter of seventh graders interviewed by Felson (1983) reported resolving their conflicts with siblings in a constructive manner. In a similar vein, Raffaelli (1992) concluded that destructive conflicts between adolescent siblings were characterized by intense negative affect, high coercion, and minimal compromise, indicating little constructive conflict resolution. It is unclear from these reports whether siblings continue to grow in social understanding and constructive conflict resolution as childhood researchers suggest.

Some research indicates that sibling conflicts can be emotionally intense and destructive, whereas other conflicts involve a give-and-take between participants that seems to spur psychological development (Bank & Kahn, 1982b; Dunn, 1988; Vandell & Bailey, 1992). Parental favoritism, differential treatment, and family stress are associated with destructive outcomes of conflicts with hostility and anger between siblings. Insecure mother–child attachment relationships and punitive disciplinary methods also are linked to destructive consequences. Reasoning and discussions about feelings and family rules, in contrast, are associated with constructive consequences in sibling conflicts and the occurrence of justification and conciliation.

Conflicts between siblings may also be important because they provide a mechanism by which children can differentiate themselves from other members of their family (Shantz & Hobart, 1989; Vandell & Bailey, 1992). Assuming sibling conflict to be an important factor in individuation, Hetherington (1988) looked at the development of children who appeared to have no conflicts with siblings; about 10% of her sample. These siblings had a close relationship with each other, but had poor relationships with peers and adults. Vandell and Bailey suggested that these children had pathologically intense, symbiotic, and restrictive sibling relationships. This sort of enmeshed sibling relationship has also been identified by Bank and Kahn (1982b).

In Hetherington's (1988) study of siblings and stepsiblings aged 9 to 15, about one-fifth had hostile relationships with destructive conflicts accompanied by high coercion and aggression or by active avoidance. Compared to children with warm, close sibling relationships, those in hostile relationships had more behavior problems, poorer peer relationships, and more school difficulties.

Gully, Dengerink, Pepping, and Bergstrom (1981) surveyed college undergraduate students regarding the degree to which they witnessed various violent behaviors directed at themselves or other family members, the degree to which they had performed violent behaviors directed toward other family members, the likelihood of their acting aggressively in a series of hypothetically stressful situations, and the amount of violent behavior they had directed toward nonfamily persons in the previous year. Previous violent behavior toward siblings, particularly as a perpetrator, was a significant predictor of the likelihood of later violent behavior.

Bank and Kahn (1982b) found violent and aggressive actions by a sibling to be a source of long-term dissatisfaction for almost 30% of the college students they studied. Similarly, Graham-Bermann et al. (1994) found that among college women, being victims of violence in childhood and adolescence was related to feelings of anxiety. In contrast, sibling perpetrators had high self esteem and no negative emotional outcomes.

CONCLUSION

Conflicts with siblings seem to be an almost inevitable part of family living as children share space and resources. Vandell and Bailey (1992) suggested that conflicts with siblings are one area where children are free to disagree with impunity, in contrast to conflicts with parents which are unwinnable, and conflicts with friends which may lead to dissolution of the friendship. It is how the conflicts are handled that determines whether they will lead to psychological growth or to psychological damage. In constructive sibling conflicts, children can learn ways to negotiate, compromise, and cooperate. However, in destructive conflicts where violence is used to deal with the aggression, there may be both physical and emotional damage. According to Bank and Kahn (1982b), in addition to the immediate issue of the conflict is an overall sibling conflict over status and power; when there is a history of sibling conflict and rivalry, residual feelings of resentment are built up that dominate the relationship.

The way parents deal with sibling conflicts can play an important role either in fostering further sibling conflict or in fostering constructive resolutions. Neither punitive actions nor a total laissez-faire approach is effective. Rather, avoiding favoritism, meeting each sibling's needs, and setting clear consistent principles and rules about what aggressive or violent actions are not permitted within the family all seem to help children learn more mature ways of dealing with conflict and develop warm sibling relationships that will last through adulthood.

However, when sibling conflicts result in physical or verbal abuse, intense negative affect, and victimization, more active interventions are needed to help children avoid negative consequences to their personality and social development.

Sibling Sexual Experiences: Normal Exploratory Behavior, Nonabusive Incest, and Abusive Incest

NORMAL SEXUAL BEHAVIOR

Normal sexual curiosity, exploration, and experimentation among siblings in childhood and adolescence can be distinguished from sexual exploitation or sexually abusive behavior, although both types of behavior may be displayed by the same sibling pair. Sexual behavior which can be termed incestuous may occur among various family members (e.g., father and daughter, cousins, siblings) and, depending on the circumstances, may be considered to be nonabusive or abusive. Distinguishing normal sexual exploratory behavior from sexually abusive behavior is difficult in itself, but the difficulty is compounded by attempting to distinguish between nonabusive and abusive incest. What is considered to be normal, what is considered incestuous, what is considered abusive or nonabusive depends in part upon the values and norms of the culture.

NORMAL SIBLING SEXUAL BEHAVIOR IN CHILDHOOD AND ADOLESCENCE

The normal developmental course of sexual behavior has been delineated by several researchers (e.g., De Jong, 1989; Litt & Martin, 1981; Rosenfeld, Bailey, Siegel, & Bailey, 1986). Development of gender identity begins by 2 to 3 years of age, as children learn to identify themselves as boys or girls. Between 3 and 6 years of age, they become aware of anatomical differences in genitals of boys and girls, with curiosity leading them to explore their own genitals and those of their siblings and peers. Masturbation is often observed in children of this age. Games like "playing doctor" or "playing mommy and daddy" are played, and may include attempts at heterosexual intercourse. Children of this age tend to identify with the same-sex parent, and may behave in a flirtatious way toward their opposite-sex parent. By middle childhood, modesty about their bodies has been learned; earlier, children seem unconcerned about displaying their naked bodies to members of the opposite sex. Normal sexual development and sexual experiences include sexual exploration and experimentation in early and middle childhood. However, with the onset of puberty and early adolescence, such sibling sexual exploration wanes, to be replaced by heterosexual peer relationships. An interesting fact in this connection is that younger siblings are more sexually active in heterosexual peer relationships at earlier ages than are older siblings, although whether the younger sibling's precocity is due to early sexual experience, modeling, increased opportunity, differential parental treatment, or other causes is not clear (Rodgers & Rowe, 1988, 1990; Rodgers, Rowe, & Harris, 1992). That some degree of sibling sexual experience occurs within most families is not in doubt. However, just which activities are considered normal will, of course, partially depend on the norms of the particular subcultural group to which the family belongs. At the present time, there is no clear cut standard that distinguishes normal and abnormal sibling sexual behavior.

INCEST

Incest may be defined broadly as sexual activity between family members who are not married to each other. It includes intimate physical contact that is sexually arousing, as well as fondling, masturbation, and intercourse (Justice & Justice, 1979). Some limit incest to sexual intercourse only, others limit it to intercourse plus attempted intercourse, still others include petting and genital touching.

Most cultures regard incest as taboo, but reasons for the taboo vary. Morality is involved if the behavior is considered to be a violation of religious law, religious standards of right and wrong, or some other ethical standard. In other cases, the taboo against incest is based on laws or societal norms concerned with couples too closely related in their genetic makeup producing inferior offspring. Alternatively, the taboo may be based on the attempt of elders in a society to prevent the occurrence of unnecessary jealousy and rivalry among close family members. The reason for the taboo may be important in determining the degree to which incest is tolerated or accepted, as well as the degree of guilt experienced by those violating the taboo.

This chapter is concerned with sibling incest, that is, those behaviors involving various degrees of sexual contact between two siblings, including attempted or completed intercourse. Although sibling incest includes homosexual as well as heterosexual behavior, most available research deals primarily with heterosexual behavior. However, sibling incest does not in itself imply sibling sexual abuse.

Abusive and Nonabusive Sibling Incest

A distinction can be made between sibling incest which is abusive and sibling incest which is nonabusive. Nonabusive incest occurs when there is sexual activity (whether homosexual or heterosexual) between two siblings who are close in age, who express mutual consent, and who share mutual enjoyment of the activity occasionally or frequently for a certain period of time. Such a definition is independent of any long-range effects, whether positive or negative.

Bank and Kahn (1982b) defined a type of sibling incest that fits the category of nonabusive incest, which they termed nurturance-oriented incest. Incest of this type often occurs by mutual consent and may contain many elements of erotic pleasure, loyalty, love, and compassion. Bank and Kahn felt that this type of sibling incest may be most satisfying when the siblings are otherwise involved in troubled and disturbing family relationships. Within this frame of reference, it is conceivable that for some siblings, incest might start early in life and continue throughout adulthood and old age with mutual satisfaction. At the present time, there is no evidence of this phenomenon but it cannot be ruled out without further investigation.

Defining abusive sibling incest is more difficult. This is not surprising given the difficulty in defining general physical and emotional abuse (see Chapter 11), since conceptions of what constitutes abuse vary with the norms of society, racial-ethnic background, socioeconomic status, who is formulating the definition (professional workers, researchers, society, family members, or siblings themselves), and so on.

From a clinical perspective, Bank and Kahn (1982b) refer to sibling abusive incest as power-oriented, sadistic, exploitative, and coercive, often involving deliberate physical or mental abuse.

Various researchers studying child sexual abuse have developed working definitions of sexually abusive behavior for use in carrying out their studies. Such definitions may also apply to abusive sibling incest. For example, Finkelhor and Hotaling (1984) regard sexual contact as abusive if it occurs (1) in a child less than 13 years of age, if the perpetrator is 5 or more years older than the victim, and in a child 13 to 16 years of age if the perpetrator is 10 years older than the victim; and (2) coercion, force, or threat are used by the perpetrator. Thus, for Finkelhor and Hotaling, whether sexual contact is judged as abusive depends on the age of the child victim, the age discrepancy between the victim and perpetrator, and whether coercion, force, or threat is used.

However, Finkelhor (1979) stated somewhat earlier that sexual contact is abusive if it occurs as the result of force, threat, deceit, or through exploitation of an authority relationship, no matter what the age of the partner.

In general, the size of the age difference between siblings, and the use of coercion, force, or threat have been used to define sexual exploitation and abuse by various researchers (e.g., Bank & Khan, 1982b; Finkelhor, 1979; O'Brien, 1991). However, Alpert (1991) makes the point that distinguishing between coercion and consent may be difficult at times. An act may appear to be based on consent but actually be based on fear. On the other hand, fear may appear to exist but genuine consent may also be involved. A careful assessment is necessary to implement the criterion of coercion in determining sexual abuse.

Kelly (1988) uses the term *violence* rather than *abuse*, but applies her definition only to women. She defines sexual violence as any physical, visual, verbal, or sexual act that is experienced by a woman or girl, at the time of occurrence or later, as a threat, invasion, or assault, that has the effect of hurting her or degrading her, or takes away her ability to control intimate contact. If this definition is applied to sibling incest, abuse would occur if a brother sexually assaulted a sister, overcoming her resistance to the point of humiliating and degrading her.

In studying sexual interactions between siblings and cousins, De Jong (1989) used four criteria to indicate sexually abusive behavior involving victims under age 14: (1) an age difference of 5 years or more between victim and perpetrator; (2) the use of force, threat, or authority by the abuser; (3) attempted penile penetration; and (4) documented injury in the victim. If one or more of these four factors is present, the behavior is considered sexually abusive. If all four factors are absent, then the behavior is considered normal sexual experimentation.

Laviola (1992) defined abusive sibling incest as the occurrence of coercion or force in the initiation and maintenance of the sexual activity. Coercion refers to any type of misuse of power or authority, bribery, or appeal to the child's trust and affection. Force refers to verbal threat of physical harm if the child does not comply, physical hitting or pinning the child down in order to perform the sexual act, or physical hitting or pinning the child down in response to the child's resistance to the sexual act.

Wiehe (1990) defines sibling sexual abusive behavior as inappropriate sexual contact, such as unwanted touching, fondling, indecent exposure, attempted penetration, intercourse, rape, or sodomy between siblings. (He also suggests that sexually abusive behavior can be identified by comparison with age-appropriate sexual behavior in terms of its frequency, duration, and purpose. But how is age-appropriate behavior determined, and for whom, the older or younger child? How frequently, for how long, and for what purpose does sexual contact have to occur before it is classified as abusive? There are no easy answers.)

Sexually abusive behavior and abusive sibling incest certainly overlap; one may consider abusive sibling incest as a special case of sexually abusive behavior involving related family members.

PREVALENCE OF NONABUSIVE AND ABUSIVE SIBLING INCEST

The lack of precise and standard definitions of sexually abusive behavior, and of nonabusive and abusive sibling incest limits the development of measuring instruments and their use in detecting the prevalence of sibling sexual activity and sexual abuse. A further difficulty is that young children have little understanding of sexual acts and may not realize the significance of the act or judge it as abusive until years later. Similarly, some sexual acts in childhood may be forgotten by adulthood. A further complication in the collection of data about taboo sexual activities is the individual's reticence about revealing participation in such acts.

Early sources of data regarding child sexual abuse were obtained from clinicians, health workers, or cases coming to the attention of police or social agencies. Later attempts to obtain information about prevalence were subject to criticisms of sampling bias when volunteer respondents were used. Consequently, the full extent of sexually abusive behavior involving children is not known, much less the prevalence of sibling sexually abusive and nonabusive sibling incest. Available findings are usually considered to be an underestimation.

A survey by David Finkelhor (1979) of sibling sexual experiences of college students in New England indicated that of 796 college undergraduates, 13% (15% of the girls and 10% of the boys) reported some type of sexual encounter with a sibling during childhood. However, Finkelhor lumped together many types of sexual activities, from exhibiting genitals to intercourse without any specific breakdown into various categories. Thus, the sibling sexual encounters comprising the overall 13% prevalence finding may include respondents whose sexual activities are considered representative of normal sibling sexual behavior, making it difficult to estimate the occurrence of sexually abusive behavior. Finkelhor indicated that about one fourth of the sexual encounter cases (approximately 3% of the total sample) involved the use of force or a large age disparity between partners. That is, about 3% of the students reported childhood sibling experiences that might be classified as sexually abusive behavior. However, that 3% may not be valid if the criteria of force and age are being applied to sexual activities that ordinarily would not be associated with abusive behavior. For example, if an older sister forces a younger brother to look at her breasts for a moment, is this abusive behavior? There is no clear way of knowing the incidence of normal sibling sexual behavior, nonabusive sibling incest, and abusive sibling incest from this study. On the other hand, Finkelhor's survey is important in that it reveals sexual contact between siblings to be relatively common, perhaps even exceeding sexual encounters between father and daughter.

Other survey studies show slightly different results. Russell (1983) interviewed 930 women over age 18 living in San Francisco; 152 women reported 186 experiences of intrafamilial sexual abuse involving different perpetrators occurring prior to age 18, with 108 of the women reporting abuse before age 14. Of the 152 women, 20 reported abuse by a brother and three by a sister (15% in all); abuse by fathers (28%), uncles (30%), and cousins (18%) was more frequent. (These 23 cases represented 2.5% of the total sample of 930, not far different from Finkelhor's 1979 findings.) When the 20 cases of completed and attempted sexual abuse by brothers were examined more closely, 27% were classified as very serious (involving vaginal, oral, or anal intercourse); 62% as serious (involving genital fondling, simulated intercourse, or digital penetration); and 12% were classified as least serious (involving sexual touching or kissing). In summary, sibling incest occurred 15% of the time compared to 28% for father–daughter relationships. These results comparing the prevalence of sibling–sibling and father–daughter relationships are opposite to those reported in the Finkelhor survey.

Wyatt's (1985) findings were obtained for a stratified random sample of 248 African-American and white adult women aged 18 to 36 in Los Angeles County. Overall, 62% of the women reported experiencing at least one incident of sexual abuse prior to age 18; results for both ethnic groups were roughly similar. However, abuse was broadly defined as ranging from mere verbal solicitations to engage in sex to intercourse, and included all acts where the perpetrator was 5 or more years older than the subject, and where force or coercion was used. Of the total cases of abuse, 3% were perpetrated by a brother or stepbrother; the incidence of father or stepfather abuse was more than twice as great. Mrazek (1981) has commented that it is not clear from the inconsistencies in existing findings whether sibling or father–daughter incest is more prevalent.

The recently completed national survey of sexual practices in the United States (Laumann, Gagnon, Michael, & Michaels, 1994) used personal interviews with a probability sample of 1,511 men and 1,921 women over the age range from 18 to 59; the researchers obtained a 79% response rate. Unfortunately, they did not focus on sexual contacts between siblings, but did ask respondents about sexual contacts with adults and adolescents over age 14 which took place when they were under age 13. "Contacts" included kissing, touching genitals, oral sex, vaginal intercourse, and anal sex. About 12% of the men and 17% of the women reported such contacts. Of the cases reported by women, 9% involved sexual contact with an older brother; 4% of men's contacts involved an older brother. These figures would suggest a lower incidence of sibling sexual contact than found in other studies, but it must be remembered that contacts between siblings when both were under age 13 were not studied.

Differences in methodology make comparisons of the existing findings difficult to interpret. However, researchers agree that existing findings probably are underestimates of the actual prevalence of sexual contact between siblings. More representative sampling methods and better techniques to probe these sensitive areas would probably yield a more accurate picture. At least, existing surveys indicate that sibling incest (without distinguishing between nonabusive and abusive behaviors) is not rare, and occurs most frequently between an older brother and younger sister.

Prevalence of Half-Sibling and Stepsibling Incest

There has been no systematic study of stepsibling incest. In Russell's (1986) study of female victims of sexual contact with a male relative, 25 reported a sexual experience with a brother. Of these 25 cases, one was with a stepbrother and one was with a half-brother. Beer (1989) extrapolated Russell's figures to suggest that roughly 3% of women in stepfamilies have experienced some sort of stepsibling sex and roughly the same percent half-sibling sex, but cautioned that the number of cases is too small to yield a reliable estimate.

Whether sexual contact between half-siblings and stepsiblings constitutes incest is open to question (Beer, 1989). Half-siblings have one parent in common, and so sexual contact between them could be considered incestuous. Stepsiblings are not related by blood, so that a sexual relationship could not be considered incestuous on that ground. However, if they are reared together in the same household, they are usually expected to observe the incest taboo. If they are reared apart, the situation is much less clear.

Cousin Incest

Sexual contact between second or third cousins is not regarded as incestuous. In the United States, the social acceptance and legality of sex and marriage between first cousins varies from state to state. The definition of close blood relationship is not defined in any standardized way, and can vary within and between countries. However, existing surveys have included sexual activity between cousins among other incestuous relationships without distinguishing between first cousins and those who are more distant.

Existing surveys have found cousin incest to be as prevalent as sibling incest (Finkelhor, 1979; Russell, 1983) or even more frequent (Wyatt, 1985), and as common as father–daughter incest (Finkelhor, 1979). Finkelhor found that 28% of all incest reported by the students was cousin incest. Russell showed that 18% and Wyatt found 23% of all incest reported by the adult women in their surveys were sexual contacts with cousins.

A study was carried out by De Jong (1989) involving 831 sexually abused children less than 14 years of age evaluated for sexual assault complaints. In this study, 49 cases of cousin incest (5.9%) and 35 cases of sibling incest (4.2%) were identified. A total of 54 male cousins abused 8 boys and 41 girls; brothers abused 3 boys and 32 girls. The victims' mean age was 6.9 years for cousins and 7.4 years for siblings. The perpetrators mean age was 16.2 years for cousins and 15.5 years for siblings, with only 16 (19%) of all perpetrators being greater than 16 years old. Of the perpetrators, 66 (79%) were greater than or equal to 5 years older than their victims.

EFFECTS OF SIBLING INCEST

When the effects of sibling incest are to be considered, both the short-term and long-term effects must be considered, and also whether the incest is abusive or nonabusive. There seem to be two viewpoints regarding the consequences of sibling sexual experiences.

One view is that sexual incest is harmless, especially if there is mutual consent. Further, incest may have a positive effect in promoting the development of the younger partners or in fulfilling needs for affiliation and warmth when parents do not fill those needs (Arndt & Ladd, 1981; Greenwald & Leitenberg, 1989; Lukianowitz, 1972; Nakashima & Zakus, 1979; Riemer, 1940; Weeks, 1976).

In an effort to separate effects of early sexual experiences from effects of experiences with others, Greenwald and Leitenberg (1989) investigated the long-term differences in 526 young adults' (188 men and 388 women) sexual behavior and adjustment subsequent to preadolescent sibling and nonsibling peer childhood sexual experiences. Of this sample 25 (5%) reported having had only a sibling sexual encounter; 61 (12%) reported having had both a sibling and a nonsibling sexual experience; 236 (45%) reported having had only a nonsibling sexual experience; and 204 (39%) reported no sexual experience with another child prior to age 13. Very few of these experiences involved force (2%) or threats of force (6%). No differences were found between the sibling, nonsibling, and no-experience groups on a variety of adult sexual behavior and sexual adjustment measures, including incidence of premarital intercourse, age at first intercourse, number of intercourse partners, sexual satisfaction, sexual arousal, and sexual dysfunctions. They concluded that adult sexual adjustment is not negatively or positively influenced by typical early childhood sexual experiences among similar-aged siblings.

The second view is that, because sexual incest is a strong taboo in society, its violation will have various negative consequences. Bank and Kahn (1982b) believe that the long-term effects of childhood sibling incest are worse for women than men, adversely affecting the woman's trust in others, her self-concept and sense of identity, her work, and her later sexual relationships (including marital problems, difficulty in obtaining sexual pleasure, and promiscuity).

Wiehe (1990) administered questionnaires to 150 adults who experienced some form of sibling abuse in childhood and adolescence and who responded to advertisements and notices placed in organizations dealing with domestic violence. Respondents' age ranged from 18 to 77, with a mean of 37 years; 89% were female, 85% white; only 24% had a high school education or less. For most, the sexual abuse was not a one-time event, but continued over a period of years, with the abuse escalating over time from inappropriate touching and sexual games to more serious forms of abuse. Five years was the age most frequently reported as when abuse began, but some recalled abuse in very early childhood. The sibling perpetrator was from 3 to 10 years older. For most, the abuse continued through adolescence; a few respondents reported sibling sexual abuse in adulthood. Parents were generally unaware of the abuse or, if they knew tended to ignore it or blame the victim. The sexual abuse incidents occurred at times when the parent was absent (the perpetrator often had a caretaking role), asleep, or otherwise occupied. The sibling perpetrators tended to use threats of physical violence to force the victim to comply and to prevent disclosure.

Wiehe (1990) concluded from victims' responses that long-range effects of sibling abusive incest exist. However, the sexual abuse usually is accompanied by some degree of physical and emotional abuse so that it is difficult to isolate the long-range effects of childhood sexual abuse from the effects of physical and emotional abuse. In addition, it is difficult to separate the effects of sibling abuse from the effects of other perpetrators. However, subjects' earlier sibling sexual abuse experiences were associated with such later problems as poor self-esteem, difficulty in relating to the opposite sex (e.g., changes in women's attitudes toward males), difficulty with male or female interpersonal relationships, tendency to repeat the victim's role in other relationships, oversensitivity to comments of others in later life as a result of being degraded earlier in life, continuing self-blame (as if they were at fault for the earlier sexual abuse), continuing anger toward the perpetrator (sometimes generalized to all men), sexual dysfunctions (e.g., avoidance, promiscuity, or inability to enjoy sex), eating disorders, alcoholism, drug abuse, depression, and flashbacks of the childhood sexual abuse which disrupted current sexual experiences. For some, effects were severe; 26% had been hospitalized for depression, 28% had substance abuse problems, and 33% had attempted suicide one or more times.

There is other evidence in the literature of harmful effects from older brother younger sister incest on the sisters' adult functioning. These effects include lowered sexual self-esteem (Finkelhor, 1980); fear of sexual assault, difficulties in sexual relationships, and preorgasmic functioning (Cole, 1982; Meiselman, 1978; Russell, 1983, 1986); depression and guilt concerning the sexual activity (Cole, 1982; Loredo, 1982); low self-esteem and repeated victimization (Cole, 1982; De Young, 1982; Meiselman, 1978; Sorrenti-Little, Bagley, & Robertson, 1984); somatization, suicide attempts, difficulties with intimate relationships, and substance abuse (Cole, 1982).

Laviola (1992) also studied the long-term effects of older brother younger sister incest on 17 women, taking into consideration the dynamics of the families of origin. Common themes were formulated from analysis of the subjects' protocols. All of the women's families of origin were described as dysfunctional in some way. The later effects of the incest experiences included mistrust of men and women, chronic low or negative self-esteem, sexual response difficulties, and intrusive thoughts of the incest.

Meiselman (1978) found that some women who had been victimized by older brothers became involved with older man who abused and mistreated them, had difficulties in marriage, or had problems dealing with their own sons.

Daie, Witztum, and Eleff (1989) reported four case studies in which even the abuser suffered from severe interpersonal and sexual problems. In three of the four cases, the incest occurred over a long period of time, and was a prolonged process in the context of a disturbed family relationship. Lasting difficulties in establishing and maintaining close relationships, especially sexual ones, were reported. In some cases, the experience of incest was so traumatic that it became an emotional trap, causing severe inhibitions in normal development of interpersonal relationships. One can speculate that the incest experience may have merely exaggerated existing personality and family difficulties.

Finkelhor (1980) retrospectively investigated differences in the regularity with which college students engaged in sexual intercourse, as well as differences in their adult sexual self-esteem, as a function of their having reported a sexual experience with a sibling or nonsibling. He found that female college students who reported a sibling sexual experience during childhood were more sexually active than either those who reported a prior nonsibling experience or those who reported no prior sexual experience with another child. For men, however, there was no difference in the frequency of sexual activity for the sibling, nonsibling, and no-experience groups. Finkelhor also found that women reporting a positive sibling sexual encounter during their childhood had higher sexual self-esteem than women who had a nonsibling sexual experience. Although this suggested that sibling sexual experiences were associated with better adult sexual adjustment for women, subjects with a sibling encounter were no different in their level of sexual self-esteem as compared to women who never had any type of childhood sexual experience. For men, there was no difference in adult sexual self-esteem for those with sibling sexual experiences as compared to those with nonsibling encounters. However, those men with a sibling experience had lower sexual self-esteem than did men without any type of childhood sexual experience.

Laumann et al. (1994) examined data from their national survey to determine whether experiences of sexual contact with an adolescent or adult prior to age 13 had later consequences. Unfortunately, there was no way to isolate effects of siblings from those of other perpetrators. However, greater percentages of both men and women with early experiences reported sexual activities over a wide variety of sexual acts and with more sex partners than were reported by those without such early experiences. Furthermore, greater percentages of those with early experiences also reported sexual difficulties in adulthood (apathy, erection problems, problems with orgasm, emotional problems, pain, lack of pleasure, anxiety, and involvement in forced sex).

Beer (1989) pointed out that a sexual relationship between siblings or stepsiblings has a damaging effect on the process of social development. In a healthy family, the children develop social skills outside the family, so that they are able to become independent, make new friends, and (in late adolescence) form romantic attachments outside the family that can lead to adult partnerships. Sex between siblings or stepsiblings results in an enmeshment of the participants within the family and prevents them from normal social development.

In sum, there appears to be a continuum of sibling sexual experiences. Sexual contact between siblings appears to be nonabusive in some cases with no negative effects, whereas sibling sexual activities in other cases appear to be abusive and associated with negative consequences in adulthood. However, the sibling sexual abuse may occur concomitantly with abuse from other perpetrators within a dysfunctional family environment, so that the extent to which the sibling abuse has independent long-range negative effects has not been determined thus far. Studies of the incidence and effects of sibling sexual experience in general populations tend to report no effects or fewer effects than clinical studies or studies of volunteers who have experienced sibling abuse. This may reflect the fact that, as Wyatt (1985) estimated, the majority of cases found in a general population involve a single incident of sexual contact between siblings, whereas the clinical cases involve a long history of abuse. The number of existing studies is limited, and all have methodological defects of some sort. Present findings indicate that the long-range effects of sibling sexual abuse are harmful whether it occurs alone or in the context of an ongoing dysfunctional family. However, long-range effects are not clear when sibling nonabusive incest occurs with siblings of equivalent age within the context of a functional family and involves mutual consent and enjoyment.

FACTORS ASSOCIATED WITH SIBLING INCEST

At present, the ultimate causes of sibling incest are not known; however, factors associated with sibling incest can be identified from existing findings. These factors include characteristics of the siblings and the sibling relationship, parent characteristics and behavior, and extrafamilial circumstances of life. Factors of low income, poor education, and minority ethnicity, which form a popular stereotype of families where sibling incest occurs, have not been found to be related. Further, no differences have been found between the various age cohorts in terms of reported sexual abuse, despite a general trend toward a society more open regarding sexual matters.

Sibling Characteristics and Relationship

The structural characteristics of the sibling constellation are very important factors in relation to sibling sexual abuse. A constellation with a younger sister and a brother who is at least 3 years older is a major factor. Although sexual abuse can start earlier or later, the peak time of onset is when the victim is about 7 years of age.

In certain situations, an older brother may abuse several younger siblings, or the oldest child may abuse a younger sibling who in turn abuses a still younger one in the family (Smith and Israel, 1987).

Abusive sexual relationships often occur in families where the prior sibling relationship involves emotional and physical abuse. Other factors in the sibling relationship, such as the attractiveness of the sister and the personality of the brother, may also be important.

Parent Characteristics and Behavior

Smith and Israel (1987) found that sibling sex experiences were associated with parents who were distant, uncaring, or inaccessible. There were times when younger daughters attempted to reveal to their mothers that sibling incest was going on, but the latter refused to believe its occurrence or blamed the daughter. The parents' own sexual behavior in the home also influenced the children's sexual activities; watching parental love-making or observing a father's abuse of the mother can stimulate imitation. Also, a parent's extramarital affair if known by the children, can lead to sibling incest. In some cases, daughters were first abused by fathers before being abused by brothers. In about a third of the families, the mothers extreme repressiveness about sex appeared to intensify the children's sexual curiosity and experimentation. Smith and Israel concluded that parental stimulation of the sexual climate in the home, whether very liberal or very repressive, is an important factor related to sibling incest.

According to Wiehe (1990), only 18% of his sample (169 subjects) indicated that their parents were aware of the existing incestuous sibling relationship between an older brother and younger sister. There were various reasons. First, at the time of the abuse, many of the victims themselves were too cognitively or emotionally immature to realize that an experience was abusive; only later did they realize what happened to them as young children. Second, the abuse often occurred in the context of authority when the parents designated an older brother as a caregiver. Often the younger sibling was instructed to obey the older brother. Third, the older brother threatened the younger sister with retaliation if she told anyone. Fourth, many victims experienced sexual pleasure during the experience, and hence felt that they contributed to the situation, and were partly to blame. Fifth, some victims did not tell their parents because the family atmosphere was such that the parents did not seem approachable, sensitive, or empathic to their needs. Hence, the victims did not feel comfortable trying to reveal such information to them. Finally, the abuse typically took place when the parents were away, sleeping, or busy in another part of the home.

Wiehe (1990) made the point that some parents do intervene appropriately, and stop the abuse. However, he feels that such parents were not represented in his volunteer sample of abused siblings. Instead, the parental responses were not effective in helping the victim or daughter, and many times, made things worse. The parents failed to protect the daughter, and the brother was free to continue his sexually abusive behavior. Parents responded by ignoring or minimizing the sexually abusive behavior (assuming it was part of normal sibling rivalry); parents did not believe their daughter; parents accepted the daughter's report of abuse but blamed her instead of the brother, making the daughter feel guilty for what occurred; parents responded inappropriately, either not knowing how to stop the abusive behavior or responding with indifference. Their own problems were so overwhelming, leading to much stress that they could not handle any problems beyond their own.

Wiehe (1990) also discussed such things as the inappropriate socialization of males; in many families boys are brought up to think they should dominate and control females, which may lead to abuse of sisters. Also, parents may have inappropriate expectations for older siblings, especially in caregiving of younger siblings in their absence. To leave younger sisters with older brothers as baby-sitters may be expecting too much in terms of moral responsibility of the older brother.

Daie et al. (1989) concluded from their analysis of clinical case studies that a number of factors contributed to the long-standing damage found: a father who was either absent or abusive; considerable age differences between exploiter and victim; the length and character of the sexual relationship; massive use of aggression and violence by the perpetrator. In addition, a family constellation that did not encourage open communication either within the family or with persons outside the family was a causative factor, as were family communications that included a double message toward sexuality, and a family constellation that encouraged identity diffusion and problems with intergenerational boundaries.

Ascherman and Safier (1990) presented a case history of sibling incest which illustrated many of the factors above. The father's work kept him away from home a great deal; the mother also worked, leaving a 16-year-old brother alone with a younger sister. The parents had a history of conflicts, and the father had a great deal of conflict with the son. When the daughter finally disclosed the incest, the mother became very upset, the brother showed no guilt or remorse but felt that the sister bore equal responsibility. However, Ascherman and Safier strongly made the point that the understanding of sibling incest is best done on a case-by-case basis, and not simply by applying some general theory. In any particular case, one should note the kind of incest, its context, the ages of participants, the family dynamics, and the individual psychopathology of family members before hypothesizing any causal factors, as causes may be different for every case.

Other Circumstances

Little is known about other circumstances affecting sibling incest. According to Wiehe (1990), the physical characteristics of the home may be important. Sharing a bedroom with a sibling at some time in childhood, or having children's bedrooms at some distance from the parents' room can contribute to a climate where abuse can occur. The peer group relationships can also be a factor; in some cases a brother and his male friends acted together to abuse a sister.

Stepsiblings

Based on his own pilot studies, Beer (1989) advanced two additional factors as possible contributors to sexual activity between stepsiblings. First, the entire atmosphere of the stepfamily is sexualized. In the traditional family, the ardor of the parents' honeymoon period will have cooled before the children arrive on the scene, whereas in the stepfamily the parents' honeymoon period goes on in the presence of children. Second, prohibitions against stepsibling sexual activity, both legally and socially, are less clear than in the case of sexual activity between full siblings. Beer interprets the indifference and hostility frequently observed between stepsiblings as their defense against the within-family forces leading to erotic attraction in the preteen or teenage years.

CONCLUSION

The causes of sibling incest (nonabusive and abusive) and its consequences are not well understood. Many theoretical and methodological
problems have limited research in this area: inadequate theories or hypotheses, small and biased samples in many studies, lack of comparison
groups in other studies, reliance on retrospective data, and so on. However, there is some commonality or convergence of findings implicating
certain factors in all the studies of with sibling incest: characteristics of
the siblings and the relationship between them, and parental treatment of
siblings whether alone or together. These factors seem to be central
whether one is trying to understand incest and abuse, or simply the
positive or negative relationships between siblings, that is, their love and
care for one another, or their violence and abuse.

CHAPTER 13

Loss of Siblings through Death

The terminal illness, dying, or death of a sibling can have a profound effect on the surviving siblings in a family, regardless of the age at which it occurs. Although siblings can be lost to one another in other ways, such as adoption, split custody arrangements, or inadvertent separations, only sibling loss through death will be considered in this chapter. Loss of a sibling in childhood is not as common in our society as it is in under-developed nations, but nevertheless it does occur in many families. The likelihood of sibling death increases until old age, when the great majority of individuals will have experienced the loss of one or more siblings.

Because sibling death can be looked on as a near-universal experience within families, a careful examination of its effects over the life span is important. What are the effects of sibling loss on personality and behavior? What are its effects on relationships both within and outside the family? What are the immediate effects? What are the long-range effects? What factors determine just how serious the effects of the loss will be?

Our earliest information about the effects of sibling loss comes from literature and the arts, followed by clinical case histories of surviving siblings whose distress was great enough to warrant some kind of psycho-therapy or special attention. Unfortunately, most existing studies involve populations biased in this way. Only more recently have researchers at-tempted to determine effects of sibling loss in general populations. These studies are also flawed, in that they do not include control groups of individuals whose siblings have not died. Despite these problems, we can attempt to draw some conclusions from them. In general, only the more recent studies are considered here. The interested reader is referred to various reviews of earlier work concerning sibling death in childhood and adolescence (Coleman & Coleman, 1984; Cook & Oltjenbruns, 1989; Davies, 1991a, 1991b; Leon, 1990; Stephenson, 1986).

Based on studies available so far, the death of a sibling is a complex experience whose effects not only depend on the nature of the death, but on the characteristics of the surviving sibling and the unique context of environmental conditions and family relationships within which it occurs. Because the surviving sibling's age and level of cognitive and emotional development are important factors, the effects of sibling loss will be considered at various stages of life: childhood, adolescence, adulthood, and old age.

LOSS IN CHILDHOOD

The death of a sibling, at whatever age it occurs, can have far-reaching effects on the individual.

To understand a child's reaction to the death of a sibling, the child's ability to understand death itself must be taken into account (Lonetto, 1980). The concept of death has three major characteristics: irreversibility, universality, and nonfunctionality. Depending on the child's stage of intellectual development and actual life experiences with death, understanding can range from notions of death as sleep (under age 5) to notions of death as final (age 9) to more abstract conceptions of death in adolescence (Stephenson, 1986). A child's seeming lack of grief over the death of a sibling may be a matter of inability to comprehend the loss. On the other hand, young children may have a more complete understanding of death than they are able to express verbally, whereas adolescents may continue to entertain notions of reversibility and personal invulnerability that are incompatible with a mature conception of death (Leon, 1990). To complicate matters further, adolescents may suppress their grief in order to appear strong to their peers.

The level of understanding, the nature of the child's personality, and the circumstances of the death will interact to determine a given child's reactions to the loss of a sibling (Bank & Kahn, 1982b; Coleman & Coleman, 1984; Stephenson, 1986). The relative birth order of the child is also important, with older children more likely to feel guilt over the death and younger children more likely to feel the burden of being a replacement. Excessive guilt reactions, distorted concepts of illness and death, death phobias, disturbed attitudes toward doctors, hospitals, and religion, and disturbances in behavior and cognitive functioning can all accompany childhood grief over a sibling's death. Parents absorbed in their own grief often add neglect to the grieving child's burden. On the other hand, parents and other family members can help the child by sharing thoughts and feelings openly and by validating the child's feelings; in such a way the family members can work through the grief to gain strength together.

Perinatal Sibling Loss

When the sibling death occurs before the birth of or early in the life of a child (Bank & Kahn, 1982b; Cain, Fast, & Erickson, 1964; Leon, 1990; Stephenson, 1986), one might expect little or no effect because there has been no opportunity for a relationship between the siblings. This is particularly true when the sibling loss takes place before a child is born, when the mother miscarries during pregnancy, or when the sibling dies at birth or shortly thereafter. Leon (1990) terms such a sibling death "invisible loss" because the surviving child rarely sees the child's body, may hear little or nothing about the pregnancy or death, and is given little opportunity to ask questions or express feelings. Sibling losses of this sort can have serious consequences for surviving siblings, although the great majority of survivors of perinatal sibling loss suffer few permanent effects (Cain et al., 1964; Leon, 1990). Leon reviewed clinical case histories of such surviving siblings, some of whom had problems that persisted into adulthood and were then transferred to their own children.

When the mother's hopes and feelings are heavily invested in a child during pregnancy, she creates an idealized image of the child which only gradually becomes modified by reality as the child develops (Leon, 1990). If the fetus or infant dies, the mother suffers not only the loss of fantasies and dreams for the child but also a blow to her sense of maternal self-worth. If she is preoccupied with her own grieving process or is unable to resolve the trauma, the impact on the surviving (or subsequent) child can be great. The child's own lack of understanding of death, the lack of information about the event, and the emotional absence of the grieving parent can interfere with the normal development of the child. Additionally, the mother can scapegoat the surviving child as a way of externalizing her guilt over the loss, can become anxiously overprotective due to her damaged sense of maternal self-worth, or can use the surviving sibling as a replacement for her loss.

Clinicians have long been familiar with the phenomenon of the replacement or substitute child (Cain et al., 1964; Legg & Sherick, 1976; Leon, 1990). The replacement child is expected to live up to an idealized image of the deceased sibling, sometimes even given the same name, no matter what the cost to his or her personality. Although willing to attempt the replacement role to ease parental grief and to secure love, the surviving sibling is doomed to an impossible task and suffers loss of self-esteem as well as survivor guilt.

Perhaps the best way for parents to avoid surviving sibling problems due to perinatal loss is to provide accurate information about the death, explaining that it was not the sibling's fault, reassuring the sibling that such a fatality won't happen to him or her, and including the sibling in the parent's grief and mourning process without expecting similar mourning behavior by the sibling (Leon, 1990).

Unexpected Sibling Death

In a retrospective study of adults who had lost a sibling in childhood, Rosen (1984–85) found that more than two-thirds of the respondents had less than a week of advance knowledge of impending death or had no notice at all. When a sibling dies unexpectedly, effects can be long lasting.

Several studies have investigated the effects of sibling loss during infancy from sudden infant death syndrome (SIDS), an unexpected death which typically leaves parents devastated and guilt-ridden. Mandell, McLain, and Reece (1988) interviewed members of 36 SIDS families 2 months after the loss. Reactions to the loss characterized 44 of the 45 surviving siblings, including changes in sleep patterns, changes in interactions with the mother, and changes in interactions with peers ranging from being quiet and withdrawn to being aggressive. In an Irish study of 78 surviving siblings of SIDS loss, the siblings' peak behavioral upset occurred in the first 3 months after the loss. However, in a follow-up almost 3 years following the loss, half of the siblings exhibited such behaviors as excessive seeking of parental affection and attention, separation anxiety, fear of being alone, and incessant curiosity about the death. In a few cases the SIDS loss in childhood had a long-term effect on sibling survivors when they themselves became parents in adulthood and manifested excessive anxiety about their own infants (Mandell, Dirks-Smith, & Smith, 1988).

Other cases of unexpected sibling death involve accidents or homicides. In a study of 20 sibling survivors of such deaths in childhood and adolescence (Applebaum & Burns, 1991), effects were severe in nature. All siblings reported symptomatology characteristic of posttraumatic stress disorder following the loss, with 45% meeting clinical diagnostic criteria for the disorder. There was no difference in level of symptoms for loss by accident and loss by homicide. The parents, who were suffering themselves, tended to be unaware of the children's symptoms; 31% of the parents met diagnostic criteria. When children have actually witnessed the homicide or accidental death of a sibling, they may be haunted by images of the scene for many years (Bank & Kahn, 1982b). Because such sibling deaths are becoming more prevalent in our increasingly violent society, the need for children to have help in dealing with the effects of loss is clear.

Sibling Loss Due to Disease

When siblings die as a result of a chronic or life-threatening disease, the dying process can extend over months or even years. Although there is more time for family members to adjust to the impending loss, the disruption in the lives of the surviving siblings can be great. Not only are the surviving siblings affected by the grave symptoms of the child's illness, but the focus of parental attention and concern on the ill child with the accompanying disturbance in normal family interaction patterns can be highly stressful.

Even when chronic illness of a sibling is not life-threatening, it can be difficult for siblings. When 27 siblings of children with diabetes, juvenile arthritis, or gastrointestinal disorders were compared to 27 matched siblings of normal children (Tritt & Esses, 1988), although no difference in self-concept was found, the siblings of ill children did differ in anxiety scores from the normal group and their parents reported more behavioral adjustment problems. More than half the siblings of ill children reported such things as changes in the relationship with the ill sibling, parents' worry about the ill child, decreased parental attention, and various other disruptions of family life.

When the sibling's illness is life-threatening, the effects on the remaining children in the family can be more severe. Two recent studies (Chesler, Allswede, & Barbarin, 1991; D.A. Stewart, Stein, Forrest, & Clark, 1992) had similar findings: Siblings almost universally expressed worry and distress about the ill child, and felt that the atmosphere in the home was one of sadness. They were aware of the parents' stresses due to the sibling's illness, but reported disruption of normal activities and less parental attention and involvement in their activities, interests, and concerns. Some feared a breakup of the family after the sibling died.

Relation of Sibling Loss to Dysfunction of Surviving Siblings

A child who has seen a sibling die may be haunted by feelings of horror, fear, and anxiety long after the event. If there has been rivalry between the siblings, feelings of guilt often predominate. On the other hand, if the siblings were extremely close, the surviving sibling often feels a loss of identity.

Many of the existing studies are anecdotal, clinical case histories, or surveys of the incidence of sibling maladjustment with inadequate controls. Cain et al. (1964) provided a detailed listing of observed reactions to the death of a sibling. The sample for the data was psychiatric patients with no comparison with a control population (e.g., the frequency of occurrence of these symptoms from a population at large who had experienced sibling loss as a child), or even specifying the frequency of occurrence of these symptoms within the psychiatric population. However, roughly one-half of the cases showed guilt reactions (suicidal thoughts, depressive withdrawal, and so on); one-third of the cases involved situations where the surviving sibling had actually had some responsibility for the death. Slightly less than one-quarter of the cases had experienced parentally enforced guilt for not mourning in an approved fashion. Almost a third equated growing up with dying, which often lead to regressive behavior, fright about minor illness, or somewhat negative attitudes toward doctors and hospitals. Approximately one-half showed immediate, prolonged, or anniversary identification with symptoms of the dead sibling (e.g., hysterical pains). One-half found themselves subject to unfavorable comparisons with the deceased. About 15% showed some major distortion of cognitive function.

Cain et al. (1964) identified a lengthy list of determinants for this type or reaction. It included the nature of the sibling's death; the age and characteristics of the sibling who died; the child's degree of actual involvement in the sibling's death; the child's preexisting relationship with the dead sibling; the immediate impact of death on the parents; the parent's handling of the initial reactions of the surviving child; the reactions of the community; the death's impact on the family structure; the availability to the child and the parents of various substitutes; the parents' enduring reactions to the sibling's death; major concurrent stresses on the child and his or her family; and the developmental level of the surviving child.

Studies of General Populations of Children Experiencing Sibling Loss

Whereas most of the information on children's disturbed reactions to the death of a sibling comes from the clinical literature, some researchers have studied grief reactions of the general population of bereaved children. From a retrospective study of 159 late adolescents and adults who had lost a sibling in childhood (55%) or adolescence (45%), Rosen (1984–85) concluded that significant prohibitions exist against adequate mourning and working through the loss. This can occur at the intrapsychic level by denial of the death, at the family level by lack of communication with the child, and at the social level by injunctions to "be strong." Although 23% of the sibling survivors were present at the time of death and 41% were informed of the death by parents, a surprising 36% learned of the death from other sources; some never spoke of the death directly with parents or did so only years later. Only about three-fourths of sibling survivors attended the funeral services.

About half of Rosen's (1984–85) respondents reported experiencing guilt at the sibling's death, ranging from guilt at being alive when the sibling had died to having negative feelings toward the sibling or wishing the sibling dead at some time in their relationship, and so on. They reported grief reactions of feeling sad, lonely, frightened, or angry following the loss, but 76% did not share their feelings with anyone. About a third reported feeling a responsibility to comfort their parents, and a third felt a responsibility to make up to their parents for the loss. The sibling survivors reported that about a third of the parents entered a period of depression and emotional withdrawal from the family following the death. Overall, in most families there was a failure to communicate feelings about the death; 62% of the sibling survivors had never discussed the death with another member of the family and felt that it was a taboo topic. Outside the home, adult friends and neighbors either were silent about the death or urged the sibling to be strong for the parents. As a result, most surviving siblings were not given social support for the grieving process and felt the need to suppress and deny feelings connected with the loss. Consequently, they had to work alone to resolve the loss, and many were able to do so only years later.

McCown (McCown, 1984; McCown & Pratt, 1985) gathered data from parents regarding reactions of 65 children aged 4 to 16 to sibling death. About the same percentage of children attended the funeral as reported by Rosen (1985–85), although the majority of those not attending were in the lower part of the age range. Parents reported that about one-fourth of the bereaved children showed problem behaviors in the year following the sibling death, with the incidence of problem behavior related to the child's age, sex, family size, funeral attendance, family communication, and the deceased sibling's sex, age, diagnosis, and place of death. There were more problems when the deceased sibling was a boy, was over 2 years of age, died of cancer rather than other conditions, and died in a hospital rather than at home. Surviving children in middle childhood showed more behavior problems than those either older or younger. In addition there were more problems in small families than in large, and when children attended the sibling's funeral (particularly among girls). Despite the existence of problems, over three-fourths of the children received no professional counseling either before or after the sibling's death. Parents mentioned problems in communicating with the child about the loss as a major factor influencing behavior problems, suggesting that the lack of communication creates difficulties both for parents and children.

Although both the Rosen (1984–85) and the McCown (McCown, 1984; McCown & Pratt, 1985) studies recruited more general populations of surviving siblings than those included in clinical studies, they were either self-selected or referred by schools, support groups, funeral directors, and the like, and were primarily middle-class whites; the Rosen and the Mc-Cown studies included rather wide age ranges. The McCown studies determined only parents' perceptions of children's problems and did not interview children directly. Rosen's subjects reported feelings about the death many years later whereas McCown interviewed parents from 2 months to a year after the death and may have sampled only early bereavement problems. Nevertheless, one can conclude that the loss of a sibling creates significant difficulty for a surprisingly large proportion of children. The proportion of bereaved children whose adjustment problems are severe enough to require clinical intervention is still unclear, as no studies have followed random samples of surviving siblings for extended longitudinal periods to determine long-term effects.

LOSS IN ADOLESCENCE

Many researchers theorize that individuals are most vulnerable to negative effects of sibling loss during adolescence, a time of life when they must deal with major physical, cognitive, emotional, and social changes as well as changes in relationships to family and peers (Balk, 1991a; Fanos & Nickerson, 1991; Martinson & Campos, 1991). The fact that nearly 80% of adolescent deaths are due to accidents, homicides, or suicides (Noppe & Noppe, 1991) adds to the stress of the loss.

Theoretically, a mature conception of death is attained by the beginning of adolescence. However, Noppe and Noppe (1991) argue that not only do adolescents' conceptions of death differ in many ways from those of mature adults, but they hold ambivalent conceptions of death that involve dialectically opposing themes. On the one hand they recognize the universality of death, but on the other hand many have a sense of personal invulnerability feeling that nothing will happen no matter what risks they take. They don't want to think about the possibility of their own deaths. Although they recognize the nonfunctionality and irreversibility of death on one level, at the same time they are drawn to notions such as resurrection, the "living dead," parallel universes of the dead, and so on. They seem unwilling to confront the idea of their own aging, decline, and disintegration into nonbeing. As a result, they tend to hold romantic and unrealistic conceptions about death. When forced to confront the reality of the loss of a sibling or peer, their intense reactions may be due to their ambivalent conceptions of death as well as to the loss itself.

The intensity of adolescent reactions to sibling loss has been demonstrated. Physical health of bereaved adolescents was lower than controls over a 4-year period (Guerriero & Fleming, 1985) and school grades suffered (Balk, 1991a). Davies (1991a) found that all 19 sibling survivors whom she interviewed reported experiences of shock, numbness, sadness, loneliness, anger, and depression immediately following the death. In a larger study, Hogan and Greenfield (1991) measured 129 adolescents' reactions to a sibling's death 3 to 84 months earlier, using 39 5-point items to assess the intensity of grief symptomatology. Although symptoms were fewer the longer the time since the sibling's death, half the group whose loss had occurred 18 months or more earlier still experienced moderate to high intensity levels. Excluding those adolescents whose siblings had died less that 18 months earlier, profiles on the Offer Self Image Questionnaire were compared for subgroups with low, moderate, and high intensity levels of grief symptomatology. The self-concept profiles were significantly different for the three groups: the low intensity group was above the national norms for all but one subscale; the moderate intensity group was below the norms for all but one subscale; and the high intensity group was well below the norms on all subscales (most noticeably for subscales assessing emotional tone, psychopathology, and the psychological self). Whether a weak self-concept present before the loss was responsible for the lingering grief symptoms, or whether the loss was responsible for the poor self-concept is not known. Theorizing that siblings act as referents in the task of developing one's identity during adolescence (Bank & Kahn, 1982b; Hogan and Greenfield, 1991), when the task is interrupted by a sibling's death, not only is the sibling lost but other siblings as well as parents may be emotionally unavailable. The bereaved adolescent is alone to find an identity and deal with grief, ruminating over survivor guilt, fearing loss of control, feeling misunderstood, feeling suicidal, and so on. Hogan and Greenfield estimated that from 25 to 50% of the adolescents they studied were at risk for long-term negative outcomes.

Following a sibling's death, 157 adolescent survivors studied by Hogan & DeSantis (1992) appeared to maintain an ongoing attachment to them, wishing to understand, reunite, and reaffirm the relationship with the sibling if they could. The authors concluded that this continuing attachment rendered the teenagers particularly vulnerable to dysfunctional outcomes.

In an endeavor to determine whether religious attitudes and beliefs helped teenagers deal with grief over a sibling's death, Balk (1991b) studied 42 surviving siblings from 14 to 19 years of age. Overall, religion or the lack of it did not make coping with the loss any easier, but the two groups differed somewhat in their reactions. The nonreligious group reported more feelings of depression, confusion, and fear, whereas the religious group reported more questions about the meaning of life, good and evil, and a shattered trust. Neither group turned to religion to help them cope.

Long-Term Effects

Several recent studies have considered the long-term effects of sibling loss during adolescence. Martinson and Campos (1991) conducted follow-up interviews with 31 young adults 7 to 9 years after a sibling died at home from cancer. Some 48% of the group had positive feelings connected with the sibling's death, 35% had mixed feelings, and only 16% saw the death negatively. Those regarding the loss as a negative influence in their lives continued to have problems in resolving the loss. They had negative memories about the sibling and recurring feelings of sadness, had difficulty discussing the death, did not see the family as a source of support and withdrew from family interaction, and tended to attribute their inadequacies and problems to the sibling's death. They saw such things as decreased parental availability, diminished family resources, disruption of normal activity, and increase in home responsibilities as leading to problems in school, loss of motivation, and greater risk-taking.

Fanos and Nickerson (1991) looked at long-term effects among 25 individuals who were between 9 and 18 years of age at the time of their sibling's death from cystic fibrosis some 10 to 20 years earlier. Effects were examined for three subgroups: preadolescents (ages 9–12), adolescents (ages 13–17) and late adolescents (age 18). Those who experienced sibling loss in adolescence had significantly more guilt, anxiety, and depression than those who were either younger or older when the death occurred. (Outcomes did not depend on birth order, family size, gender, or time since death.) This finding supports the idea that adolescence is a time when individuals are particularly vulnerable to negative outcomes of sibling loss. When Fanos and Nickerson looked at the adolescent group more closely, they found that from 50 to 100% of the group still experienced a global sense of guilt and a feeling that they were bad in some way; guilt over their relationship with their sibling while alive or over how they had handled the death; guilt that they were still alive; global anxiety; hypochondriacal concerns; somatic complaints; sleeping difficulties; excessive concerns over loved ones; and fear of intimacy with others.

Using a grounded theory method to analyze in-depth interview data, Davies (1991a) explored effects of sibling loss in adolescence among 12 survivors ranging in age from 25 to 43. Many reported that initial grief symptoms persisted for many years, although not as intensely as right after the loss. For some, pervasive feelings of loneliness and sadness characterized their outlook on life. They reported having a different perspective on life after the loss, leading to withdrawal from peers and having a sense of isolation. Davies suggested that this withdrawal from peers could be a hindrance to working through the grief, as well as to the process of identity formation through socialization.

Positive Outcomes of Sibling Loss

For many adolescents, there were positive as well as negative aspects to the sibling's death. Once the grief over the loss had been resolved, these surviving siblings realized that they had gained something from the painful experience. Three-fourths of the siblings interviewed by Davies (1991a) noted some sort of psychological growth. The sibling's death contributed to an understanding of the meaning of life, a greater seriousness of purpose, a feeling of being comfortable with their own mortality and with the deaths of others, an ability to help others, a more sensitive outlook on life, and a positive view of themselves for having weathered this crisis.

Often, adolescent siblings of cancer patients expressed the wish to help with their ill sibling's care (Chesler et al., 1991). Whether they had the opportunity to help or not, many felt that they had attained greater coping ability and maturity over the course of the sibling's illness. Based on their interviews with surviving siblings of cancer patients, similar findings were reported by Martinson and Campos (1991). Despite the pain involved in watching a sibling suffer and decline over the course of the illness, the survivors reported positive effects from the caregiving experience. These siblings recalled assisting in treatments and keeping the patient comfortable, spending time together, providing respite for parents, and participating in family decisions about treatment. Taking part in care brought the siblings into the center of family activities and counteracted the sense of isolation felt by teenagers who did not participate in care. When siblings shared in the caregiving, they were more likely to experience and share feelings with their parents as well. Overall, those who helped in caregiving were less likely to report negative effects of the loss.

Unfortunately, not all adolescents have the opportunity to participate in a dying sibling's care. When the sibling is hospitalized for an extended period over the course of an illness, not only the sibling but the parents tend to be removed from the home and sibling contact becomes difficult. Furthermore, the great majority of sibling deaths in adolescence are the result of accidents or violence and there is little or no contact with the sibling prior to death. It is in such cases where interventions to provide additional support to grieving siblings are most needed (Gaffney, Jones, and Dunne-Maxim, 1992), so that they can share feelings and learn growth-promoting behaviors to facilitate the grieving process.

According to Hogan and Greenfield (1991), sibling survivors never forget their dead siblings and never become totally free of bereavement symptomatology. Nevertheless, there seem to be divergent paths during the grieving process, depending on the self-concept of the sibling, extent of family communication, and circumstances surrounding the death: the bereaved adolescent can become a resilient survivor or can be vulnerable to long-term negative outcomes. Openness of family communication and sharing in caregiving for the dying brother or sister appear to aid surviving siblings through the grieving process by helping them to feel accepted and see themselves more positively. Davies' (1991a) findings would seem to support such a view. On one hand the loss may lead to psychological growth, but on the other, a grieving teenager who feels too far removed from the normal pursuits of the adolescent peer group may lack an important element in identify formation.

LOSS IN ADULTHOOD AND OLD AGE

Sibling death in childhood and adolescence may be particularly traumatic because of its nonnormative nature and the individual's lack of mature understanding. Although the loss of a sibling in old age is normative and is probably the most frequent death experienced by those over age 65, one might expect an easier adjustment, but this is not necessarily the case. When sibling death occurs in later adulthood, it is more readily accepted as part of the life course, but surviving siblings can still feel intense grief (Gorer, 1967; McClowry, Davies, May, Kulenkamp & Martinsin, 1987; M.S. Moss & S. Moss, 1986). Unfortunately, only a few empirical studies of the effects of sibling loss in adulthood and old age exist.

In one of the few studies examining sibling death in early and middle adulthood (Demi & Howell, 1991), a grounded theory approach was used to discover common themes in views of 17 survivors aged 26 to 50 regarding their sibling's suicide. Major themes involved the pain of losing the sibling, hiding the painful feelings from others, and efforts to resolve the loss and heal the pain. As in childhood and adolescence, suppression of painful feelings interfered with the grief work and the ultimate resolution of the loss.

A heightened sense of personal vulnerability accompanies the death of a sibling in the earlier portions of adulthood, particularly if the sibling dies unexpectedly or "off-time" with unfinished developmental tasks to complete (M.S. Moss, Lesher, & S.Z. Moss, 1986–1987; M.S. Moss & S.Z. Moss, 1983–1984, 1986; S.Z. Moss & M.S. Moss, 1989). The death of a sibling may lead to feelings of emptiness, helplessness, and hopelessness. For some adults, the sibling may have been a person central to their identity, and an important resource for emotional support or tangible assistance. The survivor may feel a sense of guilt over not having done enough for the sibling. There is a search for meaning in the sibling's death and a sense of existential incompleteness in the family. The survivor is often given little family support in mourning, as the deceased sibling's spouse and children (and parents, if still alive) are regarded as the primary mourners.

The renegotiation of family relationships following sibling death also can present difficulties. If the death occurs in the early portion of adulthood, parents are likely to be still alive and may cast the surviving sibling as a substitute for the dead one, expecting that sibling to take over the lost sibling's roles and responsibilities (M.S. Moss et al., 1986–1987). If the dead sibling was a parental favorite, some surviving siblings feel that the parent would have preferred them to die instead. Regardless of whether the parents are alive or not, relationships between the surviving siblings must change to adapt to the disruption of the sibling system. If the deceased sibling held a special role in the family (e.g., kinkeeper, financial advisor, or peacemaker), the death leaves a niche which other siblings will need to fill in some other way. Relationships with the dead sibling's spouse and children are altered. The remaining surviving siblings often become closer (S.Z. Moss & M.S. Moss, 1989).

When sibling death occurs in old age, survivors' reactions are much the same. In a study of a carefully selected sample of 20 elders with families of at least three siblings who had experienced the death of a sibling after age 60 (S.Z. Moss & M.S. Moss, 1989), a broad range of reactions to the death existed. Although the sample was small, the depth of the interviews makes the findings of considerable interest. Fully half the survivors did not find the loss hard to bear, but 30% found the loss very hard or extremely hard for them. (One elder, whose relationship with a brother had been hostile, expressed relief that he was gone.) Those who were most affected by the loss also described their relationship to the deceased sibling as close or very close. The same themes found in earlier adulthood were present in old age: loss of emotional and instrumental support, shifts in family relationships, and a sense of existential incompleteness. Because a sibling relationship extends over the whole life span, loss of a sibling represents the loss of perhaps the only one who can share memories of early life experiences and thus constitutes a loss of personal identity. However, elderly siblings' reactions were mixed regarding the theme of an increased sense of personal vulnerability toward death. Some felt that the death foreshadowed their own, and engaged in complex calculations regarding their own life expectancy or took steps to settle their own affairs in anticipation of death. There is some evidence that perceived life expectancy is affected more when a same-sex sibling dies (Marshall, 1980). Others, particularly those who were the last survivors in their family, seemed to gain a sense of their own resiliency and invulnerability in having outlived their siblings. Overall, most survivors, having learned by this age how to master losses and grief, had adjusted well to the sibling's death and felt neither guilt nor regret.

In a retrospective study of the effects of sibling loss among elders in a small Midwestern city (Cicirelli, 1989b), 99 older adults aged 61 to 91 (mean age 72.0 years) who had at least one sibling were interviewed. Collectively, these 67 women and 32 men had 246 living siblings and 204 dead siblings. Some 90% rated their own health as good or very good. Most elders mentioned the loss of the feeling of family togetherness and the sense of sadness and loneliness at being the last or nearly the last member of the sibling group. In the sense that sibling loss represents a sense of "existential incompleteness" of the family of origin (M.S. Moss & S.Z. Moss, 1986), feelings of grief for a sibling are different from feelings engendered by the loss of a parent, child, spouse, or other loved one.

The elders were also asked to rate their feelings of closeness, rivalry, and indifference to each of their siblings on a 5-point scale (Cicirelli, 1989b). Not surprisingly, feelings of closeness were significantly greater for living (M = 3.7) than for dead siblings (M = 3.0), but closeness was greater for those siblings who had died more recently. The greater the proportion of the sibling group that was dead, the closer the survivors felt to their dead siblings. There was a gender difference in feelings of well-being following the sibling loss, with women displaying more depressive symptomatology than men. Feelings of rivalry and indifference were low and did not differ for living and dead siblings. However, not only did some feelings of indifference and rivalry persist in the thoughts of the survivors, but these persisting feelings were related to greater symptoms of depression among women with dead sisters, even when effects of birth order, family size, and educational level were controlled.

CONCLUSION

Existing research into the effects of sibling death admittedly is flawed in many ways. Many studies involve only clinical cases, those sibling survivors whose bereavement sequelae were serious enough to require professional intervention. Other studies involve self-selected samples of parents and siblings drawn to such self-help groups as Compassionate Friends. Still other studies involve small samples of surviving siblings of individuals succumbing to a particular disease. Only a few studies involve surviving siblings of children and adolescents dying from accidents, violence, or suicide. Many involve such wide age ranges that it is difficult to reach conclusions about the findings. Few studies attempt to control for extraneous variables, or use comparison or control groups. The great majority of studies involve middle-and upper-class whites, so that we know little or nothing about the effects of sibling loss on individuals from the lower socioeconomic groups or from various racial-ethnic groups. For instance, how is a black teenager living in an urban ghetto affected by a sibling's shooting in a gang war? We know little about how loss of a sibling affects children in undeveloped nations where family size is large but the child death rate is high.

Most existing studies are concerned with the effect of sibling death on surviving siblings, and how lack of communication with parents is related to poor adjustment to the death. However, little is known about how relationships between the surviving siblings in the family are affected. How do they interact during the grieving period? Do they help or impede one another's adjustment? Do they draw apart or grow closer together as a result of their loss? This is an area in which further research is needed.

Despite such concerns, there are common threads running through the existing studies that suggest that the converging findings have some validity. No matter what the age at which the loss occurs, the surviving siblings of the deceased individual seem to be bypassed in the general concern over the death. The parents are the chief mourners in the first portion of life, supplanted by a spouse and children later on, with the feelings of siblings ignored by others and suppressed by the siblings themselves. The absence of open communication of feelings within the family regarding the loss appears to contribute heavily to long-term negative outcomes.

Vulnerability to the negative effects of sibling loss seems to be greatest in early childhood, when the child's understanding of death is poor. Negative effects are less during middle childhood and preadolescence, but vulnerability increases in adolescence when intensity of feelings is high. Maturity brings greater ability to deal with the loss, but even the elderly are vulnerable to feelings of existential incompleteness, loneliness, and depression when a sibling dies.

Perhaps sibling death can be understood in terms of chaos theory, where an unexpected event in childhood or adolescence can change the course of development in a negative fashion depending on the context of the death and the amount of support available to the bereaved sibling. Where family support and open communication is available, the perturbation of the child's development is lessened and the normal course of development is resumed. In other cases, it may take many years for the surviving sibling to resolve the grief and get back on course, if at all.

Siblings and Psychotherapy

Siblings with a close and warm relationship can provide companionship for one another, enhance morale, and provide psychological as well as tangible support through major life events. Not only are strong sibling ties rewarding in themselves throughout childhood and adulthood, but they lay the foundation for a more satisfying old age in which the remaining siblings from the family of origin can assist and comfort one another's last years.

However, sibling relationships are not always close and rewarding. Typical conflicts and pressures are handled routinely by the siblings themselves, given their own resources and social skills. On the other hand, sibling relationships may become disrupted to the point where therapy of some kind is needed to help restore a positive relationship.

The focus of this chapter is on the use of sibling therapy in dealing with the problems and conflicts of sibling interpersonal relationships. Sibling therapy is an attempt to resolve conflicts or solve problems existing among siblings throughout the life span. This definition is derived from the ideas put forth by Ranieri and Pratt (1978) and by Hamlin and Timberlake (1981). Although their views were stated with children and adolescents in mind, they can be extended to adults and the elderly.

In a narrow sense, the goal of sibling therapy is to improve the level of functioning of sibling group members, so that they can think, feel, and behave toward each other in a more positive manner, and coordinate their activities more effectively as a group. In a broader context, the goal of sibling therapy depends upon how this type of therapy is to be used. At the present time, there are three positions on how sibling therapy is to be used: as an adjunct to family therapy, as an adjunct to individual therapy, and as therapy independent of family and the individual.

SIBLING THERAPY AS AN ADJUNCT TO FAMILY THERAPY

Ranieri and Pratt (1978) feel that sibling therapy should be used as an adjunct to family therapy. Lewis (1988) states that sibling therapy is relevant when the family is experiencing a particular crisis and when there is no stable family structure. In these situations, sibling therapy occurs within the context of family therapy; the siblings are seen separately for a specific goal and then family therapy resumes.

As is well known, the family can be viewed as a total system with three subsystems: parent-parent, parent-child and sibling-sibling. The subsystems in the family reciprocally interact with each other; each subsystem affects and is affected by the others (P. Minuchin, 1985). The total family system involves reciprocal interaction between subsystems and between individuals within each subsystem. A balance point emerges which tends to regulate the coordination between and within the subsystems. In this sense, the overall family system has priority since the subsystems cannot deviate too far from norms necessary to maintain a balance between their interactions. Thus, the sibling subsystem is perceived as inseparable from the whole. Sibling therapy can only be perceived as an adjunct or means to helping the family. Dealing with specific problems of siblings can only make sense as a temporary step in facilitating the solution of family problems because whatever happens in the sibling subsystem will affect the other subsystems, which in turn will further modify the sibling subsystem. In the long run, one cannot view the sibling relationships in any meaningful way except within the family context. Thus, family therapy has priority over sibling therapy. Sibling therapy plays an auxiliary role in helping to resolve problems that are considered family problems. This position is consistent with that of many family therapists (P. Minuchin, 1985; S. Minuchin, 1974; S. Minuchin & Fishman, 1981).

To make this line of thinking more concrete, assume that two siblings are constantly bickering with each other. This situation leads the mother to intervene to attempt to reduce the conflict, thus involving the parent–child subsystem with the sibling-sibling subsystem. Next, the father may disagree with the mother's degree of intervention which leads to conflict between father and mother, involving the spousal subsystem. All the subsystems interact and influence each other. If the mother's intervention leads to the resolution of the siblings' conflict, the father's reaction to the mother will abate, thereby reducing the conflict in the spousal system, and so on.

It is this ongoing reciprocal interaction between all the subsystems that leads many family therapists to view sibling therapy as only a temporary focus on dealing with specific problems between siblings, but one which has the primary objective of facilitating changes in the total family system. Presumably any positive change in the sibling subsystem will have a positive effect on the total system which in turn will feed back to continue the improvement of the sibling subsystem (S. Minuchin, 1974). From this perspective, sibling therapy sessions may be carried out prior to, combined with, or after therapy sessions with the total family, or in some sequence that promises to be most effective in facilitating family therapy.

On the other hand, some practitioners of family therapy do not bother with sibling therapy. They feel that only the total family unit should have sessions together and any sibling problems that exist should be considered at the same time as other family problems are being explored. However, a compromise position might be for sibling therapy to temporarily focus on sibling relationships for the dual purpose of dealing with specific problems of siblings within the sibling subsystem, and also consider the longer range goal of facilitating change in the functioning of the total family system. This position would not make the total family system the exclusive goal, under the assumption that perhaps siblings sometimes have problems of high priority that need to be dealt with to maintain the subsystem. Any subsequent effects on the other subsystems may be either negligible or relatively minor so that treatment can be delayed.

SIBLING THERAPY AS AN ADJUNCT TO INDIVIDUAL THERAPY

When a particular sibling has unique emotional problems whose origin is relatively independent of the family and more related to his personal characteristics, then sibling therapy may be appropriate as an adjunct to individual therapy (Hamlin & Timberlake, 1981).

When the therapist's focus is on the problems of one particular sibling, perhaps therapy concerned with intrapsychic processes is more appropriate than that of a systems approach. In this case, one can conceptualize the siblings as a system rather than a subsystem. Within this system, siblings may have a great influence on each other. Siblings not only may have strong feelings toward one another, but they have their own rules for regulating behavior within the sibling system and may be quite intolerant if such rules are broken. This influence could be a contributing factor making the particular sibling's problems more difficult to treat. Their influence could encourage or reinforce the maladaptive behavior of the particular sibling. On the other hand, siblings may help alleviate a particular sibling's problems. They can encourage the necessary change and provide emotional support to help the individual improve the situation.

Lavigueur, R. Peterson, Sheese, and S. Peterson (1973) found that when siblings function as home therapists, they can help modify an individual's disruptive behavior.

In short, enlisting other siblings to participate in one sibling's treatment, given their influence on the dysfunctional individual, may facilitate the effectiveness of individual therapy. The professional therapist can train the siblings to use certain procedures with the target sibling such as behaviorally oriented techniques with appropriate reinforcement schedules (Miller & Cantwell, 1976). For example, sibling therapy sessions may influence the sibling client to develop more effective coping strategies, which in turn will help him or her to solve other personal problems being dealt with in the individual therapy.

Another possibility is that the client's siblings may have been part of the original problem. For example, a long history of sibling rivalry may exist, leaving the client with great anxiety or depression, as well as hostility toward some of his or her siblings. The use of the other siblings as informal therapists may help the client to work through these problems in groups sessions. Siblings can help the patient to gain insight into his or her problems and can provide the emotional support to deal with these problems, especially if the siblings have been part of the cause. However, this kind of therapy may not be possible with adults because other siblings may not be available. Under these conditions, the therapist can assist the adult to recall and analyze relevant experiences with siblings and work through the impact of the siblings in relation to the existing problems and conflicts. In this case, sibling therapy would operate concurrently with individual therapy in the sense of recalling past experiences and re-interpreting them.

SIBLING THERAPY USED ALONE

Lewis (1988) stated that when there is a problem between siblings, then sibling therapy alone is appropriate. Rosenberg (1980) indicated that using sibling therapy alone is appropriate when parents are unavailable or inadequate to help, and the children have the capacity to provide each other with emotional support or anchoring. Hamlin and Timberlake (1981) similarly maintain that sibling therapy can not only be used as an adjunct to family or individual therapy, but it can also be used alone.

In certain situations or problems, using sibling therapy by itself would seem more appropriate. Within the sibling subsystem, siblings may have problems or experience critical life events that affect all of them, and do not necessarily involve the parents. (From a systems viewpoint, whatever happens in one part of the system affects every other part; however, at times, the reciprocal interaction from parents to children may be insignificant.) Also, siblings may have their own unique relationships with one another; problems and conflicts emerging from sibling interactions either may not be communicated to the other family members or may have little effect on them. According to Hamlin and Timberlake (1981), sibling therapy alone is appropriate for sibling groups that have experienced a common loss (such as the death of a parent or sibling, or separations where one sibling is sent to a foster home). Sibling subgroups may be particularly helpful in reorganizing families where a member has died, divorced, or remarried, such as when a new family is being blended after remarriage, bringing together children from previous marriages, or when young siblings are moved from the home of one parent to another in families of divorce. In these cases, the siblings constitute a bridge between the original and new families; they act as a unit of continuity between the way a family was previously and what the family is now to become (Rosenberg, 1980).

A critical life event may lead to unique problems among the siblings and have a far greater impact on their interpersonal relationships within the sibling subsystem than on the total family system. In these situations, using sibling therapy alone may be appropriate to provide the focus necessary to deal with such problems. A professional therapist can work with the sibling group not only to examine the issues but to facilitate changes, depending on the special needs of the sibling subsystem (Hamlin & Timberlake, 1981). For example, a young adult male may have had an incestuous sexual relationship throughout the high school years with two sisters only a year or two younger than he. They are all now in college, and feel the need to deal with this as a problem in their lives. They would prefer working with a professional therapist as a group without communicating any knowledge of their sexual relationship to their parents, feeling the parents are quite normal and raised them in a proper manner.

In view of the above, sibling group therapy may be most helpful when major disruptions in the relationships between the siblings exist, and they are the ones primarily affected. Sibling relationships may come under strain in response to changing needs and demands of the environment. In such cases, sibling support for one another can be extremely helpful.

Through appropriate therapeutic procedures, the disruption of sibling relationships can be repaired and positive feelings and closeness among the siblings can be increased. Such strengthened relationships will further help the siblings to deal with problems in the future. In general, siblings can offer one another a support system over the life cycle to help resolve problems, conflicts, and concerns beyond what can be done within family therapy (Rosenberg, 1980).

Thus far, sibling therapy has been examined from two perspectives: sibling therapy used as an adjunct to family or individual therapy, or sibling therapy used alone. Sibling therapy can also be viewed from the perspective of the stage of life to which it is to be applied. In this view, sibling therapy in childhood and adolescence differs from sibling therapy in adulthood and old age.

SIBLING THERAPY IN CHILDHOOD AND ADOLESCENCE

The potential for conflict among siblings in childhood and adolescence is enormous. Siblings may experience differential treatment or favoritism of siblings by parents or parental conflicts may lead to sibling conflicts. Sibling differences in natural abilities may lead to jealousies. There may be mutual sibling aggression and violence, sibling physical, emotional, or sexual abuse, or lack of mutual trust or loyalty. There may be lack of attachment or bonding between siblings, distress over one sibling's illness or disability, miscommunications and perceptual stereotypes, low self-esteem related to negative feelings toward one another, and so on.

According to Ranieri and Pratt (1978), sibling therapy provides an environment without parents, giving the siblings more freedom to express their feelings and explore their relationships without the need to justify such feelings to their parents and without fear of punishment. In childhood and adolescence, many problems and conflicts are best dealt with when parents are not present. For example, opposite sex siblings would find it difficult to discuss any sexual interest in each other with parents present. Having parents present might lead to inhibition and repression of the siblings' problem rather than open discussion and an attempt to understand their feelings. Siblings may feel more free to express their feelings in each other's presence because they feel a sense of security through their familiarity with their brothers and sisters and their knowledge of what to expect from them. In such an environment, they can be less defensive and make more rapid progress in their treatment.

In the process of sharing thoughts and feelings about each other (through use of such techniques as dialogue, role play, art therapy, and so on), young siblings gain insight into the dynamics of their relationship. For example, they can learn about how they might unintentionally hurt each other emotionally, or how they may ignore the interest of another sibling when they attempt to manipulate parents for their own ends. They may learn how bickering and hostile feelings toward another sibling may merely be a cover-up for deeper feelings of jealousy.

Sibling differences in feelings and thoughts may be related to siblings' constellation factors. Gender, age, and birth order may be partially responsible for negative feelings due to differences in power, privileges, or responsibilities that are often associated with these sibling status variables. Children may feel special needs associated with their sibling status position that are being overlooked or ignored by insensitive siblings.

In addition, sibling group therapy provides an opportunity for siblings to express positive feelings about one another. They may feel that such feelings will be misunderstood if expressed in an everyday environment or they may feel embarrassed about expressing them. When such feelings are not expressed, siblings can feel that only indifference or hostility exists, which hampers their relationship.

The professional therapist would normally also guide the siblings to examine their roles within the group to identify any dysfunctional roles (such as the scapegoat, the pet or ideal child, the bully, and so on) that need to be recognized openly by everyone for their disruptive influence on the group in order to provide the impetus for modifying such roles. Also, the professional therapist needs to help the siblings define the boundary issues between the sibling, parental, and parent–child subsystems of the family. The siblings need to determine their degree of privacy, loyalties, and responsibilities to one another as distinct from those pertaining to parents.

Once the siblings have gained understandings and insights into their problems and conflicts, then the process of reworking relationships begins, using and further developing problem solving and interpersonal relationship skills.

In summary, when sibling therapy provides a context without parents, it creates an environment where siblings can share their thoughts and feelings about each other, gain insights about themselves and their relationship, recognize any dsyfunctional roles that are being enacted, and clarify the boundaries of their sibling relationship to determine their responsibilities toward each other in relation to their responsibilities toward parents.

The challenge for the therapist is to find out the nature of the sibling relationship, whether it is close or distant, how it developed, and how it can be modified through psychotherapy (Bank & Kahn, 1982a, 1982b).

As a beneficial side effect, treatment of sibling problems may be a way of enhancing social skills that can be used with peers, as well as in coping with family problems such as parental alcoholism or the loss of parent through death or divorce. Siblings can also help one another to learn appropriate ways of interacting socially.

Therapy of this sort can facilitate the siblings' development, which in turn influences overall family functioning. Most of the time, siblings from the same family are brought together to deal with common problems. However, some professional therapists (e.g., Jesse, 1988; McGuire & Tolan, 1988) have carried out sibling therapy by bringing together siblings from different families who have similar problems of adjustment.

Limitations of Sibling Therapy in Childhood and Adolescence

According to Hamlin and Timberlake (1981), there are certain limitations to sibling therapy when applied to children and adolescents. Some parents may be reluctant to allow their children to participate in sibling therapy for fear that the therapist will ally him- or herself with their children and against the parents. Some therapists may resist using sibling therapy because they do not feel comfortable dealing with young children. Many therapists prefer therapy where verbal expression is involved. However, with young children, it may be necessary to use play therapy, role play, art expressions, and the like. Also, when dealing with reconstituted families, therapists often feel that it is too difficult to bring together full siblings, half-siblings, stepsiblings, and possibly adopted siblings who may live in different homes; therapists may feel that such siblings are too dissimilar for therapy to accomplish very much. This is unfortunate because serious problems in sibling relationships often exist in blended families.

Schibuk (1989) has observed that many therapists working with older individuals use a systems approach, whereas play therapy derives more from an intrapsychic approach. This theoretical inconsistency may lead some therapists to avoid young children and the play therapy involved.

Both therapists and parents may resist sibling therapy to protect other siblings when one child is being treated, feeling that to involve siblings in the problems of the untreated child may affect them negatively.

Accordingly to Lewis (1988), there are other reasons for not using sibling group therapy with young children. Young children can hide their fears behind a high activity level; children are unpredictable; they may not rely on language for communication to the extent desired by therapists; working with children may revive therapists' fears of unresolved problems in childhood; some therapists may have had little exposure to or care for children, having no children of their own. Therapists may lack knowledge of child development and the significance of play, leading to misinterpretations of children's behavior; and working with children may lead to siding with them against parents, generating parent resentment of therapists.

SIBLING THERAPY IN ADULTHOOD AND OLD AGE

A minority of sibling pairs have been either completely apathetic toward each other or have had very troubled relationships in adulthood and old age. Some 22% of the sibling relationships studied by Gold (1989b) fell into the hostile and apathetic types, although Scott (1990) identified only 5% in a replication, all of whom were apathetic. It appears that sibling relationships are more difficult for half-siblings and stepsiblings than for full siblings; a significantly greater proportion reported having a sibling with whom they did not get along (White & Riedmann, 1992b).

Apathetic siblings may never have developed a very strong sibling bond in childhood, and simply drifted apart in adulthood. Such factors as a wide age difference, little contact during the formative years, or general family disorganization can contribute to a weak bond.

A hostile or conflict-filled sibling relationship in adulthood usually has its roots in childhood (Bank & Kahn, 1982a, 1982b; Dunn & Kendrick, 1982b). Although some degree of conflict between siblings early in life can be considered a healthy experience in learning how to deal with disagreements, extensive or deep-seated conflict can have serious negative effects. Perceived unequal or unfair treatment by a parent, unfavorable comparisons to a sibling, spousal conflicts or divorce, parental violence or child abuse, sibling violence, and sibling sexual abuse can all have effects that persist in the form of poor sibling relationships throughout life or major psychological problems.

Even when early sibling rivalry and other problems have seemingly been transcended in adulthood, they can resurface when critical life events occur. Recent studies (Bedford, 1990; Connidis, 1992) found that for many siblings such events are accompanied by changes in the sibling relationship. Critical events found by these researchers to influence the sibling relationship included marriage or divorce, changing interests, employment change, relocation to a new area, illness and death, family arguments, changing frequency of contact, and so on. Such changes may be positive for some sibling dyads and negative for others, depending on the circumstances. One sibling's marriage resulted in a less close relationship for a third of the sibling pairs studied by Bedford. This is understandable if the new spouse is not liked by the other siblings, but even if the spouse is liked, the marriage can disrupt the flow of a formerly close sibling relationship. On the other hand, marriage to a spouse who is well liked can bring siblings closer together. Negotiating congenial relationships with a sibling's spouse is often difficult and can be source of bitter sibling conflict. Similarly, difficulties involving children of siblings can escalate into major family fights. Divorce and widowhood often bring siblings closer, but also can lead to estrangement, particularly if one sibling feels that the other is somehow at fault. Employment stress or job loss also can affect the sibling relationship. Bedford cited the case of a sister who felt "stressed out" at work and asked her sister for help. The stressed sister was so appreciative of the help that she changed her behavior toward the helping sister, who responded favorably, and the sisters drew closer. Often severe medical problems or a brush with death will bring siblings closer, but they can do the opposite. Bedford reported the case of sisters where one sister recovered from mental problems and drug dependency. The other sister was overtly happy for her but then felt unneeded and their relationship deteriorated. The important conclusion to be drawn is that sibling relationships are not fixed and unchanging, but can be influenced by events both internal and external to the relationship.

When siblings participate in family businesses together, the potential for conflict and acrimony is great because family issues are interwoven with business themes of power, control, and responsibility (Carroll, 1988); not only can disagreements disrupt the business partnership but they can damage the sibling relationship beyond repair.

Family issues such as inheritance also can threaten family relationships in midlife. Whether problems concerning inheritance involves such major issues as unequal bequests to adult children, failure to reward the sacrifice of a caregiving adult child, unusual bequests, or such minor issues of who should get Mother's tea set or Father's tie pin, they can lead to violent conflict and sibling estrangement.

Among the elderly, many problems special to the age group are predominant, such as the need to deal with deterioration due to aging, the need to improve self-care, the need to relieve symptoms of anxiety or depression, and the need to encourage activity. In old age as well as at younger ages, lack of care or concern on the part of a sibling or lack of appreciation for help and support can lead to bitterness and withdrawal.

One can conclude that, no matter what stage of life or critical life event, the sibling relationship can be a stage for conflict as old rivalries or dysfunctional family relationships are played out.

Some problems that warrant sibling therapy in adulthood and old age are critical life events that are common to or affect all the siblings, such as the death of a sibling, parent, or close relative, the separation from a sibling who has been hospitalized in a terminal ward, committed to a nursing home, hospice, or sanitarium, the separation from a sibling who has moved far away, the divorce of a sibling, and the placement of parents in a residential treatment or care facility. In short, losses due to death and long term or permanent separations of siblings from one another may lead to a common grieving experience that siblings can best work out together.

Where siblings have persisting strong conflicts or rivalries, or where there has been a history of abuse or wrongdoing, sibling therapy can be used to attempt to mend the bond in adulthood or old age. Most siblings feel a need to mend their relationships as they grow older. In addition, in many situations the sibling relationship becomes important in dealing with the mental health problems of the elderly (Cicirelli, 1988). Conflicts and estrangements persisting from childhood or from the time of later critical incidents (Dunn, 1984), long-term sibling dependencies, or reactivated rivalries and aggressions can all come to necessitate therapy in old age.

(It should be mentioned, however, that in some cases the damage done by an abusive sibling early in life was so great and long-lasting that it may be better to help the abused sibling escape the relationship and reach some understanding and peace of mind as an individual rather than to attempt to repair the sibling relationship.)

Few guidelines exist for treatment of the elderly client who has problems involving siblings. Therapeutic approaches range from probing sibling relationships in the course of psychoanalysis (Rosner, 1985), to individual therapy (Bank, 1988; Bank & Kahn, 1982a, 1982b; Kahn, 1983), to inclusion of siblings in family therapy (Kahn & Bank, 1981; Palazzoli, 1985), and family counseling (Herr & Weakland, 1979). Therapy can include all living siblings, or only a subgroup of siblings. If the siblings are close-knit, they can be seen as a group, otherwise it may be more effective to see a sibling individually (Church, 1986; Harris, 1988; Kahn, 1983; Kahn & Bank, 1981). Bank recommends proceeding by attempting to transfer the emotional intensity from the difficulties in the sibling relationship to a context of parental failure, so that the sibling can see the parents' role in the genesis of the sibling problem.

The use of reminiscence as an approach to therapy with older people has gained favor in recent years as an outgrowth of its use in the life review process. While reminiscence in itself is simply talking or thinking about the past, in the life review past experiences are analyzed, evaluated, and reintegrated in relation to present events, values, and attitudes in order to resolve old conflicts, come to grips with past mistakes, and achieve integrity in the latter portion of life (Butler, 1963; Molinari & Reichlin, 1985; Osgood, 1985).

Reminiscence is an approach that could be used profitably with siblings. Because they share a long and unique history, reminiscing about earlier times together is an activity in which siblings spontaneously engage at many points in the life span, although it seems to become more frequent and valuable in old age. Indeed, most communication between elderly siblings centered around discussion of family events and concerns and around old times (Cicirelli, 1985a), with old times discussed more frequently with siblings than with adult children. The fewer the remaining siblings in the family, the greater the extent of the reminiscing. As the surviving members of their families of origin, siblings can use reminiscences of old times together to clarify events and relationships that took place in early years and to place them in mature perspective. Ross and Milgram (1982) observed that sharing recollections of childhood experiences appeared to be a source of comfort and pride for the elderly, evoking the warmth of early family life and contributing to a sense of integrity that life had been lived in harmony with the family. Elderly participants in Gold's (1986) interview study reported that reminiscing about sibling relationships during the course of the interview helped them to put their current relationships with siblings into a meaningful context, helped them to understand present events, and helped them to appreciate the significant of sibling relationships in their lives.

One can also speculate on the use of reminiscence of nonshared sibling experiences as a complementary procedure in helping elderly siblings to understand one another. If each sibling in a group were to reminiscence about an early family event that was not shared (or was interpreted differently), the sharing and discussion of such events could help to integrate isolated childhood events for each of them, and make earlier experiences more meaningful and insightful.

Whether or not older siblings feel a need or desire to enter therapy to remedy a troubling sibling relationship, engaging in informal reminiscence together can help siblings come to a better understanding of their common or different pasts and a greater appreciation of their relationships. Certainly the persistence of the sibling relationship and its value for the individual should not be underestimated.

Sibling therapy with a group of adult siblings has been a rare occurrence. It is difficult to get such a group together, and adults of this age are more prone to be highly individualistic. Although Kahn and Lewis's (1988) book provides a number of examples of sibling therapy in adulthood and old age, few of these involve attempts to work with siblings as a group.

Group therapy with elderly siblings can be used to explore siblings' feelings and increase their sensitivity toward one another's needs. Group reminiscing would certainly help siblings to deal with conflicts which have their origins in early family life. In general, group therapy would give elderly siblings support, guidance, or insight into themselves, would help them learn to communicate more effectively with each other, and would allow them to air feelings about each other. Many times, group therapy can be short term and informally carried out. Siblings' problems and previously unexpressed emotions can be shared, and they can concentrate on dealing with relationship difficulties, problems of independence, self-esteem, loneliness, or death in the family.

From the perspective discussed earlier in this chapter, sibling therapy as an adjunct to family therapy could still be a viable option with the old. The family of origin would no longer exist (except for siblings), but members of the family of procreation could participate (along with spouses of the elderly siblings) in dealing with problems between the elderly siblings that threaten relationships in the family of procreation.

Sibling therapy as an adjunct to individual therapy could also be used. If the remaining living siblings could be brought together for such therapeutic sessions, they probably would still have an important influence on the problems of a particular sibling. Certainly, they could provide support and guidance.

Sibling therapy used alone would appear to have its greatest application with the elderly. In many cases, the only members of the family of origin remaining are some siblings, and with their tendency to want to reminiscence at this stage of life, they might welcome the opportunity to be brought together for a series of sessions. Thus far, sibling therapy has been little used with the elderly; it would seem a fertile area for practitioners as well as for researchers.

CHAPTER 15

Epilogue

At present, research on sibling relationships across the life span has not yet provided a coherent body of knowledge. The study of sibling relationships is still a young field of research, awaiting the discovery of new aspects of sibling relationships to fill the gaps in present knowledge, the further verification of phenomena already discovered, and the formulation of theories of sibling relationships that have explanatory power across the life span.

INTEGRATING RESEARCH ACROSS THE LIFE SPAN

If an understanding of sibling relationships across the life span is to be accomplished, it is important to recognize that at present two groups of sibling researchers are working in relative isolation, those concerned with childhood and adolescence, and those concerned with adulthood and old age. There is a need to integrate these two bodies of knowledge, as well as to facilitate greater collaboration between researchers working at different ends of the life span.

Researchers working in different segments of the life span have either been working on the same topics or phenomena almost independently of each other, with no attempt to integrate their findings across the life span, or they have been working on different topics, with no inclination on the part of those working in childhood and adolescence to extend their research endeavors forward to adulthood and old age, and no inclination on the part of those working in adulthood and old age to extend their research backward to childhood and adolescence.

An added problem is that these different research groups tend to employ different research methodologies, due primarily to differences in the age of the subjects and their accessibility for study. As a result, researchers working in different portions of the life span tend to ask different research questions and deal with different topics, phenomena, problems, and issues. The differing concerns of researchers studying childhood and adolescence and those studying adulthood and old age are illustrated below.

Phenomena Occurring in Only One Part of the Life Span

Certain sibling phenomena occur primarily in childhood and adolescence, such as older siblings providing caretaking for younger siblings, siblings residing in the same home with a dysfunctional sibling, and older siblings' violence and abuse toward younger siblings. In adulthood and old age, siblings may be involved in cooperative business relationships, or in the aging and dissolution of sibling relationships. Although such phenomena do not occur exclusively in either the early or late portions of the life span, in most cases they do occur in only one or two segments. Therefore, it is not surprising that researchers working in different segments of the life span carry out studies in these areas in relative independence of one another. However, greater communication between the two camps would surely stimulate the formulation of research questions and encourage the use of methods and procedures that could enable comparison of findings across the life span.

Phenomena Now Investigated in Only One Part of the Life Span

Researchers working in childhood and adolescence have been preoccupied with certain topics and phenomena. For example, some have been concerned with sibling sexual activity and sibling incest, which certainly occurs with greater frequency in the earlier stages of life. Although it is quite possible that incestuous sexual activity between some siblings may continue throughout the life span, researchers have not considered this possibility, made any attempt to detect its occurrence, or considered its positive or negative effects.

The study of sibling relationships within both family and extrafamilial contexts has been undertaken primarily in the childhood and adolescence portion of the life span. This interesting work needs to be extended to include adulthood and old age. As suggested by the narrative type of study presented in Chapter 7 of this book, adult sibling relationships are strongly influenced by the wider kinship context in which they take place.

Again, the recent interest in explaining sibling individual differences in terms of nonshared genetic factors and environments (or experiences) has resulted in studies carried out in childhood and adolescence. It would seem important to extend this kind of research to adulthood and old age, given the fact that certain critical nonnormative life events (such as chronic illness or widowhood) occur more frequently with increasing age. along with increases in individual differences as one gets older.

Researchers working in childhood and adolescence have been concerned with studying the mild to moderate conflicts between siblings hypothesized to lead to constructive outcomes and further social development, as well as with studying more severe conflict (perhaps accompanied by violence or abuse) that leads to negative outcomes and disruption of development. Researchers working in adulthood and old age have been preoccupied with the decline in conflict with age and the increase in sibling closeness and helping behavior. However, sibling conflicts continue to occur in adulthood, some severe enough to shatter family relationships. Conflict research needs to be extended to the latter segment of the life span, with attention to the strategies used by adults in dealing with sibling conflicts.

In childhood and adolescence, the reciprocal influence of sibling relationships and friendships on each other has been studied to some extent, whereas in adulthood and old age, sibling relationships have been compared to friendships to determine their similarities and differences (i.e., whether certain sibling relationships are friendships). Both types of research could profitably be extended over the entire life span. It would be important to know, for example, whether social development of children is facilitated by certain siblings who are also perceived as close friends or hampered by other siblings who are viewed as mere acquaintances. Similarly, in adulthood, it would be important to know how strong sibling relationships affect peer friendships, and vice versa.

In adulthood and old age, one area of research has been concerned with studying how siblings work as a team or coordinated subsystem to provide caregiving to elderly parents. This topic has important implications for sustained high-quality care for the elderly. One might inquire whether similar team caregiving occurs in other cultures or whether it occurs in childhood and adolescence in relation to an ill or disabled sibling. If so, under what conditions does it occur, and what are its consequences for sibling relationships and individual development?

In adulthood and old age, siblings relationships sometimes blend with working or business relationships as siblings become partners in a business or work together in the same occupation. Sometimes the same phenomenon occurs in adolescence, when siblings play on the same sports team, operate a baby-sitting or lawn care service, organize a band or singing group together, and so on. Yet such activities have never been investigated. It would be interesting to know how siblings' family and business relationships affect each other, and what the long-range effects are when siblings begin a working or business relationship at an early age.

In adulthood and old age, the influence of spouses and in-laws on sibling relationships adds a new dimension to studying sibling relationships within the family or the larger kinship context. However, a similar phenomenon can also be found in late adolescence when one sibling develops a strong bond with a potential mate or marries early in life. Research could certainly be extended in this direction.

Same Phenomena Studied Independently in Both Parts of the Life Span

Describing phenomena associated with normative changes in sibling relationships and determining their causes is work that has been undertaken in childhood, adolescence, adulthood, and old age. However, there has been little effort to integrate studies to obtain a better picture of the overall developmental course. At present, the greatest gap in knowledge about the course of sibling relationships across the life span is in young adulthood. This area would be a natural meeting place for researchers of both camps to meet and carry out research studies. The bridging of such a gap would go a long way toward determining the lifetime course of sibling relationships more clearly. Collaboration on longitudinal studies or even cross-sectional studies across various parts of the life span would be extremely helpful in answering other questions about the course of sibling relationships. For example, does sibling rivalry change over time to sibling closeness, or does it proceed to sibling indifference? Or do these components coexist in varying degrees for different siblings and under different conditions across the life span?

The effect of a sibling's death on other siblings in the family has been studied both in childhood and adolescence and in adulthood and old age but many more studies are needed in both segments of the life span. For example, are the effects of the death of a 7-year-old sibling on a 5-year-old child comparable to the effects of the death of a 90-year-old sibling on an 88-year-old elder? Such comparative work is now nonexistent. Death of a sibling is an extremely important critical life event whether it occurs in the earlier or later parts of the life span. However, the timing of this event can lead to quite different effects.

The influence of siblings on one another's development, adjustment, and interpersonal relations has been of interest to researchers in both segments of the life span. However, in adulthood and old age, the emphasis has been more on siblings as helping agents than on siblings as agents of socialization. But is this an arbitrary distinction? Is there an overlap? Does socialization include helping? Does helping lead to socialization? If helping is different, does it occur more frequently or in a different form with different implications in each part of the life span? Again, this is an area in which further integration of existing knowledge across the life span is needed.

Finally, there has been considerable comparison of cross-cultural differences in sibling relationships, especially comparisons between industrialized and nonindustralized countries. Such studies have included both children and adults, but typically focus on different phenomena in the two types of cultures. Yet there are huge gaps in existing knowledge. To remedy this situation would require not only the collaboration of researchers concentrating on different segments of the life span, but collaborations extending across a variety of cultures. Fortunately, modern communication systems can make such collaborations more easy.

Methodological Differences

As compared to researchers in adulthood and old age, researchers in childhood and adolescence have made greater use of laboratory experiments, naturalistic field studies, and observational studies in the attempt to better understand the process of sibling interactions and the dynamics of sibling relationships. Also, they have used larger and more representative samples and exercised greater control over sibling structure variables. Workers in the early portion of the life span have the opportunity to work with siblings who are easily accessible to study (easy to identify in school settings, living in close proximity, and willing to participate in research). All these are more difficult to accomplish in adulthood and old age. Also, sibships in the earlier portions of the life span are more likely to be unbroken by sibling death than those later in life. In many cases, carrying out a sibling research study in childhood and adolescence involves only the effort of obtaining the approval of a school system where both a population and sample is available.

Researchers in adulthood and old age are not that fortunate. It is true that in old age, subjects can be found in hospitals, retirement villages, nursing homes, hospices, and so on, but they are limited in number, frail, and many times without sufficient mental competence to participate in research. Finally, these subjects do not necessarily represent a healthy, normal population. Their siblings are likely to be deceased or to live at a distance. In middle age, siblings are often busy with their careers and children, are spread out geographically, and more important, are either not interested or are too busy to participate in research. The identification of subjects, gaining their approval to participate in research, and making arrangements for them to come to university laboratories either individually or as a group for research studies is quite difficult. Even naturalistic field studies, especially if carried out longitudinally, are not welcomed by subjects if they suspect any invasion of their privacy.

Thus, researchers working in adulthood and old age are much more limited in the size and representativeness of their samples, the types of questions that can be investigated, the types of designs that can be used, and the methods of data collection that are appropriate to the situation. Researchers in adulthood and old age consequently have depended mostly on face-to-face or telephone interviews, mailed questionnaires, case studies of normal or pathological cases, and such qualitative approaches as use of diaries, biographies, and so on.

Thus, many differences in the research efforts in the two portions of the life span are the result of the greater methodological restrictions upon research with adults and elders. However, collaboration may help to overcome some of these problems. For example, researchers from other segments of the life span working together could target the same population in which children are recruited from infancy to young adulthood for various studies. Researchers in adulthood and old age could simultaneously attempt to recruit the parents and grandparents of these younger people. Such a coordinated effort may lead to better public relations for recruiting, and lead to pooling of financial resources, making more money available to pay subjects as an incentive to participate in such studies. In addition, the dynamics of the larger family system could be better understood.

In sum, researchers from both parts of the life span need better communication to exchange ideas and stimulate one another's research work. They also need a greater collaborative effort to fill gaps in existing knowledge of sibling relationships and to integrate this knowledge across the life span.

Common Problems for Researchers across the Life Span

Among the existing problems for researchers in both parts of the life span is the lack of concern for studying increasingly prevalent types of siblings found in modern families, that is, half-siblings, stepsiblings, adoptive siblings, and fictive siblings. Researchers need to focus their efforts on understanding relationships involving these types of siblings, in addition to relationships in the traditional family with full siblings. The latter are likely to be in the minority in the 21st century.

As yet, very little is known about sibling dynamics, the process by which siblings influence or socialize one another. Certainly, this process is somewhat different when siblings are young and living in the same household than when they are adults living apart from each other.

Most researchers today emphasize the study of sibling relationships within the context of the family, and yet most present research is carried out with the two-child, two-parent, middle-class, white family. Little is knows about siblings in families with three or more siblings, single-parent families, lower-class or upper-class families, and black, Asian, Hispanic, or other minority families. Findings of present studies are limited, and yet these results tend to be overgeneralized to apply to other types of families.

Studies of sibling structure (constellation) variables in relation to cognitive and personality characteristics have been criticized in the past for leading to weak and inconsistent results. As such, they have been abandoned by many researchers. However, the sibling structure framework has rarely been applied in an appropriate manner. Instead of studying the effects of one component or a few components at a time (such as sibling gender and sibling birth order), the interactive effects of all the components should be studied as they relate to sibling characteristics and sibling interactions. At the very least, sibling structure variables provide a framework within which sibling studies relating other variables should be carried out. Certainly, different sets of family and social expectations exist for the behavior of an older daughter and a younger son, for example. The description of individual differences using sibling structure characteristics and their associated experiences can be a starting point in research. Explanations of individual differences can then follow from such descriptive results in all portions of the life span.

When studying sibling relationships within the context of the family from a life span perspective, researchers need to think in terms of the larger kin network rather than the nuclear family alone. The existence and importance of various family members change over time. For example, in childhood, sibling relationships may be heavily influenced by parents; in adulthood, the sibling relationships may be more influenced by their spouses than by parents; in old age, the sibling relationships may be more influenced by their adult children.

Also, in studying the dynamics of sibling relationships either within the dyad alone or in the context of family or kin, researchers need to pay more attention to the communication and language patterns that characterize the ongoing process. The surface has barely been scratched in this area, and yet understanding sibling communication is crucial to understanding sibling interactions, whether in childhood and adolescence or in adulthood and old age.

The communication network of the family needs to be studied in more detail to delineate the role of siblings in the network, their degree of congruence in family members' perceptions, the role of spouses, the role of intergenerational family members parents in the network, and differences in perceived experiences and behaviors associated with sibling structure (e.g., does a preponderance of males or females in the sibship lead to undue influence on or isolation of siblings of the minority gender?).

One aim of sibling therapy is to improve the quality of sibling relationships. However, little research has been done to evaluate the effectiveness of various approaches to sibling therapy that are either now in use or have been advocated. Evaluation studies are needed to determine which therapies are most effective in regard to what problems and under what conditions. Such studies may be tedious and costly but without knowing the effectiveness of a therapy, an approach may be used that is wasteful of time and money and that also has negative long-range consequences. If Rowe (1994) is correct in that sibling behavior and relationships are primarily determined by genetic factors, then neither family intervention nor sibling therapy will be of much help. This needs to be determined.

Also, there is the question of just how siblings' experiences (both shared and nonshared) interact with their shared and nonshared genetic potential to produce individual differences in characteristics and behaviors. (Although nonshared environments and experiences are sometimes used synonymously, they mean something quite different, and need to be separated when designing a study. Nonshared environments may exist when different siblings in the same family environment are inadvertently exposed to different aspects of that environment; nonshared experiences can occur when two siblings dealing with the same aspect of the family environment but experience different interpretations of it. This point is not always made clear in studies dealing with nonshared environment.)

The problems involved in coordinating sibling research across the life span could be dealt with in a more effective manner if researchers had a guiding theory that applied to such a diversity of phenomena. Such a possibility is discussed below.

ATTACHMENT THEORY: A UNIFYING THEORY FOR LIFE SPAN SIBLING RESEARCH

At present, no theory exists that can account for changes in sibling relationships across the life span, sibling closeness, sibling caregiving and helping, sibling violence and abuse, and so on. Certain theories have applications to particular topics pertaining to sibling behavior and relationships, but none can account for sibling behavior and relationships across the whole life span from infancy to death.

A life span attachment theory (i.e., the integration of traditional infant attachment theory with its extension to adult attachment) is proposed here as one way to account for many diverse phenomena pertaining to siblings and sibling relationships.

In recent years, there has been great interest in the expansion of attachment theory to apply to adult attachments. Work in this area includes a concern for attachment styles (secure attachment and varieties of insecure attachment) developed in the mother–child relationship in infancy, stored as an internal working model in childhood, and applying to later relationships. Briefly, the nature of the early mother–child relationship is the source of either a secure or insecure attachment to the mother. If a sensitive and responsive reciprocal relationship between infant and mother exists, then a secure attachment will form, and this attachment style will be applied in turn to the formation of relationships with siblings and others. (On the other hand, if the mother treats the infant in an inconsistent, erratic, or irresponsible manner, then various types of insecure or disturbed attachments will form and transfer to relationships with siblings and others.)

Recent theorists in the developmental, social-personality, and clinical areas have been concerned with the transfer of attachment styles from childhood to adulthood. The style of the child's original attachment relationship to the mother exists as an internal working model within the child, and serves as a prototype for interpersonal relationships and multiple attachments in adulthood. In addition to Ainsworth's (1972) original three styles of infant attachment (secure, insecure-avoidant, insecure-resistant), additional styles have been identified. The central idea is that the way in which children learned to relate to the mother early in life is the way in which they prefer to relate to others in adulthood, resulting in varying degrees of happiness or maladjustment in adult life depending on whether the original attachment was secure or insecure (see Sperling and Berman, 1994, for further discussion of these approaches.)

The present author's adult attachment theory (Cicirelli, 1983, 1987, 1989a, in press) is somewhat different in that its original concern was only with the continuation of the unique or nonreplaceable attachment to the parent (usually the mother) throughout the life span in order to account for the sustained motivation of an adult child to protect the existence of the attachment figure by providing sustained help and care to a frail elderly parent. (The author's work focused on secure attachments; however, he agrees that insecure attachments also exist for a subgroup of individuals.) That is, a secure childhood attachment to a parent continues to endure in adulthood, sustained by a continuing reciprocal sensitive and responsive relationship between parent and adult child. However, the degree of secure attachment can vary throughout adult life, depending upon the circumstances of life and the continued reciprocity with the mother.

A second aspect of the author's theory applies to siblings. The secure or insecure attachment of the child to the mother serves as a prototype for the attachment style manifested in sibling relationships.

Thus, a secure or insecure (disturbed) attachment between siblings can be used to account for positive or negative sibling relationships in different parts of the life span. For example, secure attachments might explain siblings' help to one another while a disturbed attachment might explain sibling violence or sexual abuse. In general, different attachment styles used in multiple attachments with different siblings may help explain the quality of interpersonal relations between them. Thus, life span attachment theory has the potential to explain diverse phenomena occurring in sibling relationships across the life span.

Finally, insecure or disturbed attachments are perhaps more unstable than secure attachments. For example, a child's insecure–ambivalent attachment to a sibling may be expressed in greater vacillation in behavior toward that sibling. This may provide initial conditions that are highly sensitive to change, especially if unexpected familial or extrafamilial critical life events occur. In such a case, the direction of change over time in the sibling relationship may be unpredictable. Such phenomena might be interpreted in terms of chaos theory and tested in longitudinal studies. The work of Gottman (1991) in applying chaos theory to family changes over time could serve as a beginning for integrating the latter with attachment theory.

References

Abramovitch, R., Corter, C., & Lando, B. (1979). Sibling interaction in the home. *Child Development, 50,* 997–1003.

Abramovitch, R., Corter, C., & Pepler, D. (1980). Observations of mixed-sex sibling dyads. *Child Development, 51,* 1268–1271.

Abramovitch, R, Corter, C., Pepler, D. J., & Stanhope, L. (1986). Sibling and peer interaction: A final follow-up and a comparison. *Child Development, 57,* 217–229.

Abramovitch, R., Pepler, D., & Corter, C. (1982). Patterns of sibling interaction among preschoolage children. In M. E. Lamb & B. Sutton-Smith (Eds.), *Sibling relationships: Their nature and significance across the life span* (pp. 61–86). Hillsdale, N.J.: Erlbaum.

Abramovitch, R., Stanhope, L., Pepler, D., & Corter, C. (1987). The influence of Down's syndome in sibling interaction. *Journal of Child Psychology and Psychiatry, 28,* 865–879.

Adam, B. S., & Livingston, R. (1993). Sororocide in preteen girls: A case report and literature review. *Acta Paedopsychiatrica: International Journal of Child and Adolescent Psychiatry, 56,* 47–51.

Adams, B. N. (1968). *Kinship in an urban setting.* Chicago: Markham.

Adelson, L. (1972). The battering child. *Journal of the American Medical Association, 222,* 159–161.

Adler, A. (1959). *Understanding human nature.* New York: Fawcett.

Ainsworth, M. L. (1972). Attachment and dependency: A comparison. In J. L Gerwirtz (Ed.), *Attachment and dependency* (pp. 97–137). New York: Wiley.

Ainsworth, M. L. (1989). Attachments beyond infancy. *American Psychologist, 44,* 709–716.

Aldous, J. (1987). New views on the family life of the elderly and the near-elderly. *Journal of Marriage and the Family, 49,* 227–234.

Alpert, J. L. (1991, August). *Sibling, cousin, and peer child sexual abuse: Clinical implications.* Paper presented at the American Psychological Association convention, San Francisco.

Anderson, E. T., Hetherington, E. M., Reiss, D., & Howe, G. (1994). Parents' nonshared treatment of siblings and the development of social competence during adolescence. *Journal of Family Psychology, 8,* 303–320.

Antonucci, T. C. (1994). Attachment in adulthood and aging. In M. B. Sperling and W. B. Berman (Eds.), *Attachment in adults: Clinical and developmental perspectives* (pp. 256–272). New York: Guilford Press.

Appelbaum, D. R., & Burns, G. L. (1991). Unexpected childhood death: Posttraumatic stress disorder in surviving siblings and parents. *Journal of Clinical Child Psychology, 20,* 114–120.

Arndt, W. B., & Ladd, B. (1981). Sibling incest as an index of Oedipal conflict. *Journal of Assessment, 45,* 52–58.

225

Ascherman, L. I., & Safier, E. J. (1990). Sibling incest: A consequence of individual and family dysfunction. *Bulletin of the Menninger Clinic, 54,* 311–322.

Auletta, R., & DeRosa, A. P. (1991). Self-concepts of adolescent siblings of children with mental retardation. *Perceptual and Motor Skills, 73,* 211–214.

Avioli, P. S. (1989). The social support functions of siblings in later life: A theoretical model. *American Behavioral Scientist, 33,* 45–57.

Azmitia, M., & Hesser, J. (1993). Why siblings are important agents of cognitive development: A comparison of siblings and peers. *Child Development, 64,* 430–444.

Bagenholm, A., & Gilbert, C. (1991). Psychosocial effects on siblings of children with autism and mental retardation. *Journal of Mental Deficiency Research, 35,* 291–307.

Bahr, S. J. (1989). Prologue: A developmental overview of the aging family. In S. J. Bahr & E. T. Peterson (Eds.), *Aging and the family* (pp. 1–11). Lexington, MA: Lexington Press.

Balk, D. E. (1991a). Death and adolescent bereavement: Current research and future directions. *Journal of Adolescent Research, 6,* 7–27.

Balk, D. E. (1991b). Sibling death, adolescent bereavement, and religion. *Death Studies, 15,* 1–20.

Baltes, P. B. (1987). Theoretical propositions of life-span developmental psychology: On the dynamics between growth and decline. *Developmental Psychology, 23,* 611–626.

Bank, S. P. (1988). The stolen birthright: The adult sibling in individual therapy. In M. D. Kahn & K. G. Lewis (Eds.), *Siblings in therapy: Life span and clinical issues* (pp. 341–355). New York: W. W. Norton.

Bank, S. (1992). Remembering and reinterpreting sibling bonds. In F. Boer & J. Dunn (Eds.), *Children's sibling relationships: Developmental and clinical issues* (pp. 139–151). Hillsdale, NJ: Lawrence Erlbaum Associates.

Bank, S. P. & Kahn, M. D. (1982a). Intense sibling loyalties. In M. Lamb & B. Sutton-Smith (Eds.), *Sibling relationships: Their nature and significance across the life span* (pp. 251–266). Hillsdale, NJ: Erlbaum.

Bank, S. P., & Kahn, M. D. (1982b). *The sibling bond.* New York: Basic Books.

Basso, E. B. (1984). A husband for his daughter, a wife for her son: Strategies for selecting a set of in-laws among the Kalapalo. In K. M. Kensinger (Ed.), *Marriage practices in lowland South America* (pp. 33–44). Urbana, IL: University of Illinois Press.

Beals, A. R., & Eason, M. A. (1993). Siblings in North America and South Asia. In C. W. Nuckolls (Ed.), *Siblings in South Asia: Brothers and sisters in cultural context* (pp. 71–101). New York: Guilford Press.

Bedford, V. H. (1989a). A comparison of thematic apperceptions of sibling affiliation, conflict, and separation at two periods of adulthood. *International Journal of Aging and Human Development, 28,* 53–66.

Bedford, V. H. (1989b). Understanding the value of siblings in old age. *American Behavioral Scientist, 33,* 33–44.

Bedford, V. H. (1990, July). Changing affect toward siblings and the transition to old age. *Proceedings of the Second International Conference on the Future of Adult Life.* Leeuwenhorst, The Netherlands.

Beer, W. R. (1989). *Strangers in the house: The world of stepsiblings and half-siblings* (pp. 63–85). New Brunswick, NJ: Transaction Publishers.

Begun, A. L. (1989). Sibling relationships involving developmentally disabled people. *American Journal on Mental Retardation, 93,* 566–574.

Bengtson, V. L., & Mangen, D. J. (1988). Family intergenerational solidarity revisited: Suggestions for future management. In D. J. Mangen, V. L. Bengtson, & P. H. Landry, Jr. (Eds.), *Measurement of intergenerational relations* (pp. 222–238). Newbury Park, CA: Sage.

Berndt, T. J., & Bulleit, T. N. (1985). Effects of sibling relationships on preschoolers' behavior at home and at school. *Developmental Psychology, 21,* 761–767.

Boer, F. (1990). *Sibling relationships in middle childhood*. Leiden: DSWO University of Leiden Press.

Borland, D. C. (1989). The sibling relationship as a housing alternative to institutionalization in later life. In L. Ade-Ridder & C. B. Hennon (Eds.), *Lifestyles of the elderly* (pp. 205–219). New York: Human Sciences Press.

Bowlby, J. (1979). *The making and breaking of affectional bonds*. London: Tavistock.

Bowlby, J. (1980). *Attachment and loss: Vol. 3. Loss, stress, and depression*. New York: Basic Books.

Boyce, G. C., & Barnett, W. S. (1993). Siblings of persons with mental retardation: A historical perspective and recent findings. In Z. Stoneman & P. W. Berman (Eds.), *The effects of mental retardation, disability, and illness on sibling relationships: Research issues and challenges* (pp. 145–184). Baltimore: Paul H. Brookes Publishing Company.

Brady, E. M., & Noberini, M. R. (1987, August). *Sibling support in the context of a model of sibling solidarity*. Paper presented at the 95th Annual Meeting of the American Psychological Association, New York.

Bretherton, I. (1992). Attachment and bonding. In V. G. Van Hasselt & M. Hersen (Eds.), *Handbook of social development: A lifespan perspective* (pp. 133–155). New York: Basic Books.

Brody, E. M. (1985). Parent care as a normative family stress. *The Gerontologist, 25*, 19–29,

Brody, E. M. (1990). *Women in the middle: Their parent care years*. New York: Springer-Verlag.

Brody, E. M., Hoffman, C., Kleban, M. H., & Schoonover, C. B. (1989). Caregiving daughters and their local siblings: Perceptions, strains, and interactions. *Gerontologist, 29*, 529–538.

Brody, E. M., Kleban, M. H., Hoffman, C., & Schoonover, C. B. (1988). Adult daughters and parent care: A comparison of one-, two-, and three-generation households. *Home Health Care Services Quarterly, 9*, 19–45.

Brody, E. M., Litvin, S. J., Albert, S. M., & Hoffman, C. J. (1994). Marital status of daughters and patterns of parent care. *Journal of Gerontology: Social Sciences, 49*, S95–103.

Brody, E. M, & Schoonover, C. B. (1986). Patterns of parent care when adult daughters work and when they do not. *The Gerontologist, 26*, 372–381.

Brody, G. H., & Stoneman, Z. (1987). Sibling conflict: Contributions of the siblings themselves, the parent-sibling relationships, and the broader family system. *Journal of Children in Contemporary Society, 19*, 39–53.

Brody, G. H., & Stoneman, Z. (1990). Sibling relationships. In E. S. Irving & G. H. Brody (Eds.), *Methods of family research: Biographies of research projects. Vol. 1. Normal projects* (pp. 189–212). Hillsdale, NJ: Lawrence Erlbaum Associates.

Brody, G. H., & Stoneman, Z. (1993). Parameters for inclusion in studies on sibling relationships: Some heuristic suggestions. In Z. Stoneman & P. W. Berman (Eds.), *The effects of mental retardation, disability, and illness on sibling relationships: Research issues and challenges* (pp. 275–286). Baltimore: Paul H. Brookes Publishing Company.

Brody, G. H., Stoneman, Z., & Burke, M. (1987). Child temperaments, maternal differential behavior, and sibling relationships. *Developmental Psychology, 23*, 354–362.

Brody, G. H., Stoneman, Z., Davis, C. H., & Crapps, J. M. (1991). Observations of the role relations and behavior between older children with mental retardation and their younger siblings. *American Journal on Mental Retardation, 95*, 527–536.

Brody, G. H., Stoneman, Z., MacKinnon, C. E. & MacKinnon, R. (1985). Role relationships and behavior beween preschool-aged and school-aged sibling pairs. *Developmental Psychology, 21*, 124–129.

Brody, G. H., Stoneman, Z., & McCoy, J. K. (1994). Contributions of family relationships and child temperaments to longitudinal variations in sibling relationship quality and sibling relationship styles. *Journal of Family Psychology, 8*, 274–286.

Brody, G. H., Stoneman, Z, McCoy, J. K., & Forehand, R. (1992). Contemporaneous and longitudinal associations of sibling conflict with family relationships assessments and family discussions about sibling problems. *Child Development, 63*, 391–400.

Brown, J. R., & Dunn, J. (1992). Talk with your mother or your sibling? Developmental changes in early family conversations about feelings. *Child Development, 63,* 336–349.

Brown, S. C. (1991). Conceptualizing and defining disability. In S. Thompson-Hoffman & I. C. Storck (Eds.), *Disability in the United States: A portrait from national data.* New York: Springer-Verlag.

Bryant, B. K. (1982). Sibling relationships in middle childhood. In M. E. Lamb & B. Sutton-Smith (Eds.), *Sibling relationships: Their nature and significance across the life span* (pp. 87–121). Hillsdale, NJ: Erlbaum.

Bryant, B. K. (1989). The child's perspective of sibling caretaking and its relevance to understanding social-emotional functioning and development. In P. G. Zukow (Ed.), *Sibling interaction across cultures: Theoretical and methodological issues* (pp. 143–164). New York: Springer-Verlag.

Bryant, B. K. (1992). Sibling caretaking: Providing emotional support during middle childhood. In F. Boer & J. Dunn (Eds.), *Children's sibling relationships: Developmental and clinical issues* (pp. 55–69). Hillsdale, NJ: Lawrence Erlbaum Associates.

Bryant, B., & Crockenberg, S. (1980). Correlates and dimensions of prosocial behavior: A study of female siblings with their mothers. *Child Development, 51,* 529–544.

Buhrmester, D. (1992). The developmental courses of sibling and peer relationships. In F. Boer & J. Dunn (Eds.), *Children's sibling relationships: Developmental and clinical issues* (pp. 19–40). Hillsdale, NJ: Lawrence Erlbaum Associates.

Buhrmester, D., & Furman, W. (1987). The development of companionship and intimacy. *Child Development, 58,* 1101–1113.

Buhrmester, D., & Furman, W. (1990). Perceptions of sibling relationships during middle childhood and adolescence. *Child Development, 61,* 1387–1398.

Butler, R. N. (1963). The life review: An interpretation of reminiscence in the aged. *Psychiatry, 26,* 65–76.

Butcher, K. F., & Case, A. (1994). The effect of sibling sex composition on women's education and earnings. *Quarterly Journal of Economics, 109,* 531–563.

Cain, A. C., Fast, I., & Erickson, M. E. (1964). Children's disturbed reactions to the death of a sibling. *American Journal of Orthopsychiatry, 34,* 741–745.

Cantor, M. (1979). Neighbors and friends: An overlooked resource in the informal support system. *Research on Aging, 1,* 434–463.

Carroll, R. (1988). Siblings in the family business. In M. D. Kahn & K. G. Lewis (Eds.), *Siblings in therapy: Life span and clinical issues* (pp. 379–398). New York: Norton.

Chee, T. S. (1979). Social change and the Malay family. In E. C. Y. Kuo & A. K. Wong (Eds.), *The contemporary family in Singapore: Structure and change* (pp. 88–114). Singapore: University of Singapore Press.

Chesler, M. A., Allswede, J., & Barbarin, O. O. (1991). Voices from the edge of the family: Siblings of children with cancer. *Psychosocial Oncology, 9,* 19–42.

Church, M. (1986). Issues in psychological therapy with elderly people. In I. Hanley & M. Gilhooly (Eds.), *Psychological therapies for the elderly* (pp. 1–21). London: Croom Helm.

Cicirelli, V. G. (1972). The effect of sibling relationships on concept learning of young children taught by child teachers. *Child Development, 43,* 282–287.

Cicirelli, V. G. (1973). Effects of sibling structure and interaction on children's categorization style. *Developmental Psychology, 9,* 132–139.

Cicirelli, V. G. (1974). Relationship of sibling structure and interaction to younger sib's conceptual style. *Journal of Genetic Psychology, 125,* 37–49.

Cicirelli, V. G. (1975). Effects of mother and older sibling on the problem solving behavior of the younger child. *Developmental Psychology, 11,* 749–756.

Cicirelli, V. G. (1977). Relationship of siblings to the elderly person's feelings and concerns. *Journal of Gerontology, 32*, 317–322.

Cicirelli, V. G. (1978). The relationship of sibling structure to intellectual abilities and achievement. *Review of Educational Research, 48*, 365–379.

Cicirelli, V. G. (1979, May). *Social services for elderly in relation to the kin network.* Report to the NRTA-AARP Andrus Foundation.

Cicirelli, V. G. (1980a). Relationship of family background variables to locus of control in the elderly. *Journal of Gerontology, 35*, 108–115.

Cicirelli, V. G. (1980b). Sibling influence in adulthood: A life span perspective. In L. W. Poon (Ed.), *Aging in the 1980's* (pp. 455–462). Washington, DC: American Psychological Association.

Cicirelli, V. G. (1981). *Helping elderly parents: Role of adult children.* Boston: Auburn House.

Cicirelli, V. G. (1982). Sibling influence throughout the lifespan. In M. E. Lamb, & B. Sutton-Smith (Eds.), *Sibling relationships: Their nature and significance across the lifespan* (pp. 267–284). Hillsdale, NJ: Erlbaum.

Cicirelli, V. G. (1983). Adult children's attachment and helping behavior to elderly parents: A path model. *Journal of Marriage and the Family, 45*, 815–822.

Cicirelli, V. G. (1984). Marital disruption and adult children's perception of their sibling's help to elderly parents. *Journal of Family Relations, 33*, 613–621.

Cicirelli, V. G. (1985a). The role of siblings as family caregivers. In W. J. Sauer & R. T. Coward (Eds.), *Social support networks and the care of the elderly* (pp. 93–107). New York: Springer-Verlag.

Cicirelli, V. G. (1985b). Sibling relationships throughout the life cycle. In L. L'Abate (Ed.), *The handbook of family psychology and therapy. Vol. 1* (pp 177–214). Homewood, IL: Dorsey Press.

Cicirelli, V. G. (1987, July). *Attachment theory and sibling psychological support in old age.* Paper presented to the IXth Biennial Meetings of the International Society for the Study of Behavioural Development, Tokyo.

Cicirelli, V. G. (1988). Interpersonal relationships among elderly siblings: Implications for clinical practice. In M. Kahn & K. G. Lewis (Eds.), *Siblings in therapy* (pp. 435–456), New York: W. W. Norton.

Cicirelli, V. G. (1989a). Feelings of attachment to siblings and well being in later life. *Psychology and Aging, 4*, 211–216.

Cicirelli, V. G. (1989b, July). *Influence of siblings' death on subjective well-being in old age.* Paper presented at the Xth Biennial Meetings of the International Society for the Study of Behavioural Development, Jyvaskyla, Finland.

Cicirelli, V. G. (1990). Family support in relation to health problems of the elderly. In T. H. Brubaker (Ed.), *Family relationships in later life* (2nd ed., pp. 218–228). Newbury Park, CA: Sage.

Cicirelli, V. G. (1991). Sibling relationships in adulthood. In S. P. Pfeifer & M. B. Sussman (Eds.), *Families: Intergenerational and generational connections* (pp. 291–310). New York: Haworth Press.

Cicirelli, V. G. (1992a). The influence of siblings upon beliefs and decision making. In *Family caregiving: Autonomous and paternalistic decision making.* (pp. 173–188). Newbury Park, CA: Sage.

Cicirelli, V. G. (1992b). Siblings as caregivers in middle and old age. In J. E. Dwyer & R. T. Coward (Eds.), *Gender, families, and elder care* (pp. 84–101). Newbury Park, CA: Sage.

Cicirelli, V. G. (1993a). Intergenerational communication in the mother-daughter dyad regarding caregiving decisions. In N. Coupland & J. F. Nussbaum (Eds.), *Discourse and lifespan identity* (pp. 215–236). Newbury Park, CA: Sage.

Cicirelli, V. G. (1993b). The individual in the family life cycle. In L. L'Abate (Ed.), *Handbook of developmental psychology and psychopathology* (2nd ed., pp. 27–43). New York: Wiley and Sons.

Cicirelli, V. G. (1993c). The longest bond: The sibling life cycle. In L. L'Abate (Ed.), *Handbook of developmental psychology and psychopathology* (2nd ed., pp. 44–59). New York: Wiley.

Cicirelli, V. G. (1994a). Sibling relationships in cross-cultural perspective. *Journal of Marriage and the Family, 56,* 7–20.

Cicirelli, V. G. (1994b, November). *Sibling relationships over the life course.* Paper presented at the 49th Annual Scientific Meeting of the Gerontological Society of America, Atlanta.

Cicirelli, V. G. (in press). Sibling relationships in middle and old age. In G. Brody (Ed.), *Sibling relationships: Their causes and consequences.* (Advances in Applied Development series.) Norwood, NJ: Ablex.

Cicirelli, V. G., Coward, R. T., Dwyer, J. W. (1992). Siblings as caregivers for impaired elders. *Research on Aging, 14,* 331–350.

Clark, M. & Anderson, B. (1967). *Culture and aging: An anthropological study of older Americans.* Springfield, IL: C. C. Thomas.

Cleveland, D. W., & Miller, N. (1977). Attitudes and life commitments of older siblings of mentally retarded adults: An exploratory study. *Mental Retardation, 15,* 38–41.

Cole, E. (1982). Sibling incest: The myth of benign sibling incest. *Women and Therapy, 1,* 79–89.

Coleman, F. W., & Coleman, W. S. (1984). Helping siblings and other peers cope with dying. In H. Wass & C. A. Corr (Eds.), *Childhood and death* (pp. 129–150). Cambridge: Hemisphere Press.

Coleman, P. (1986). Issues in the therapeutic use of reminiscence with elderly people. In I. Hanley & M. Gilhooly (Eds.), *Psychological therapies for the elderly* (pp. 41–64). London: Croom Helm.

Conger, K. J., & Conger, R. D. (1994). Differential parenting and change in sibling differences in delinquency. *Journal of Family Psychology, 8,* 287–302.

Connidis, I. A. (1989). Siblings as friends in later life. *American Behavioral Scientist, 33,* 81–93.

Connidis, I. A. (1992). Life transitions and the adult sibling tie: A qualitative study. *Journal of Marriage and the Family, 54,* 972–982.

Connidis, I. A. (1994). Sibling support in older age. *Journal of Gerontology: Social Sciences, 49,* S309–317.

Connidis, I. A., & Davies, L. (1990). Confidants and companions in later life: The place of family and friends. *Journal of Gerontology: Social Sciences, 45,* 141–149.

Cook, A. S., & Oltjenbruns, K. A. (1989). *Dying and Grieving.* New York: Holt, Rinehart, & Winston.

Cornell-Pedrick, C. P., & Gelles, R. J. (1982). Adolescent to parent violence. *Urban and Social Change Review, 15,* 8–14.

Coward, R. T., & Dwyer, J. W. (1990). The association of gender, sibling network composition, and patterns of parent care by adult children. *Research on Aging, 12,* 158–181.

Craft, M. J., Lakin, J. A., Oppliger, R. A., Clancy, G. M., & Vanderlinden, D. W. (1990). Siblings as change agents for promoting the functional status of children with cerebral palsy. *Developmental Medicine and Child Neurology, 32,* 1049–1057.

Crocker, W. H. (1984). Canela marriage: Factors in change. In K. M. Kensinger (Ed.), *Marriage practices in lowland South America* (pp. 63–98). Urbana: University of Illinois Press.

Cumming, E., & Henry, W. (1961). *Growing old.* New York: Basic Books.

Daie, N., Witztum, E., & Eleff, M. (1989). Long-term effects of sibling incest. *Journal of Clinical Psychiatry, 50,* 428–431.

Daniels, D. (1986). Differential experiences of siblings in the same family as predictors of adolescent sibling personality differences. *Journal of Personality and Social Psychology, 51,* 339–346.

Daniels, D., Dunn, J., Furstenberg, F. F., & Plomin, R. (1985). Environmental differences within the family and adjustment differences within pairs of adolescent siblings. *Child Development, 56,* 764–774.

Davies, B. (1991a). Long term outcomes of adolescent sibling bereavement. *Journal of Adolescent Research, 6,* 83–96.

Davies, B. (1991b). Responses of children to the death of a sibling. In D. Papadatos & C. Papadatos (Eds.), *Children and death. Series in death education, aging, and health care* (pp. 125–133). New York: Hemisphere.

Deal, J. E., Halverson, C. F., Jr., & Wampler, K. S. (1994). Sibling similarity as an individual differences variable: Within-family measures of shared environment. In E. M. Hetherington, D. Reiss, & R. Plomin (Eds.), *Separate social worlds of siblings: The impact of nonshared environment on development* (pp. 205–218). Hillsdale, NJ: Erlbaum.

Dean-Oswald, H. (1985). Sri Lankan families. In D. Storer (Ed.), *Ethnic family values in Australia* (pp. 227–261). Sydney, Australia: Prentice-Hall.

de Jong, A. R. (1989). Sexual interactions among siblings and cousins: Experimentation or exploitation? *Child Abuse & Neglect, 13,* 271–279.

de Young, M. (1982). *The sexual victimization of children.* London: McFarland.

Demi, A. S., & Howell, C. (1991). Hiding and healing: Resolving the suicide of a parent or sibling. *Archives of Psychiatric Nursing, 5,* 350–356.

de Munck, V. C. (1990). Cross-sibling relationships and the dowry in Sri Lanka. *Ethnos, 55,* 56–73.

de Munck, V. C. (1993). The dialectics and norms of self interest: Reciprocity among cross-siblings in a Sri Lankan Muslim community. In C. W. Nuckolls (Ed.), *Siblings in South Asia: Brothers and sisters in cultural context* (pp. 143–162). New York: Guilford Publications.

Derne, S. (1993). Equality and hierarchy between adult brothers: Culture and sibling relations in North Indian urban joint families. In C. W. Nuckolls (Ed.), *Siblings in South Asia: Brothers and sisters in cultural context* (pp. 165–189). New York: Guilford Press.

Dole, G. E. (1984). The structure of Kuikuru marriage. In K. M. Kensinger (Ed.), *Marriage practices in lowland South America* (pp. 45–62). Urbana, IL: University of Illinois Press.

Duck, S. (1992). *Human relationships* (2nd ed.). Newbury Park, CA: Sage.

Dunn, J. (1984). Sibling studies and the developmental impact of critical incidents. In P. B. Baltes & O. G. Brim (Eds.), *Life span development and behavior* (Vol. 6, pp. 335–353). Orlando, FL: Academic Press.

Dunn, J. (1985). *Sisters and brothers.* Cambridge, MA: Harvard University Press.

Dunn, J. (1988). *The beginnings of social understanding.* Cambridge, MA: Harvard University Press.

Dunn, J. (1989). Siblings and the development of social understanding in early childhood. In P. G. Zukow (Ed.), *Sibling interaction across cultures: Theoretical and methodological issues* (pp. 106–116). New York: Springer-Verlag.

Dunn, J. (1992). Introduction. In F. Boer & J. Dunn (Eds.), *Children's sibling relationships: Developmental and clinical issues* (pp. xiii–xvi). Hillsdale, NJ: Erlbaum.

Dunn, J. (1993). Perspectives on siblings: A developmental psychologist's view. In C. W. Nuckolls (Ed.), *Siblings in South Asia: Brothers and sisters in cultural context* (pp. 235–240). New York: Guilford Press.

Dunn, J., Beardsall, L., & Slomkowski, C. (1993). *Predicting perceived self-competence in early adolescence: A longitudinal analysis of siblings.* Manuscript submitted for publication.

Dunn, J., & Kendrick, C. (1981). Social behavior of young siblings in the family context: Differences between the same-sex and different-sexed dyads. *Child Development, 52,* 1265–1273.

Dunn, J., & Kendrick, C. (1982a). Siblings and their mothers: Developing relationships within the family. In M. E. Lamb & B. Sutton-Smith (Eds.), *Sibling relationships: Their nature and significance across the life span* (pp. 39–60). Hillsdale, NJ: Erlbaum.

Dunn, J., & Kendrick, C. (1982b). *Siblings: Love, envy, and understanding.* Cambridge, MA: Harvard University Press.

Dunn, J, & Kendrick, C. (1982c). The speech of two- and three-year olds to infant siblings: "Baby talk" and the context of communication. *Journal of Child Language, 9,* 579–595.

Dunn, J., & McGuire, S. (1994). Young children's nonshared experiences: A summary of studies in Cambridge and Colorado. In E. M. Hetherington, D. Reiss, & R. Plomin (Eds.), *Separate social worlds of siblings: The impact of nonshared environment on development* (pp. 111–128). Hillsdale, NJ: Erlbaum.

Dunn, J., & Munn, P. (1985). Becoming a family member: Family conflict and the development of social understanding in the second year. *Child Development, 56,* 480–492.

Dunn, J., & Munn, P. (1986a). Sibling quarrels and maternal intervention: Individual differences in understanding and aggression. *Journal of Child Psychology & Psychiatry, 27,* 583–595.

Dunn, J., & Munn, P. (1986b). Siblings and the development of prosocial behaviour. *International Journal of Behavior Development, 9,* 265–284.

Dunn, J., & Munn, P. (1987). Development of justifications in disputes with mother and sibling. *Developmental Psychology, 23,* 791–798.

Dunn, J., Plomin, R., & Daniels, D. (1986). Consistency and change in mothers' behavior towards young siblings. *Child Development, 57,* 348–356.

Dunn, J., & Shatz, M. (1989). Becoming a conversationalist despite (or because of) having a sibling. *Child Development, 60,* 399–410.

Dunn, J., Slomkowski, C., & Beardsall, L. (1994). Sibling relationships from the preschool period through middle childhood and early adolescence. *Developmental Psychology, 30,* 321–324.

Dunn, J., Slomkowski, C., Beardsall, L., & Rende, R. (1994). Adjustment in middle childhood and early adolescence: Links with earlier and contemporary sibling relationships. *Journal of Child Psychology & Psychiatry, 35,* 491–504.

Dunn, J., & Stocker, C. (1989). The significance of differences in siblings' experiences within the family. In K. Kreppner & R. M. Lerner (Eds.), *Family systems and life-span development* (pp. 289–301). Hillsdale, NJ: Erlbaum.

Dunn, J., Stocker, C., & Plomin, R. (1990a). Assessing the relationship between young siblings: A research note. *Journal of Child Psychology and Psychiatry and Allied Disciplines, 31,* 983–991.

Dunn, J., Stocker, C., & Plomin, R. (1990b). Nonshared experiences within the family: Correlates of behavior problems in middle childhood. *Development and Psychopathology, 2,* 113–126.

Dwyer, J. W., Henretta, J. C., Coward, R. T., & Barton, A. (1992). Changes in the helping behaviors of adult children as caregivers. *Research on Aging, 14,* 351–375.

Dyson, L. L. (1989). Adjustment of siblings of handicapped children: A comparison. *Journal of Pediatric Psychology, 14,* 215–229.

Dyson, L., Edgar, E., & Crnic, K. (1989). Psychological predictors of adjustment by siblings of developmentally disabled children. *American Journal on Mental Retardation, 94,* 292–302.

East, P. L., & Rook, K. S. (1992). Compensatory patterns of support among children's peer relationships: A test using school friends, nonschool friends, and siblings. *Developmental Psychology, 28*, 163–172.

Eggebeen, D. J. (1992). Changes in sibling configurations for American pre-school children. *Social Biology, 39*, 27–44.

Erikson, E. H. (1968). *Identity, youth, and crisis.* New York: Norton.

Ervin-Tripp, S. (1989). Sisters and brothers. In P. G. Zukow (Ed.), *Sibling interaction across cultures: Theoretical and methodological issues* (pp. 184–195). New York: Springer-Verlag.

Essman, C. S. (1977). Sibling relations as socialization for parenthood. *Family Coordinator, 26*, 259–262.

Fanos, J. H., & Nickerson, B. G. (1991). Long-term effects of sibling death during adolescence. *Journal of Adolescent Research, 6*, 70–82.

Feinberg, R. (1983). The meaning of "sibling" on Anuta. In M. Marshall (Ed.), *Siblingship in Oceania: Studies in the meaning of kin relations* (pp. 105–148). Lanham, MD: University Press of America.

Feld, S. L. (1988). *Violence as a strategy of the weak against the strong: The case of siblings.* Durham, NH: Family Research Laboratory, University of New Hampshire Press.

Felson, R. B. (1983). Aggression and violence between siblings. *Social Psychology Quarterly, 46*, 271–285.

Felson, R., & Russo, N. (1988). Parental punishment and sibling aggression. *Social Psychology Quarterly, 51*, 11–18.

Finkelhor, D. (1979). *Sexually victimized children.* New York: Free Press.

Finkelhor, D. (1980). Sex among siblings: A survey on prevalence, variety, and effects. *Archives of sexual behavior, 9*, 171–194.

Finkelhor, D. H., & Hotaling, G. T. (1984). Sexual abuse in the national incidence study of child abuse and neglect: An appraisal. *Child Abuse and Neglect, 8*, 23–33.

Ford, D. H., & Lerner, R. M. (1992). *Developmental systems theory: An integrative approach.* Newbury Park, CA: Sage.

Furman, W., & Buhrmester, D. (1982). The contribution of peers and siblings to the parenting process. In M. Kostelnik (Ed.), *Child Nurturance: Vol. 2. Patterns of supplementary parenting* (pp. 69–100). New York: Plenum.

Furman, W., & Buhrmester, D. (1985). Children's perceptions of the qualities of sibling relationships. *Child Development, 56*, 448–461.

Furman, W., Jones, L., Buhrmester, D., & Adler, T. (1989). Children's, parents', and observers' perspectives on sibling relationships. In P. G. Zukow (Ed.), *Sibling interaction across cultures: Theoretical and methodological issues* (pp. 165–183). New York: Springer-Verlag.

Gaffney, D. A., Jones, E. T., & Dunne-Maxim, K. (1992). Support groups for sibling suicide survivors. *Crisis, 13*, 76–81.

Gamble, W. C., & E. J. Woulbroun (1993). Measurement considerations in the identification and assessment of stressors and coping strategies. In Z. Stoneman & P. W. Berman (Eds.), *The effects of mental retardation, disability, and illness on sibling relationships: Research issues and challenges* (pp. 287–319). Baltimore: Paul H. Brookes.

Glaser, B. C. (1978). *Theoretical sensitivity.* Mill Valley, CA: Sociology Press.

Glaser, B. C., & Strauss, A. L. (1967). *The discovery of grounded theory.* New York: Aldine.

Goetting, A. (1986). The developmental tasks of siblingship over the life cycle. *Journal of Marriage and the Family, 48*, 703–714.

Gold, D. T. (1986). *Sibling relationships in retrospect: A study of reminiscence in old age.* Doctoral dissertation. Northwestern University, Evanston, IL. [*Dissertation Abstracts International, 47*, 2274A.]

Gold, D. T. (1987, August). *Generational solidarity: Sibling ties in late life.* Paper presented at the meeting of the American Psychological Association, New York.

Gold, D. T. (1989a). Generational solidarity. *American Behavioral Scientist, 33,* 19–32.

Gold, D. T. (1989b). Sibling relationships: A typology. *International Journal of Aging and Human Development, 28,* 37–51.

Gold, D. T. (1990). Late-life sibling relationships: Does race affect typological distribution? *The Gerontologist, 30,* 741–748.

Gold, D. T., Woodbury, M. A., & George, L. K. (1990). Relationship classification using grade of membership analysis: A typology of sibling relationships in later life. *Journal of Gerontology: Social Sciences, 45,* S43–S51.

Goodale, J. C. (1983). Siblings as spouses: The reproduction and replacement of Kaulong society. In M. Marshall (Ed.), *Siblingship in Oceania: Studies in the Meaning of Kin Relations* (pp. 275–305). Lanham, MD: University Press of America.

Gorer, G. (1967). *Death, grief, and mourning.* Garden City, NY: Doubleday.

Gottman, J. M. (1991). Chaos and regulated change in familiies: A metaphor for the study of transition. In P. A. Cowan & M. Hetherington (Eds.), *Family transitions* (pp. 247–272). Hillsdale, NJ: Erlbaum.

Graham-Bermann, S. A., Cutler, S. E., Litzenberger, B. W., & Schwartz, W. E. (1994). Perceived conflict and violence in childhood sibling relationships and later emotional adjustment. *Journal of Family Psychology, 8,* 85–97.

Greenwald, E., & Leitenberg, H. (1989). Long-term effects of sexual experiences with siblings and nonsiblings during childhood. *Archives of Sexual Behavior, 18,* 389–399.

Griffiths, D. L., & Unger, D. G. (1994). Views about planning for the future among parents and siblings of adults with mental retardation. *Family Relations, 43,* 221–227.

Grossman, F. K. (1972). *Brothers and sisters of retarded children: An exploratory study.* Syracuse, NY: Syracuse University Press.

Guerriero, A. M., & Fleming, S. J. (1985, June). *Adolescent bereavement: A longitudinal study.* Paper presented at the Annual Meeting of the Canadian Psychological Society, Halifax, Nova Scotia.

Gully, K., Dengerink, H. A., Pepping, M., & Bergstrom, D. (1981). Research note: Sibling contribution to violent behavior. *Journal of Marriage and the Family, 43,* 333–337.

Hamlin, E. R., & Timberlake, E. M. (1981). Sibling group treatment. *Clinical Social Work Journal, 9,* 101–110.

Harris, E. G. (1988). My brother's keeper: Siblings of chronic patients as allies in family treatment. In M. D. Kahn & K. G. Lewis (Eds.), *Siblings in therapy: Life span and clinical issues* (pp. 314–337). New York: Norton.

Hartup, W. W. (1975). The origins of friendships. In M. Lewis & L. A. Rosenblum (Eds.), *The origins of behavior. Vol. 4: Friendship and peer relations* (pp. 11–26). New York: Wiley.

Hecht, J. A. (1983). The cultural contexts of siblingship in Pukapuka. M. Marshall (Ed.), *Siblingship in Oceania: Studies in the meaning of kin relations* (pp. 53–77). Lanham, MD: University Press of America.

Herr, J. J., & Weakland, J. H. (1979). *Counseling elders and their families: Practical techniques for applied gerontology.* New York: Springer-Verlag.

Hetherington, E. M. (1988). Parents, children, and siblings six years after divorce. In R. A. Hinde & J. Stevenson-Hinde (Eds.), *Relationships within families: Mutual influences* (pp. 311–331). New York: Oxford University Press.

Hinde, R. A. (1981). The bases of a science of interpersonal relationships. In S. Duck & R. Gilmore (Eds.), *Personal relationships (Vol. 1): Studying personal relationships* (pp. 1–22). New York: Academic Press.

Hoff-Ginsberg, E., & Krueger, W. M. (1991). Older siblings as conversational partners. *Merrill-Palmer Quarterly, 37*, 465–481.

Hoffman, L. W. (1991). The influence of the family environment on personality: Accounting for sibling differences. *Psychological Bulletin, 110*, 187–203.

Hogan, N., & DeSantis, L. (1992). Adolescent sibling bereavement: An ongoing attachment. *Qualitative Health Research, 2*, 159–177.

Hogan, N. S., & Greenfield, D. B. (1991). Adolescent sibling bereavement symptomatology in a large community sample. *Journal of Adolescent Research, 6*, 97–112.

Howe, N. (1991). Sibling-directed internal state language, perspective-taking, and affective behavior. *Child Development, 62*, 1503–1512.

Howe, N., & Ross, H. S. (1990). Socialization, perspective-taking, and the sibling relationship. *Developmental Psychology, 26*, 160–165.

Hoyt, D. R., & Babchuk, N. (1983). Adult kinship-networks: The selective formation of intimate ties with kin. *Social Forces, 62*, 84–101.

Huntsman, J. (1983). Complementary and similar kinsmen in Tokelau. In M. Marshall (Ed.), *Siblingship in Oceania: Studies in the Meaning of Kin Relations* (pp. 79–103). Lanham, MD: University Press of America.

Huston, T. L., & Robins, E. (1982). Conceptual and methodological issues in studying close relationships. *Journal of Marriage and the Family, 44*, 902–925.

Jackson, J. E. (1984). Vaupes marriage practices. In K. M. Kensinger (Ed.), *Marriage practices in lowland South America* (pp. 156–179). Urbana, IL: University of Illinois Press.

Jacob, T., Tennenbaum, D., Seilhamer, R. A., Bargiel, K., & Sharon, T. (1994). Reactivity effects during naturalistic observations of distressed and nondistressed families. *Journal of Family Psychology, 8*, 354–363.

Jesse, R. C. (1988). Children of alcoholics: Their sibling world. In M. D. Kahn & K. G. Lewis (Eds.), *Siblings in therapy: Life span and clinical issues* (pp. 228–252). New York: Norton.

Johnson, C. L. (1982). Sibling solidarity: Its origin and functioning in Italian-American families. *Journal of Marriage and the Family, 44*, 155–167.

Johnson, C. L. (1985). *Growing up and growing old in Italian-American families*. New Brunswick, NJ: Rutgers University Press.

Johnson, C. L. (1988). Relationships among family members and friends in later life. In R. Milardo (Ed.), *Families and social networks* (pp. 168–189). Newbury Park, CA: Sage Publications.

Johnson, C. L., & Catalano, D. J. (1981). Childless elderly and their family supports. *The Gerontologist, 21*, 610–618.

Justice, B., & Justice, R. (1979). *The broken taboo: Sex in the family*. New York: Human Sciences Press.

Kahn, M. D. (1983). Sibling relationships in later life. *Medical Aspects of Human Sexuality, 17*, 94–103.

Kahn, M. D., & Bank, S. (1981). In pursuit of sisterhood. *Family Process, 20*(1), 85–95.

Kahn, M. D., & Lewis, K. G. (Eds.)(1988). *Siblings in therapy: Life span and clinical issues*. New York: W. W. Norton.

Kaplan, J. O. (1984). Dualisms as an expression of differences and danger: Marriage exchange and reciprocity among the Piaroa of Venezuela. In K. M. Kensinger (Ed.), *Marriage practices in lowland South America* (pp. 127–155). Urbana, IL: University of Illinois Press.

Kaplan, L., Hennon, C. B., & Ade-Ritter, L. (1993). Splitting custody of children between parents: Impact on the sibling system. *Families in Society, 74*, 131–144.

Kasl, S. V., & Berkman, L. F. (1981). Some psychosocial influences on the health status of the elderly: The perspective of social epidemiology. In J. L. McGaugh & S. B. Kiesler (Eds.), *Aging: Biology and behavior* (pp. 345–377). New York: Academic.

Kausler, D. H. (1991). *Experimental psychology, cognition, and human aging* (2nd ed.). New York: Springer-Verlag.

Kelley, H. H., Berscheid, E., Christensen, A., Harvey, J. H., Huston, T. L., Levinger, G., McClintock, E., Peplau, L. A., & Peterson, D. R. (1983). Analyzing close relationships. In H. H. Kelley, E. Berscheid, A. Christensen, J. H. Harvey, T. L. Huston, G. Levinger, E. McClintock, L. A. Peplau, & D. R. Peterson (Eds.), *Close relationships* (pp. 20–67). New York: W. H. Freeman.

Kelly, L. (1988). *Surviving sexual violence*. Minneapolis: University of Minnesota Press.

Kempton, T., Armistead, L., Wierson, M., & Forehand, R. (1991). Presence of a sibling as a potential buffer following parental divorce: An examination of young adolescents. *Journal of Clinical Psychology, 20*, 434–438.

Kendrick, C., & Dunn, J. (1983). Sibling quarrels and maternal responses. *Developmental Psychology, 19*, 62–70.

Kensinger, K. M. (1984). An emic model of Cashinahua marriage. In K. M. Kensinger (Ed.), *Marriage practices in lowland South America* (pp. 221–251). Urbana, IL: University of Illinois Press.

Kirkpatrick, J. (1983). Meanings of siblingship in Marquesan society. In M. Marshall (Ed.), *Siblingship in Oceania: Studies in the meaning of kin relations* (pp. 17–51). Lanham, MD: University Press of America.

Kivett, V. R. (1985). Consanguinity and kin level: Their relative importance to the helping networks of older adults. *Journal of Gerontology: Social Sciences, 40*, 228–234.

Koch, H. L. (1954). The relation of "primary mental abilities" in five- and six-year-olds to sex of child and characteristics of his sibling. *Child Development, 25*, 209–223.

Koch, H. L. (1955). The relation of certain family constellation characteristics and the attitudes of children toward adults. *Child Development, 26*, 13–40.

Koch, H. L., (1956). Some emotional attitudes of the young child in relation to characteristics of the sibling. *Child Development, 27*, 393–426.

Kolenda, P. (1993). Sibling relations and marriage practices: A comparison of North, Central, and South India. In C. W. Nuckolls (Ed.), *Siblings in South Asia: Brothers and sisters in cultural context* (pp. 103–141). New York: Guilford Press.

Kracke, W. H. (1984). Kagwahiv moieties: Form without function? In K. M. Kensinger (Ed.), *Marriage practices in lowland South America* (pp. 99–124). Urbana, IL: University of Illinois Press.

Krauss, M. W., Seltzer, M. M., & Goodman, S. J. (1992). Social support networks of adults with mental retardation who live at home. *American Journal on Mental Retardation, 96*, 432–441.

Lamb, M. E. (1978a). Interactions between 18-month-olds and their preschool-aged siblings. *Child Development, 49*, 51–59.

Lamb, M. E. (1978b). The development of sibling relationships in infancy: A short term longitudinal study. *Child Development, 49*, 1189–1196.

Lamb, M. E. (1982). Sibling relationships across the lifespan: An overview and introduction. In M. E. Lamb & B. Sutton-Smith (Eds.), *Sibling relationships: Their nature and significance across the life span* (pp. 1–11). Hillsdale, NJ: Erlbaum.

Lamb, M. E. (1988). Social and emotional development in infancy. In M. H. Bornstein & M. E. Lamb (Eds.), *Developmental psychology: An advanced textbook* (2nd ed., pp. 359–410). Hillsdale, NJ: Lawrence Erlbaum.

Lambert, B. (1983). Equivalence, authority and complementarity in Butaritari-Makin sibling relationships (Northern Gilbert Islands). In M. Marshall (Ed.), *Siblingship in Oceania:*

Studies in the Meaning of Kin Relations (pp. 149–200). Lanham, MD: University Press of America.

Laumann, E. O., Gagnon, J. H., Michael, R. T., & Michaels, S. (1994). *The social organization of sexuality: Sexual practices in the United States.* Chicago: University of Chicago Press.

Lavigueur, H., Peterson, R., Sheese, J., & Peterson, L. (1973). Behaviour treatment in the home: Effects on untreated sibling and long-term follow-up. *Behavioral Therapy, 4,* 431–441.

Laviola, M. (1992). Effects of older brother-younger sister incest: A study of the dynamics of 17 cases. *Child Abuse & Neglect, 16,* 409–421.

LeClere, F. B., & Kowalewski, B. M. (1994). Disability in the family: The effects on children's well-being. *Journal of Marriage and the Family, 56,* 457–468.

Lee, G. R., & Ihinger-Tallman, M. (1980). Sibling interactions and morale. *Research on Aging, 2,* 367–391.

Lee, T. R., Mancini, J. A., & Maxwell, J. W. (1990). Sibling relationships in adulthood: Contact patterns and motivations. *Journal of Marriage and the Family, 52,* 431–440.

Legg, C., & Sherick, I. (1976). The replacement child: A developmental tragedy. *Child Psychiatry and Human Development, 7,* 113–125.

Leigh, G. K. (1982). Kinship interaction over the family life span. *Journal of Marriage and the Family, 44,* 197–208.

Leon, I. G. (1990). *When a baby dies: Psychotherapy for pregnancy and newborn loss.* New Haven, CT: Yale University Press.

Lerner, M. J., Somers, D. G., Reid, D., Chiriboga, D., & Tierney, M. (1991). Adult children as caregivers: Egocentric biases in judgments of sibling contributions. *The Gerontologist, 31,* 746–755.

Lewis, K. G. (1988). Symptoms as sibling messages. In M. D. Kahn & K. G. Lewis (Eds.), *Siblings in therapy: Life span and clinical issues* (pp. 255–272). New York: Norton.

Litwak, E. (1985). *Helping the elderly: The complementary roles of informal networks and formal systems.* New York: Guilford.

Litt, I. F., & Martin, J. A. (1981). Development of sexuality and its problems. In M. Levine, W. D. Carey, A. C. Crocker, & R. T. Gross (Eds.), *Developmental-behavioral pediatrics* (pp. 633–649). Philadelphia: W. B. Saunders.

Lobato, D. J. (1983). Siblings of handicapped children: A review. *Journal of Autism and Developmental Disorders, 13,* 347–364.

Lobato, D. J. (1990). *Brothers, sisters, and special needs.* Baltimore, MD: Paul H. Brookes.

Lobato, D. J., Faust, D., & Spirato, A. (1988). Examining the effects of chronic disease and disability on children's sibling relationships. *Journal of Pediatric Psychology, 13,* 389–407.

Loevinger, J. C. (1976). *Ego development.* San Francisco: Jossey-Bass.

Lonetto, R. (1980). *Children's conceptions of death.* New York: Springer-Verlag.

Lonner, W. J. (1979). Issues in cross-cultural psychology. In A. A. Marsella, R. G. Tharp, & T. J. Ciborowski (Eds.), *Perspectives on cross-cultural psychology* (pp. 17–45). New York: Academic Press.

Lopata, H. (1973). *Widowhood in an American city.* Cambridge, MA: Schenkman.

Loredo, C. M. (1982). Sibling incest. In S. M. Sgroi (Ed.), *Handbook of clinical intervention in child sexual abuse* (pp. 177–188). Lexington, MA: Lexington Press (and D. C. Heath).

Lukianowitz, N. (1972). Incest: II. Other types of incest. *British Journal of Psychiatry, 120,* 301–313.

Lyon, P. J. (1984). Change in Wachipaeri marriage patterns. In K. M. Kensinger (Ed.), *Marriage practices in lowland South America* (pp. 252–263). Urbana, IL: University of Illinois Press.

Mandelbaum, D. G. (1970). *Society in India. Vol. I: Continuity and change.* Berkeley: University of California Press.

Mandell, F., Dirks-Smith, T., & Smith, M. F. (1988). The surviving child in the SIDS family. *Pediatrician, 15,* 217–221.

Mandell, F., McLain, M., & Reece, R. (1988). The sudden infant death syndrome: Siblings and their place in the family. *Annals of the New York Academy of Sciences, 533,* 129–131.

Marshall, M. (1983a). Introduction: Approaches to siblingship in Oceania. In M. Marshall (Ed.), *Siblingship in Oceania: Studies in the Meaning of Kin Relations* (pp. 1–16). Lanham, MD: University Press of America.

Marshall, M. (1983b). Sibling sets as building blocks in Greater Trukese society. In M. Marshall (Ed.), *Siblingship in Oceania: Studies in the Meaning of Kin Relations* (pp. 201–224). Lanham, MD: University Press of America.

Marshall, V. W. (1980). *Last chapters: A sociology of aging and dying.* Monterey, CA: Brooks/ Cole.

Martinson, I. M., & Campos, R. G. (1991). Adolescent bereavement: Long-term responses to sibling's death from cancer. *Journal of Adolescent Research, 6,* 54–69.

Matthews, S. H. (1987). Provision of care to old parents: Division of care among adult children. *Research on Aging, 9,* 45–60.

Matthews, S. H. (1988, October). *Gender and the division of filial responsibility.* Paper presented at the conference on Gender Roles through the Life Course, Ball State University, Muncie, Indiana.

Matthews, S. H., Delaney, P. J., & Adamek, M. E. (1989). Male kinship ties: Bonds between adult brothers. *American Behavioral Scientist, 33,* 58–69.

Matthews, S. H., & Rosner, T. T. (1988). Shared filial responsibility: The family as the primary caregiver. *Journal of Marriage and the Family, 50,* 185–195.

Matthews, S. H., & Sprey, J. (1989). Older family systems: Intra- and intergenerational relations. In J. A. Mancini (Ed.), *Aging parents and adult children* (pp. 63–77). New York: D. C. Heath & Company.

Matthews, S. H., Werkner, J. E., & Delaney, P. J. (1989). Relative contributions of help by employed and unemployed sisters to their elderly parents. *Journal of Gerontology: Social Sciences, 44,* S36–S44.

McClowry, S. G., Davies, E. B., May, K. A., Kulenkamp, E. H., & Martinson, I. M. (1987). The empty space phenomenon: The process of grief in the bereaved family. *Death Studies, 11,* 361–374.

McCown, D. E. (1984). Funeral attendance, cremation, and young siblings. *Death Education, 8,* 349–363.

McCown, D. E., & Pratt, C. (1985). Impact of sibling death on children's behavior. *Death Studies, 9,* 323–335.

McGhee, J. L. (1985). The effects of siblings on the life satisfaction of the rural elderly. *Journal of Marriage and the Family, 47,* 85–91.

McGuire, D. E., & Tolan, P. (1988). Clinical interventions with large family systems: Balancing interests through siblings. In M. D. Kahn & K. G. Lewis (Eds.), *Siblings in therapy: Life span and clinical issues* (pp. 115–134). New York: Norton.

McHale, S. M., & Gamble, W. C. (1987). Sibling relationships and the adjustment of children with disabled brothers. *Journal of Children in Contemporary Society, 19,* 131–158.

McHale, S., & Gamble, W. (1989). Sibling relationships of children with disabled and non-disabled brothers and sisters. *Developmental Psychology, 25,* 421–429.

McHale, J., Sloan, J., & Simeonsson, R. (1986). Sibling relationships of children with autistic, mentally retarded, and non-handicapped brothers and sisters. *Journal of Autism and Mental Disorders, 16,* 399–413.

McNeill, D., & Freiberger, P. (1993). *Fuzzy logic.* New York: Simon & Schuster.

Meiselman, K. C. (1978). *Incest: A psychological study of causes and effects with treatment considerations.* San Francisco, CA: Jossey-Bass.

Miller, N. B., & Cantwell, D. P. (1976). Siblings as therapists: A behavioral approach. *American Journal of Psychiatry, 133,* 447–550.

Minuchin, P. (1985). Families and individual development: Provocations from the field of family therapy. *Child Development, 56,* 289–305.

Minuchin, S. (1974) *Families and family therapy.* Cambridge, MA: Harvard University Press.

Minuchin, S., & Fishman, H. C. (1981). *Family therapy techniques.* Cambridge, MA: Harvard University Press.

Molinari, V., & Reichlin, R. E. (1985). Life review reminiscence in the elderly: A review of the literature. *International Journal of Aging and Human Development, 230,* 81–92.

Montemayor, R., & Hanson, E. (1985). A naturalistic view of conflict between adolescents and their parents and siblings. *Journal of Early Adolescence, 5,* 23–30.

Montgomery, R. J. V., & Kamo, Y. (1989). Parent care by sons and daughters. In J. A. Mancini (Ed.), *Aging parents and adult children* (pp. 213–230). Lexington, MA: Lexington Books.

Moss, M. S., Lesher, E. L., & Moss, S. Z. (1986–87). Impact of the death of an adult child on elderly parents: Some observations. *Omega, 17,* 209–218.

Moss, M. S., & Moss, S. Z. (1983–84). The impact of parental death on middle aged children. *Omega, 14,* 65–75.

Moss, M. S., & Moss, S. Z. (1986). Death of an adult sibling. *International Journal of Family Psychiatry, 7,* 397–418.

Moss, S. Z., & Moss, M. S. (1989). Death of an elderly sibling. *American Behavioral Scientist, 33,* 94–106.

Mrazek, P. B. (1981). The nature of incest: A review of contributing factors. In Mrazek, P. B., & Kempe, C. H. (Eds.), *Sexually abused children and their families* (pp. 97–107). Exeter, UK: Pergamon.

Munn, P., & Dunn, J. (1988). Temperament and the developing relationship between siblings. *International Journal of Behavioral Development, 12,* 433–451.

Nakashima, I. I., & Zakus, G. (1979). Incestuous families. *Pediatric annals, 8,* 300–308.

Nash, A. (1988). Ontogeny, phylogeny, and relationships. In S. W. Duck (Ed.), *Handbook of personal relationships* (pp. 121–141). New York: Wiley.

Nelson, H. B., & Martin, C. A. (1985). Increased child abuse in twins. *Child Abuse & Neglect, 9,* 501–505.

Noppe, L. D., & Noppe, I. C. (1991). Dialectical themes in adolescent conceptions of death. *Journal of Adolescent Research, 6,* 28–42.

Nuckolls, C. W. (1993). An introduction to the cross-cultural study of sibling relations. In C. W. Nuckolls (Ed.), *Siblings in South Asia: Brothers and sisters in cultural context* (pp. 19–41). New York: Guilford Press.

Nye, F. I., & Berardo, F. M. (1973). *The family: Its structure and interaction.* New York: Macmillan.

O'Brien, M. J. (1991). Taking sibling incest seriously. In M. Patton (Ed.), *Family sexual abuse* (pp. 75–92). Newbury Park, CA: Sage.

O'Bryant, S. L. (1988). Sibling support and older widows' well-being. *Journal of Marriage and the Family, 50,* 173–183.

Ochs, E. (1982). Talking to children in Western Samoa. *Language in Society, 11,* 77–104.

Osgood, N. J. (1985). *Suicide in the elderly: A practitioner's guide to diagnosis and mental health intervention.* Rockville, MD: Aspen.

Palazzoli, M. S. (1985). The problem of the sibling as the referring person. *Journal of Marital and Family Therapy, 11,* 21–34.

Patterson, G. R. (1986). The contribution of siblings to training for fighting: A microsocial analysis. In D. Olweus, J. Block, & M. Radke-Yarrow (Eds.), *Development of antisocial and prosocial behavior: Research, theories, and issues* (pp. 235–261). Orlando, FL: Academic Press.

Pepler, D. J. Abramovitch, R., & Corter, C. (1981). Sibling interaction in the home: A longitudinal study. *Child Development, 52,* 1344–1347.

Pepper, S. C. (1942). *World hypotheses: A study in evidence.* Berkeley, CA: University of California Press.

Perlmutter, M. (1988). Cognitive potential throughout life. In J. E. Birren & V. L. Bengtson (Eds.), *Emergent theories of aging* (pp. 247–268). New York: Springer-Verlag.

Phinney, J. S. (1985). The structure of 5-year-olds' verbal quarrels with peers and siblings. *Journal of Genetic Psychology, 147,* 47–60.

Plomin, R., Chipuer, H. M., & Neiderhiser, J. M. (1994). Behavioral genetic evidence for the importance of nonshared environment. In E. M. Hetherington, D. Reiss, & R. Plomin (Eds.), *Separate social worlds of siblings: The impact of nonshared environment on development* (pp. 1–31). Hillsdale, NJ: Erlbaum.

Plomin, R., & Foch, J. (1981). Sex differences and individual differences. *Child Development, 52,* 383–385.

Prochaska, J. M., & Prochaska, J. O. (1985). Children's views of the causes and "cures" of sibling rivalry. *Child Welfare, 64,* 427–433.

Pulakos, J. (1990). Correlations between family environment and relationships of young adult siblings. *Psychological Reports, 67,* 1283–1286.

Raffaelli, M. (1992). Sibling conflict in early adolescence. *Journal of Marriage and the Family, 54,* 652–663.

Ranieri, R. F., & Pratt, T. C. (1978). Sibling therapy. *Social Work, 23,* 418–419.

Reay, M. (1975–76). When a group of men takes a husband. *Anthropological Forum, 4,* 77–96.

Reiss, D., Plomin R., Hetherington, E. M., Howe, G. W., Rovine, M., Tryon, A., & Hagan, M. S. (1994). The separate worlds of teenage siblings: An introduction to the study of nonshared environment and adolescent development. In E. M. Hetherington, D. Reiss, & R. Plomin (Eds.), *Separate social worlds of siblings: The impact of nonshared environment on development* (pp. 63–109). Hillsdale, NJ: Erlbaum.

Riegel, K. F. (1979). *Foundations of dialectical psychology.* New York: Academic Press.

Riemer, S. (1940). A research note on incest. *American Journal of Sociology, 45,* 554–565.

Rodgers, J. L., & Rowe, D. C. (1988). Influence of siblings on adolescent sexual behavior. *Developmental Psychology, 24,* 722–728.

Rodgers, J. L., & Rowe, D. C. (1990). Adolescent sexual activity & mildly deviant behavior. Sibling and friendship effects. *Journal of Family Issues, 11,* 274–293.

Rodgers, J. L., Rowe, D. C., & Harris, D. F. (1990). Sibling differences in adolescent sexual behavior: Inferring process models from family composition patterns. *Journal of Marriage and the Family, 54,* 142–152.

Roscoe, B., Goodwin, M., & Kennedy, D. (1987). Sibling violence and agonistic interactions experienced by early adolescents. *Journal of Family Violence, 2,* 121–138.

Rosen, H. (1984–85). Prohibitions against mourning in childhood sibling loss. *Omega, 14,* 307–316.

Rosenberg, E. (1980). Therapy with siblings in reorganizing families. *International Journal of Family Therapy, 2,* 139–158.

Rosenberg, G. S., & Anspach, D. F. (1973). Sibling solidarity in the working class. *Journal of Marriage and the Family, 35,* 108–113.

Rosenfeld, A., Bailey, R., Siegel, B., & Bailey, G. (1986). Determining incestuous contact between parent and child: Frequency of children touching parent's genitals in a nonclinical population. *Journal of the American Academy of Child Psychiatry, 25,* 481–484.

Rosner, S. (1985). On the place of siblings in psychoanalysis. *Psychoanalytic Review, 72,* 457–477.

Ross, H. G., & Milgram, J. I. (1982). Important variables in adult sibling relationships: A qualitative study. In M. E. Lamb & B. Sutton-Smith (Eds.), *Sibling relationships: Their nature and significance across the lifespan* (pp. 225–249). Hillsdale, NJ: Erlbaum.

Ross, H. S., Filyer, R. E., Lollis, S. P., Perlman, M., & Martin, J. L. (1994). Administering justice in the family. *Journal of Family Psychology, 8,* 254–273.

Rovine, M. J. (1994). Estimating nonshared environment using sibling discrepancy scores. In E. M. Hetherington, D. Reiss, & R. Plomin (Eds.), *Separate social worlds of siblings: The impact of nonshared environment on development* (pp. 63–109). Hillsdale, NJ: Erlbaum.

Rowe, D. C. (1994). *The limits of family influence.* New York: Guilford Press.

Rowe, D. C., & Plomin, R. (1981). The importance of nonshared (E1) environmental influences in behavioral development. *Developmental Psychology, 17,* 527–531.

Rubinstein, R. L. (1983). Siblings in Malo culture. In M. Marshall (Ed.), *Siblingship in Oceania: Studies in the meaning of kin relations* (pp. 307–334). Lanham, MD: University Press of America.

Russell, D. E. (1983). The incidence and prevalence of intrafamilial and extrafamilial sexual abuse of female children. *Child Abuse & Neglect, 7,* 133–146.

Russell, D. E. H. (1986). *The secret trauma: Incest in the lives of girls and women.* New York: Basic Books.

Salthouse, T. A. (1991). *Theoretical perspectives on cognitive aging.* Hillsdale, NJ: Erlbaum.

Samuels, H. R. (1980). The effect of an older sibling on infant locomotor exploration of a new environment. *Child Development, 51,* 607–609.

Scarr, S., & Grajek, S. (1982). Similarities and differences among siblings. In M. E. Lamb & B. Sutton-Smith (Eds.), *Sibling relationships: Their nature and significance across the life span* (pp. 357–381). Hillsdale, NJ: Erlbaum.

Schachter, F. F. (1982). Sibling deidentification and split-parent identification: A family tetrad. In M. E. Lamb & B. Sutton-Smith (Eds.), *Sibling relationships: Their nature and significance across the life span* (pp. 123–151). Hillsdale, NJ: Erlbaum.

Schachter, F. (1985). Sibling deidentification in the clinic: Devil vs. angel. *Family Process, 24,* 415–427.

Schachter, F. F., & Stone, R. K. (1987). Comparing and contrasting siblings: Defining the self. *Journal of Children in Contemporary Society, 19,* 55–75.

Schibuk, M. (1989). Treating the sibling subsystem: An adjunct of divorce therapy. *American Journal of Orthopsychiatry, 59,* 226–237.

Schooler, C. (1972). Birth order effects. *Psychological Bulletin, 78,* 161–175.

Schneider, D. M. (1983). Conclusions. In M. Marshall (Ed.), *Siblingship in Oceania: Studies in the meaning of kin relations* (pp. 389–404). Lanham, MD: University Press of America.

Schvaneveldt, J. D., & Ihinger, M. (1979). Sibling relationships in the family. In W. R. Burr, R. Hill, R. I. Nye, & I. L. Reiss (Eds.), *Contemporary theories about the family. Vol. I. Research-based theories* (pp. 453–467). New York: Free Press.

Scott, J. P. (1983). Siblings and other kin. In T. H. Brubaker (Ed.), *Family relationships in later life* (pp. 47–62). Beverly Hills, CA: Sage.

Scott, J. P. (1990). Sibling interaction in later life. In T. H. Brubaker (Ed.), *Family relationships in later life* (2nd ed., pp. 86–99). Newbury Park, CA: Sage.

Seltzer, G. B., Begun, A., Seltzer, M. M., & Krauss, M. W. (1991). The impacts of siblings on adults with mental retardation and their aging mothers. *Family Relations, 40,* 310–317.

Seltzer, M. M., & Krauss, M. W. (1989). Aging parents with adult mentally retarded children: Family risk factors and sources of support. *American Journal on Mental Retardation, 94,* 303–312.

Seltzer, M. M., & Krauss, M. W. (1993). Adult sibling relationships of persons with mental retardation. In Z. Stoneman & P. W. Berman (Eds.), *The effects of mental retardation, disability, and illness on sibling relationships: Research issues and challenges* (pp. 99–115). Baltimore, MD: Paul H. Brookes.

Seymour, S. (1993). Sociocultural contexts: Examining sibling roles in South Asia. In C. W. Nuckolls (Ed.), *Siblings in South Asia: Brothers and sisters in cultural context* (pp. 45–69). New York: Guilford Press.

Shanas, E. (1973). Family-kin networks and aging in cross-cultural perspective. *Journal of Marriage and the Family, 35,* 505–511.

Shanas, E., Townsend, P., Wedderburn, D., Friis, H., Milhoj, D., & Stehouwer, J. (1968). *Older people in three industrial societies.* New York: Atherton.

Shantz, C. U. (1987). Conflicts between children. *Child Development, 58,* 283–305.

Shantz, C. U., & Hobart, C. J. (1989). Social conflict and development: Peers and siblings. In T. J. Berndt & G. W. Ladd (Eds.), *Peer relations in child development* (pp. 71–94). New York: Wiley.

Shapiro, J. R. (1984). Marriage rules, marriage exchange, and the definition of marriage in lowland South American societies. In K. M. Kensinger (Ed.), *Marriage practices in lowland South America* (pp. 1–30). Urbana, IL: University of Illinois Press.

Simons, R. L. (1983–84). Specificity and substitution in the social networks of the elderly. *International Journal of Aging and Human Development, 18,* 121–139.

Smith, H., & Israel, E. (1987). Sibling incest: A study of the dynamics of 25 cases. *Child Abuse & Neglect, 11,* 101–108.

Smith, T. E. (1984). School grades and responsibility for younger siblings: An empirical study of the "teaching function." *American Sociological Review, 49,* 248–260.

Smith, T. E. (1990a). Academic achievement and teaching younger siblings. *Social Psychology Quarterly, 53,* 352–363.

Smith, T. E. (1990b). Time and academic achievement. *Journal of Youth and Adolescence, 19,* 539–558.

Smith, T. E. (1992). Time use and change in academic achievement: A longitudinal follow-up. *Journal of Youth and Adolescence, 21,* 725–747.

Smith, T. E. (1993). Growth in academic achievement and teaching younger siblings. *Social Psychology Quarterly, 56,* 77–85.

Sorensen, A. P., Jr. (1984). Linguistic exogamy and personal choice in the northwest Amazon. In K. M. Kensinger (Ed.), *Marriage practices in lowland South America* (pp. 180–193). Urbana, IL: University of Illinois Press.

Sorrenti-Little, L., Bagley, C., & Robertson, S. (1984). An operational definition of the long-term harmfulness of sexual relations with peers and adults by young children. *Canadian Child, 9,* 45–57.

Sperling, M. B., & Berman, W. H. (Eds.)(1994). *Attachment in adults: Clinical and developmental perspectives.* New York: Guilford.

Spitze, G., & Logan, J. (1990). Sons, daughters, and intergenerational social support. *Journal of Marriage and the Family, 52,* 420–430.

Steinmetz, S. K. (1977). *The cycle of violence: Assertive, aggressive, and abusive family interaction.* New York: Praeger.

Steinmetz, S. K. (1982). A cross-cultural comparison of sibling violence. *International Journal of Family Psychiatry, 2,* 337–351.

Steinmetz, S. K. (1987). Family violence: Past, present, and future. In M. B. Sussman & S. K. Sussman (Eds.), *Handbook of marriage and the family* (pp. 725–765). New York: Plenum.

Stephenson, J. (1986). Grief of siblings. In T. A. Rando (Ed.), *Parental loss of a child* (pp. 321–338). Champaign, IL: Research Press.

Stewart, D. A., Stein, A., Forrest, G. C., & Clark, D. M. (1992). Psychosocial adjustment of children with chronic life-threatening diseases. *Journal of Child Psychology and Psychiatry and Allied Disciplines, 33,* 779–789.

Stewart, R. B. (1983). Sibling attachment relationships: Child-infant interaction in the strange situation. *Developmental Psychology, 19,* 192–199.

Stewart, R. B., & Marvin, R. S. (1984). Sibling relations: The role of conceptual perspective taking in the ontogeny of sibling caregiving. *Child Development, 55,* 1322–1332.

Stewart, R. B., Mobley, L. A., Van Tuyl, S. S., & Salvador, M. A. (1987). The firstborns' adjustment to the birth of a sibling. A longitudinal assessment. *Child Development, 58,* 341–355.

Stocker, C., Dunn, J., & Plomin, R. (1989). Sibling relationships: Links with child temperament, maternal behavior, and family structure. *Child Development, 60,* 715–727.

Stocker, C., & McHale, S. (1992). The nature and family correlates of preadolescents' perceptions of their sibling relationships. *Journal of Personal and Social Relationships, 9,* 179–195.

Stoller, E. P. (1985). Exchange patterns in the informal support networks of the elderly: The impact of reciprocity on morale. *Journal of Marriage and the Family, 47,* 335–348.

Stoller, E. P. (1990). Males as helpers: The role of sons, relatives, and friends. *The Gerontologist, 30,* 228–235.

Stoller, E. P., Forster, L. E., Duniho, T. S. (1992). Systems of parent care within sibling networks. *Research on Aging, 14,* 28–49.

Stoneman, Z., & Brody, G. H. (1984). Research with families of severely handicapped children: Theoretical and methodological considerations. In J. Blacher (Ed.), *Severely handicapped young children and their families: Research in review* (pp. 179–214). San Diego, CA: Academic Press.

Stoneman, Z., & Berman, P. W. (Eds.)(1993). *The effects of mental retardation, disability, and illness on sibling relationships: Research Issues and Challenges.* Baltimore: Paul H. Brookes.

Stoneman, Z., Brody, G. H., Davis, C. H., & Crapps, J. M. (1987). Mentally retarded children and their older same-sex siblings: Naturalistic in-home observations. *American Journal on Mental Retardation, 92,* 290–298.

Stoneman, Z., Brody, G. H., Davis, C. H., & Crapps, J. M. (1988). Childcare responsibilities, peer relations, and sibling conflict: Older siblings of mentally retarded children. *American Journal on Mental Retardation, 93,* 174–183.

Stoneman, Z., & Crapps, J. M. (1990). Mentally retarded individuals in family care homes: Relationships with the family of origin. *American Journal on Mental Retardation, 94,* 420–430.

Straus, M. A. (1971). Some social antecedents of physical punishment: A linkage theory interpretation. *Journal of Marriage and the Family, 33,* 658–663.

Straus, M. A. (1974). Leveling, civility, and violence in the family. *Journal of Marriage and the Family, 36,* 13–29.

Straus, M. A. (1979). Measuring intrafamily conflict and violence: The Conflict Tactics Scale. *Journal of Marriage and the Family, 41,* 75–88.

Straus, M. A., & Gelles, R. J. (1986). Societal change and change in family violence from 1975 to 1985 as revealed by two national surveys. *Journal of Marriage and the Family, 48,* 465–479.

Straus, M. A., Gelles, R. J., & Steinmetz, S. K. (1980). *Behind closed doors: Violence in the American family.* Garden City, NY: Anchor.

Strauss, A. (1987). *Qualitative analysis for social scientists.* New York: Cambridge University Press.

Suggs, P. K. (1989). Predictors of association among older siblings: A black/white comparison. *American Behavioral Scientist, 33,* 70–80.

Sutton-Smith, B., & Rosenberg, B. G. (1970). *The sibling.* New York: Holt, Rinehart, & Winston.

Teti, D. M. (1992). Sibling interaction. In V. G. Van Hasselt & M. Hersen (Eds.), *Handbook of social development: A lifespan perspective* (pp. 201–226). New York: Plenum Press.

Teti, D. M., Gibbs, E. D., & Bond, A. (1989). Sibling interaction, birth spacing, and intellectual linguistic development. In P. G. Zukow (Ed.), *Sibling interaction across cultures: Theoretical and methodological issues* (pp. 117–141). New York: Springer-Verlag.

Toman, W. (1976). *Family constellation: Its effects on personality and social behavior (3rd ed.).* New York: Springer-Verlag.

Tonti, M. (1988). Relationships among adult siblings who care for their aged parents. In M. D. Kahn & K. G. Lewis (Eds.), *Siblings in therapy: Life span and clinical issues* (pp. 417–434). New York: Norton.

Tooley, K. (1977). The young child as victim of sibling attack. *Social Casework, 58,* 25–28.

Townsend, P. (1957). *The family life of old people: An inquiry in East London.* Glencoe, IL.: Free Press.

Trawick, M. (1990). *Notes on love in a Tamil family.* Berkeley, CA: University of California Press.

Tritt, S. G., & Esses, L. M. (1988). Psychosocial adaptation of siblings of children with chronic medical illnesses. *American Journal of Orthopsychiatry, 58,* 211–220.

Troll, L. E. (1975). *Early and middle adulthood.* Monterey, CA: Brooks/Cole.

Troll, L. E., Miller, S., & Atchley, R. (1978). *Families of later life.* Belmont, CA: Wadsworth.

Usdansky, M. L. (August 30, 1994). "Blended," "extended" now all in the family. *USA Today,* pp. 1A, 3A.

Vandell, D. L. (1987). Baby sister/baby brother: Reactions to the birth of a sibling and patterns of early sibling relations. *Journal of Children in Contemporary Society, 19,* 13–37.

Vandell, D. L., & Bailey, M. D. (1992). Conflicts between siblings. In C. U. Shantz & W. W. Hartup (Eds.), *Conflict in child and adolescent development* (pp. 242–269). New York: Cambridge University Press.

Vandell, D. L., Minnett, A. M., & Santrock, J. W. (1987). Age differences in sibling relationships during middle childhood. *Journal of Applied Developmental Psychology, 8,* 247–257.

Volling, B. L., & Belsky, J. (1992). The contribution of mother-child and father-child relationships to the quality of sibling interactions: A longitudinal study. *Child Development, 63,* 1209–1222.

Walberg, H. J., & Marjoribanks, K. (1976). Family environment and cognitive development. *Review of Educational Research, 46,* 527–552.

Wallden, J. (1990). *Sibling position and mental capacity—Reconsidered.* Project Metropolitan Research Report No. 31. Stockholm: Department of Sociology, University of Stockholm, S–10691.

Watson-Gegeo, K. A., & Gegeo, D. W. (1989). The role of sibling interaction in child socialization. In P. G. Zukow (Ed.), *Sibling interaction across cultures: Theoretical and methodological issues* (pp. 54–76). New York: Springer-Verlag.

Weeks, R. B. (1976). The sexually exploited child. *Southern Medical Journal, 69,* 848–852.

Weisner, T. S. (1982). Sibling interdependence and child caretaking: A cross-cultural view. In M. E. Lamb & B. Sutton-Smith (Eds.), *Sibling relationships: Their nature and significance across the lifespan* (pp. 305–327). Hillsdale, NJ: Erlbaum.

Weisner, T. S. (1987). Socialization for parenthood in sibling caretaking societies. In J. B. Lancaster, J. Altman, A. Rossi, & L. Sherrod (Eds.), *Parenting across the life span* (pp. 237–270). New York: Aldine De Gruyter.

Weisner, T. S. (1989a). Comparing sibling relationships across cultures. In Zukow, P. G. (Ed.), *Sibling interaction across cultures: Theoretical and methodological issues* (pp. 11–25). New York: Springer-Verlag.

Weisner, T. S. (1989b). Cultural and universal aspects of social support for children: Evidence from the Abaluyia of Kenya. In D. Belle (Ed.), *Children's social networks and social supports* (pp. 70–90). New York: Wiley Interscience.

Weisner, T. S. (1993a). Ethnographic and ecocultural perspectives on sibling relationships. In Z. Stoneman & P. W. Berman (Eds.), *The effects of mental retardation, disability, and illness on sibling relationships* (pp. 51–83). Baltimore, MD: Paul H. Brookes.

Weisner, T. S. (1993b). Overview: Sibling similarity and difference in different cultures. In C. W. Nuckolls (Ed.), *Siblings in South Asia: Brothers and sisters in cultural context* (pp. 1–18). New York: Guilford Press.

Weisner, T. S., & Gallimore, R. (1977). My brother's keeper: Child and sibling caretaking. *Current Anthropology, 18,* 169–191.

Weisner, T. S., Gallimore, R., & Jordan, C. (1988). Unpackaging cultural effects on classroom learning: Native Hawaiian peer assistance and child-generated activity. *Anthropology & Education Quarterly, 19,* 327–353.

Wenger, M. (1989). Work, play, and social relationships among children in a Giriama community. In D. Belle (Ed.), *Children's social networks and social supports* (pp. 91–115). New York: Wiley Interscience.

White, L. K., & Riedmann, A. (1992a). Ties among adult siblings. *Social Forces, 71,* 85–102.

White, L. K., & Riedmann, A. (1992b). When the Brady bunch grows up: Step/half- and fullsibling relations in adulthood. *Journal of Marriage and the Family, 54,* 197–208.

Whittemore, R. D., & Beverly, E. (1989). Trust in the Mandinka: The cultural context of sibling care. In P. G. Zukow (Ed.), *Sibling interaction across cultures: Theoretical and methodological issues* (pp. 26–53). New York: Springer-Verlag.

Whitten, N. E., Jr., & Whitten, D. S. (1984). The structure of kinship and marriage among the Canelos Quichua of east-central Ecuador. In K. M. Kensinger (Ed.), *Marriage practices in lowland South America* (pp. 194–220). Urbana, IL: University of Illinois Press.

Wiehe, V. R. (1990). *Sibling abuse: Hidden physical, emotional, and sexual trauma.* Lexington, MA: Lexington Books.

Wishart, J. G. (1986). Siblings as models in early infant learning. *Child Development, 57,* 1232–1240.

Wong, A. K. (1979). The National Family Planning Programme and changing family life. In E. C. Y. Kuo & A. K. Wong (Eds.), *The contemporary family in Singapore: Structure and change* (pp. 211–238). Singapore: University of Singapore Press.

Wong, A. K., & Kuo, E. C. Y. (1979). The urban kinship network in Singapore. In E. C. Y. Kuo & A. K. Wong (Eds.), *The contemporary family in Singapore: Structure and change* (pp. 17–39). Singapore: University of Singapore Press.

Wyatt, G.E. (1985). The sexual abuse of Afro-American and White-American women in childhood. *Child Abuse & Neglect, 9,* 507–519.

Yanagisako, S. J. (1985). *Transforming the past: Tradition and kinship among Japanese-Americans.* Stanford, CA: Stanford University Press.

Zajonc, R. B., & Markus, G. B. (1975). Birth order and intellectual development. *Psychological Review, 82,* 74–88.

Zarit, S. H., Reever, K. E., & Bach-Peterson, J. (1980). Relatives of the impaired elderly: Correlates of feelings of burden. *The Gerontologist, 26,* 260–266.

Zetlin, A. G. (1986). Mentally retarded adults and their siblings. *American Journal on Mental Retardation, 91,* 217–225.

Zukow, P. G. (1989). Communicating across disciplines: On integrating psychological and ethnographic approaches to sibling research. In P. G. Zukow (Ed.), *Sibling interaction across cultures: Theoretical and methodological issues* (pp. 1–9). New York: Springer-Verlag.

Author Index

Abramovitch, R., 42, 50, 110, 114, 142, 157, 161, 163, 164
Adam, B. S., 158
Adamek, M. E., 56, 125, 126, 135
Adams, B. N., 55, 57, 58, 66, 73, 81, 114
Ade-Ritter, L., 48
Adelson, L., 165
Adler, A., 6
Adler, T., 77
Ainsworth, M. L., 43, 223
Albert, S. M., 130
Aldous, J., 123, 131
Allswede, J., 189, 195
Alpert, J. L., 174
Anderson, B., 53
Anderson, E. T., 7
Anspach, D. F., 53
Antonucci, T. C., 120
Appelbaum, D. R., 188
Armistead, L., 48
Arndt, W. R., 177
Ascherman, L. I., 183
Atchley, R., 57
Auletta, R., 144
Aviola, P. S., 115, 120, 122
Azmitia, M., 35, 113

Babchuk, N., 116
Bach-Peterson, J., 133
Bagenhold, A., 144
Bagley, C., 178
Bahr, S. J., 72
Bailey, G., 170
Bailey, M. D., 151, 152, 159, 160, 161, 163, 164, 166, 167
Bailey, R., 170

Balk, D. E., 192, 193
Baltes, P. B., 15, 20
Bank, S. P., 5, 43, 55, 56, 57, 59, 60, 110, 153, 154, 162, 166, 167, 171, 172, 177, 186, 187, 189, 193, 207, 209, 211, 212
Barbarin, O. O., 189, 195
Bargiel, K., 37
Barnett, W. S., 141
Barton, A., 124
Basso, E. B., 79
Beals, A. R., 80, 82
Beardsall, L., 77, 111
Bedford, V. H., 56, 60, 61, 62, 99, 117, 118, 120, 122, 160, 209
Beer, W. R., 28, 162, 175, 176, 180, 183
Begun, A. L., 146, 148
Belsky, J., 161, 163, 164
Bengtson, V. L., 66
Berardo, F. M., 90
Bergstrom, D., 167
Berkman, L. F., 117
Berman, P. W., 138
Berman, W. H., 223
Berndt, T. J., 163
Berscheid, E., 3
Beverly, E., 77
Boer, F., 49
Bond, A., 76
Borland, D. C., 118
Bowlby, J., 43, 66
Boyce, G. C., 141
Brady, E. M., 120
Bretherton, I., 43
Brody, E. M., 123, 124, 126, 128, 129, 130, 131, 132, 133, 134, 135
Brody, G. H., 18, 49, 50, 139, 142, 153, 159, 161, 162, 163, 164

247

Brown, J. R., 44, 110
Brown, S. C., 137
Bryant, B. K., 44, 50, 76, 111, 112, 113, 161
Buhrmester, D., 35, 44, 50, 72, 77, 157, 159
Bulleit, T. N., 163
Burke, M., 49, 50
Burns, G. L., 188
Butcher, K. F., 64, 65, 95
Butler, R. N., 64, 211

Cain, A. C., 187, 190
Campos, R. G., 192, 194, 195
Cantor, M., 121
Cantwell, D. P., 204
Carroll, R., 57, 210
Case, A., 64, 65, 95
Catalano, D. J., 116
Chee, T. S., 83
Chesler, M. A., 189, 195
Chipuer, H. M., 51, 52
Chiriboga, D., 125
Christensen, A., 3
Church, M., 211
Cicirelli, V. G., 3, 5, 16, 18, 20, 21, 24, 32, 35,
    45, 53, 54, 55, 56, 57, 58, 59, 60, 61,
    63, 64, 66, 67, 72, 73, 74, 81, 112, 113,
    115, 116, 117, 119, 121, 122, 124, 126,
    127, 128, 131, 132, 135, 160, 198, 211,
    212, 223
Clancy, G. M., 138
Clark, D. M., 189
Clark, M., 53
Cleveland, D. W., 145
Cole, E., 178
Coleman, F. W., 186
Coleman, P., 64
Coleman, W. S., 186
Conger, K. J., 50
Conger, R. D., 50
Connidis, I. A., 55, 57, 58, 61, 62, 99, 118,
    121, 209
Cook, A. S., 186
Cornell-Pedrick, C. P., 165
Corter, C., 42, 50, 110, 114, 142, 157, 161,
    163, 164
Coward, R. T., 117, 121, 122, 124, 126, 128,
    129, 134
Craft, M. J., 138
Crapps, J. M., 142, 145
Crnic, K., 141, 142
Crockenberg, S., 50, 161
Crocker, W. H., 79, 83

Cumming, E., 63
Cutler, S. E., 163, 164, 165, 167

Daie, N., 179, 182
Daniels, D., 50, 52
Davies, B., 186, 193, 194, 195, 196
Davies, E. B., 196
Davies, L., 55, 58
Davis, C. H., 142
De Jong, A. R., 170, 172, 176
de Munck, V. C., 80, 82
De Young, M., 178
Deal, J. E., 34
Dean-Oswald, H., 80, 82
Delaney, P. J., 56, 60, 125, 126, 130, 135
Demi, A. S., 196
Dengerink, H. A., 167
Derne, S., 80, 82
DeRosa, A. P., 144
DeSantis, L., 193
Dirks-Smith, T., 188
Dole, G. E., 79
Duck, S., 3
Duniho, T. S., 128, 129
Dunn, J., 5, 7, 18, 34, 42, 43, 44, 48, 49, 50,
    51, 52, 76, 77, 78, 85, 110, 111, 114,
    115, 153, 154, 161, 162, 163, 164, 165,
    166, 209, 211
Dunne-Maxim, K., 196
Dwyer, J. W., 117, 121, 122, 124, 126, 128,
    129, 134
Dyson, L. L., 141, 142

Eason, M. A., 80, 82
East, P. L., 111
Edgar, E., 141, 142
Eggebeen, D. J., 27
Eleff, M., 179, 182
Erickson, M. E., 187, 190
Erikson, E. H., 15
Ervin-Tripp, S., 42, 70, 78, 79, 112, 113
Esses, L. M., 189
Essman, C. S., 114

Fanos, J. H., 192, 194
Fast, I., 187, 190
Faust, D., 139, 140
Feinberg, R., 80
Feld, S. L., 156
Felson, R. B., 152, 157, 162, 163
Filyer, R. E., 162

Finkelhor, D., 172, 174, 176, 178, 179
Fishman, H. C., 202
Fleming, S. J., 193
Foch, J., 52
Ford, D. H., 21, 22
Forehand, R., 48, 162
Forrest, G. C., 189
Forster, L. E., 128, 129
Freiberger, P., 23
Friis, H., 53
Furman, W., 35, 44, 50, 77, 157, 159
Furstenberg, F. F., 50, 52

Gaffney, D. A., 196
Gagnon, J. H., 175, 179
Gallimore, R., 83, 111
Gamble, W. C., 35, 140, 143, 159, 161
Gegeo, D. W., 71, 77, 79
Gelles, R. J., 157, 158, 159, 160, 164, 165
George, L. K., 60
Gibbs, E. D., 76
Gilbert, C., 144
Glaser, B. C., 87
Goetting, A., 57, 109, 115, 116, 123, 134
Gold, D. T., 56, 59, 60, 64, 66, 74, 81, 116,
        117, 118, 120, 122, 209, 212
Goodale, J. C., 82
Goodman, S. J., 145
Goodwin, M., 160, 164
Gorer, G., 196
Gottman, J. M., 224
Gracek, S., 33, 49, 52, 67
Graham-Bermann, S. A., 163, 164, 165, 167
Greenfield, D. B., 193, 196
Greenwald, E., 177
Griffiths, D. L., 148
Grossmann, F. K., 144
Guerriero, A. M., 193
Gully, K., 167

Hagan, M. S., 29, 34, 51
Halverson, C. F., Jr., 34
Hamlin, E. R., 201, 203, 204, 205, 208
Hanson, E., 160
Harris, D. F., 170
Harris, E. G., 211
Hartup, W. W., 3
Harvey, J. H., 3
Hecht, J. A., 71
Hennon, C. B., 48
Henretta, J. C., 124

Henry, W., 63
Herr, J. J., 211
Hesser, J., 35, 113
Hetherington, E. M., 7, 29, 34, 48, 51, 161,
        162, 166
Hinde, R. A., 3
Hobart, C. J., 152, 153, 154, 166
Hoff-Ginsburg, E., 113
Hoffman, C., 124, 129, 130
Hoffman, L. W., 50
Hogan, N. S., 193, 196
Hotaling, G. T., 172
Howe, G. W., 7, 29, 34, 51
Howe, N., 110
Howell, C., 196
Hoyt, D. R., 116
Huntsman, J., 80
Huston, T. L., 3

Ihinger, M., 5, 114
Ihinger-Tallman, M., 63
Israel, R., 181

Jackson, J. E., 72, 77
Jacob, T., 37
Jesse, R. C., 208
Johnson, C. L., 57, 66, 81, 83, 116, 120
Jones, E. T., 196
Jones, L., 77
Jordan, C., 83
Justice, B., 170
Justice, R., 170

Kahn, M. D., 5, 43, 55, 56, 57, 59, 60, 110,
        153, 154, 162, 166, 167, 171, 172, 177,
        186, 187, 189, 193, 207, 209, 211, 212
Kamo, Y., 128, 129, 133
Kaplan, J. O., 79
Kaplan, L., 48
Kasl, S. V., 117
Kausler, D. H., 15, 23
Kelley, H. H., 3
Kelly, L., 172
Kempton, T., 48
Kendrick, C., 42, 43, 110, 114, 161, 164, 209
Kennedy, D., 160, 164
Kensinger, K. M., 79
Kirkpatrick, J., 71, 77
Kivett, V. R., 115, 116
Kleban, M. H., 124, 129
Koch, H. L., 30
Kolenda, P., 80, 82

Kowalewski, B. M., 138
Kracke, W. H., 79
Krauss, M. W., 145, 146, 148
Krueger, W. M., 113
Kulenkamp, E. H., 196
Kuo, E. C. Y., 83

Ladd, B., 177
Lakin, J. A., 138
Lamb, M. R., 5, 18, 67, 114, 163, 165
Lambert, B., 77, 80, 82
Lando, B., 42, 50, 110, 114, 142, 157, 161,
    163
Laumann, E. O., 175, 179
Lavigueur, H., 204
Laviola, M., 173, 178
LeClere, F. B., 138
Lee, G. R., 63
Lee, T. R., 119
Legg, C., 187
Leigh, G. K., 60
Leitenberg, H., 177
Leon, I. G., 28, 186, 187, 188
Lerner, M. J., 125
Lerner, R. M., 21, 22
Lesher, E. L., 197
Levinger, G., 3
Lewis, K. G., 202, 204, 208, 212
Litt, I. F., 170
Litvin, S. J., 130
Litwak, E., 121
Litzenberger, B. W., 163, 164, 165, 167
Livingston, R., 158
Lobato, D. J., 139, 140, 141
Loevinger, J. C., 22
Logan, J., 134
Lollis, S. P., 162
Lonetto, R., 186
Lonner, W. J., 70
Lopata, H., 115, 116
Loredo, C. M., 178
Lukianowitz, N., 177
Lyon, P. J., 79, 83

MacKinnon, C. E., 159, 164
MacKinnon, R., 159, 164
Mancini, J.A., 119
Mandelbaum, D. G., 74
Mandell, R., 188
Mangen, D. G., 66
Marjoribanks, K., 64

Markus, G. B., 46, 73, 76, 112
Marshall, M., 3, 70, 71, 80, 82
Marshall, V. W., 198
Martin, C. A., 158
Martin, J. A., 170
Martin, J. L., 160
Martinson, I. M., 192, 194, 195, 196
Marvin, R. S., 43, 110
Matthews, S. H., 56, 60, 125, 126, 129, 130,
    131, 132, 135
Maxwell, J. W., 119
May, K. A., 196
McClintock, E., 3
McClowry, S. G., 196
McCown, D. E., 191, 192
McCoy, J. K., 50, 162, 163
McGhee, J. L., 63
McGuire, D. E., 208
McGuire, S., 51
McHale, J., 142, 144
McHale, S. M., 35, 140, 143, 157, 159, 161
McLain, M., 188
McNeill, D., 23
Meiselman, K. C., 178, 179
Michael, R. T., 175, 179
Michaels, S., 175, 179
Milgram, J. I., 55, 56, 64, 212
Milhoj, D., 53
Miller, N. B., 145, 204
Miller, S., 57
Minnett, A. M., 45
Minuchin, P., 202
Minuchin, S., 7, 202, 203
Mobley, L. A., 165
Molinari, V., 64, 211
Montemayor, R., 160
Montgomery, R. J. V., 128, 129, 133
Moss, M. S., 197, 198
Moss, S. Z., 197, 198
Mrazek, P. B., 175
Munn, P., 44, 49, 50, 162, 163, 166

Nakashima, I. I., 177
Nash, A., 67
Neiderhizer, J. M., 51, 52
Nelson, H. B., 158
Nickerson, B. G., 192, 194
Noberini, M. R., 120
Noppe, I. C., 192
Noppe, L. D., 192
Nuckolls, C. W., 74, 80, 82
Nye, F. I., 90

O'Brien, M. J., 172
O'Bryant, S. L., 63, 117
Ochs, E., 79
Oltjenbruns, K. A., 186
Oppliger, R. A., 138
Osgood, N. H., 64, 211

Palazzoli, M. S., 211
Patterson, G. R., 157
Peplau, L. A., 3
Pepler, D. J., 42, 50, 110, 114, 142, 157, 161, 163, 164
Pepper, S. C., 23
Pepping, M., 167
Perlman, M., 162
Perlmutter, M., 15
Peterson, D. R., 3
Peterson, L., 204
Peterson, R., 204
Phinney, J. S., 159
Plomin, R., 7, 29, 34, 49, 50, 51, 52, 161, 163
Pratt, C., 191, 192
Pratt, T. C., 201, 202, 206
Prochaska, J. M., 157, 159, 164
Prochaska, J. O., 157, 159, 164
Pulakos, J., 55

Raffaelli, M., 152, 160, 166
Ranieri, R. F., 201, 202, 206
Reay, M., 82
Reece, R., 188
Reever, K. E., 133
Reichlin, R. E., 64, 211
Reid, D., 125
Reiss, D., 7, 29, 34, 51
Rende, R., 77, 111
Riedmann, A., 54, 55, 56, 61, 116, 131, 209
Riegel, K. F., 23
Riemer, S., 177
Robertson, S., 178
Robins, E., 3
Rodgers, J. L., 50, 114, 170
Rook, K. S., 111
Roscoe, B., 170, 174
Rosen, H., 188, 190, 191, 192
Rosenberg, B. G., 5, 30, 47, 73, 163, 164
Rosenberg, E., 204, 205
Rosenberg, G. S., 53
Rosenfeld, A., 170
Rosner, S., 211
Rosner, T. T., 125, 126, 131, 132, 135
Ross, H. G., 55, 56, 64, 212

Ross, H. S., 110, 162
Rovine, M., 29, 34, 51
Rowe, D. C., 50, 51, 114, 170, 222
Rubinstein, R. L., 71
Russell, D. E. H., 174, 175, 176, 178
Russo, N., 157, 162

Safier, E. J., 183
Salthouse, T. A., 15
Salvador, M. A., 165
Samuels, H. R., 43
Santrock, J. W., 45
Scarr, S., 33, 49, 52, 67
Schachter, F. F., 47, 153
Schibuk, M., 5, 208
Schneider, D. M., 70, 80, 82
Schooler, C., 46
Schoonover, C. G., 124, 129, 130
Schvaneveldt, 5, 114
Schwartz, W. E., 163, 164, 165, 167
Scott, J. P., 57, 60, 115, 116, 209
Seilhamer, R. A., 37
Seltzer, G. B., 146, 148
Seltzer, M. M., 145, 146, 148
Seymour, S., 78, 80, 82, 83
Shanas, E., 53
Shantz, C. U., 151, 152, 153, 154, 157, 166
Shapiro, J. R., 79
Sharon, T., 37
Shatz, M., 44
Sheese, J., 204
Sherick, I., 187
Siegel, B., 170
Simeonsson, R., 142, 144
Simons, R. L., 121
Sloan, J., 142, 144
Slomkowski, C., 77, 111
Smith, H., 181
Smith, M. F., 188
Smith, T. E., 76, 112
Somer, D. G., 125
Sorensen, A. P., Jr., 79
Sorrenti-Little, L., 178
Sperling, M. B., 223
Spirato, A., 139, 140
Spitze, G., 134
Sprey, J., 125, 132
Stanhope, L., 42, 50, 142, 157, 161
Stehouwer, J., 53
Stein, A., 189
Steinmetz, S. K., 157, 158, 159, 160, 164

Stephenson, J., 186, 187
Stewart, D. A., 189
Stewart, R. B., 43, 110, 165
Stocker, C., 7, 34, 49, 50, 52, 157, 161, 163
Stoller, E. P., 120, 128, 129
Stone, R. K., 47
Stoneman, Z., 18, 49, 50, 138, 139, 142, 145,
    153, 159, 161, 162, 163, 164
Straus, M. A., 35, 157, 158, 159, 160, 164
Strauss, A. L., 87
Suggs, P. K., 116, 117, 120
Sutton-Smith, B., 5, 30, 47, 73, 163, 164

Tennenbaum, D., 37
Teti, D. M., 42, 51, 76
Tierney, M., 125
Timberlake, E. M., 201, 203, 204, 205, 208
Tolan, P., 208
Toman, W., 47
Tonti, M., 133, 134
Tooley, K., 165
Townsend, P., 53, 115
Trawick, M., 80, 82
Tritt, S. G., 189
Troll, L. E., 57, 115
Tryon, A., 29, 34, 51

Unger, D. G., 148
Usdansky, M. L., 11, 28

Van Tuyl, S. S., 165
Vandell, D. L., 45, 151, 152, 159, 160, 161,
    163, 164, 165, 166, 167

Vandenlinden, D. W., 138
Volling, B. L., 161, 163, 164

Walberg, H. J., 64
Wallden, J., 75
Wampler, K. S., 34
Watson-Gegeo, K. A., 71, 77, 79
Weakland, J. H., 211
Weeks, R. B., 177
Weisner, T. S., 3, 70, 71, 74, 75, 77, 78, 79, 80,
    81, 82, 83, 84, 85, 109, 111
Wenger, M., 71, 77, 83
Werkner, J. E., 60, 130
White, L. K., 54, 55, 56, 61, 116, 131, 209
Whittemore, R. C., 77
Whitten, D. S., 79
Whitten, N. E., Jr., 79
Wiehe, V. R., 142, 154, 164, 173, 177, 178,
    181, 182, 183
Wierson, M., 48
Wishart, J. G., 113
Wong, A. K., 83
Woodbury, M. A., 60
Woulbroun, E. J., 140
Wyatt, G. E., 175, 176, 180

Yanagisako, S. J., 83

Zajonc, R. B., 46, 73, 76, 112
Zakus, G., 177
Zarit, S. H., 133
Zetlin, A. G., 146, 148
Zukow, P. G., 70

Subject Index

Abuse
  definitions and distinctions, 155–157
  prevalence, 157–158
  sexual, 170–175
Aggression
  definitions and distinctions, 155–157
  prevalence, 157–158
Attachment, 43, 66–67, 222–224

Caregiving for elderly parents
  associated factors, 128–132
  decision making, 127–28
  effects on adult siblings
    affection and life satisfaction, 134–135
    conflict and issues of fairness, 131–133
    stress and burden, 133–134
  help from various siblings, 123–126
  use of formal services, 126–127
Caretaking
  cross-cultural comparisons, 75–79
  in adulthood and old age, 117–118, 145–146, 148
  in childhood, 111–112, 140
Communication and contact between siblings, 54–55, 58, 101
Conflict
  associated factors, 160–163
  management of, 152, 164–165
  meaning of, 151–152
  outcomes, 153–154
    associated factors, 165–167
  problems in studying, 155
Contextualism, 21
Critical life events, 48
Cross-cultural comparisons
  caretaking in childhood, 75–79, 112–113
  definition of siblings, 71–72

Cross-cultural comparisons (cont.)
  effects of cultural change, 82–84
  marriage arrangements, 79–81
  relationships in adulthood, 81–82
  universality, 69–70
Crossover roles, 140

Death, see Loss
Deidentification, 47
Development and aging, 15
Developmental changes
  in adulthood and old age, 60–63
  in childhood and adolescence, 41, 44–45
  in conflict, violence, and abuse, 159–160
Dialectical logic, 23
Differential parenting, 49

Family
  business, 57
  solidarity, 66
  systems approach, 49, 51
    sibling dyads in, 25
    partial systems, 24
Fuzzy logic, 23

Gender effects, 55–58, 63–65, 140, 145
Genetic differences, 49

Half-siblings
  definition, 3
  incest, 175–176
  relationships in adulthood, 55, 56
  relationships in childhood, 48, 49, 183
Help to siblings
  in adulthood and old age, 115–119
  in childhood and adolescence, 110–111

Help to siblings (*cont.*)
  interactions, 110–111
  motivation, 110, 119–120
Hermeneutic approach
  study procedure, 88
  background characteristic of family
    members, 89
  family climate, 90–91
  feelings of closeness
    siblings, 96
    spouses, 99
  impact and common interests, 98
  influence of sibling structure, 92–95
  sibling communication and contact,
    101
    existence and frequency, 101
    indirect parental switchboard system,
      102
    influence of spouses on combination
      system, 104
    reasons for communication, 103
    social communication system, 102
    task communication system, 102
  siblings' perceptions of one another, 95–
    98, 99–101
  spouses' perceptions of siblings, 99

Identification of siblings for study
  populations and samples, 27, 71–72
  sibling dyads, 32–33
Incest
  abusive, 170–175
    associated factors, 180–183
    definitions and distinctions, 171–173
    effects, 176–180
    prevalence, 173–176
    nonabusive, 171–172
Invisible death, 187

Kinship, 17

Life span perspective, 13
Life span sibling research,
  common problems for researchers, 220–
    221
  integration across the life span, 216–218
  methodological differences due to age,
    219–220
Life span time frame, 14

Loss of sibling
  in adolescence
    concept of death, 192
    experience of loss, 192–194
    long-term effects, 194–195
    positive outcomes, 195–196
  in adulthood and old age
    existential incompleteness, 197
    personal vulnerability, 197
  in childhood
    concept of death, 196
    effects, 185, 189–193
    perinatal loss, 187
    unexpected death, 188
  lack of communication, 191, 196
  prohibition against mourning, 190–191
  types of studies, 185, 190

Management of conflict, 152, 164–165
Mechanistic world view, 22
Mental retardation, illness and disability
  caretaking in childhood, 141
  definitions, 137–138
  effects on normal sibling
    in adolescence, 143–144
    in adulthood, 144–146
    in childhood, 140–143
  effects on retarded sibling, 146–147
  future care following parents' death, 148
  interactions in adulthood, 145–146
  methodological problems, 138–139
Methods of data collection
  ethnography, 38
  experiments, 34
  interviews and questionnaires, 35
  observations, 36–37
  sources of sibling data, 38–40
  test and self reports, 35
Mismatched feelings, 96
Models of support, 120–122
Modeling behavior, 113–114

Nonshared environments, 52

Organicism, 21
Outcomes of conflict, 153–154

Path analysis
  nonrecursive, 23
  recursive, 23

Perinatal sibling loss, 187
Person and context, 20
Prohibition against mourning, 190–191
Prototype concept, 23

Quasi-contextualism, 21

Reference group theory, 64
Relationships between siblings
    across life span, 32–33
    companionship, 57
    dimensions
        affectional closeness, 55
        indifference, 56–57
        rivalry, 56
    effects on well-being, 63–65
    explanations of,
        in adulthood and old age, 65–67
        in childhood and adolescence, 46–52
    formation, 42
    friendship, 57
    importance, 5
    meaning, 4
    typologies, 59–60, 146–147
Reminiscence, 64
Replacement child, 187–188

Scapegoating of surviving sibling, 187
Shared environments, 52
Sibling
    meaning and definition of, 3, 71–72
    types, 3, 71–72
    unfinished or incomplete sibling sets,
        30
Sibling characteristics,
    constellation, 17
    demographic changes, 10
    meaning, 5
    influence of siblings on, 6
    structure, 29

Sibling sexual behavior (also see Incest)
    normal
        effect of older siblings, 114
        exploratory behavior, 169
    incest
        abusive, 170–183
        cousin incest, 176
        nonabusive, 170–171
Sibling structure (constellation), 17, 29, 72–
    75
Sibling therapy
    goals, 201
    in adulthood and old age,
    in child and adolescence, 206–208
    limitations,
        in childhood and adolescence, 208
        in adulthood and old age, 209–213
    uses of sibling therapy
        adjunct to family therapy, 201
        adjunct to individual therapy, 203
        sibling therapy used alone, 204
Socialization for adult roles, 114
Stepsiblings
    definition, 3
    relationships in adulthood, 55–56
    relationships in childhood and adoles-
        cence, 48–49, 183
    sexual abuse and incest, 175–176, 183
Structure and process, 20
Substitution hierarchy, 148

Teaching, 112–113
Typologies of sibling relationships
    in adulthood and old age, 59–
        60
    in mental retardation, 146–147

Unexpected sibling death, 188

Violence
    definitions and distinctions, 155–157
    prevalence, 157–158